Black, British and De-Churched

To Darren, for your loving support and wise counsel.

Black, British and De-Churched

Message to the Mainstream

E. P. Louis

scm press

© E. P. Louis 2025

Published in 2025 by SCM Press

Editorial office
3rd Floor, Invicta House,
110 Golden Lane,
London EC1Y 0TG, UK
www.scmpress.co.uk

SCM Press is an imprint of Hymns Ancient & Modern Ltd
(a registered charity)

Hymns Ancient & Modern® is a registered trademark of
Hymns Ancient & Modern Ltd
13A Hellesdon Park Road, Norwich,
Norfolk NR6 5DR, UK

All rights reserved. No part of this publication may be reproduced,
stored in a retrieval system, or transmitted,
in any form or by any means, electronic, mechanical,
photocopying or otherwise, without the prior permission of
the publisher, SCM Press.

The Author has asserted their right under the Copyright, Designs and
Patents Act 1988 to be identified as the Author of this Work

Except where indicated, Scripture quotations are from The ESV® Bible (The Holy Bible,
English Standard Version®), copyright © 2001 by Crossway, a publishing ministry of Good
News Publishers. Used by permission. All rights reserved.
Where indicated, Bible extracts are from the Authorized Version of the Bible (The King
James Bible), the rights in which are vested in the Crown, and are reproduced by permission
of the Crown's Patentee, Cambridge University Press.

British Library Cataloguing in Publication data

A catalogue record for this book is available
from the British Library

ISBN: 978-0-334-06694-1

EU GPSR Authorised Representative
LOGOS EUROPE, 9 rue Nicolas Poussin, 17000, LA ROCHELLE, France
E-mail: Contact@logoseurope.eu

No part of this book may be used or reproduced in any manner for the
purpose of training artificial intelligence technologies or systems.

Typeset by Regent Typesetting

Contents

Foreword by Robert Beckford   vii

1. Black Consciousness and Christian Faith   1
2. Black Man's Religion?   31
3. Out of Kemet?   59
4. The Black Face of the Early Church   81
5. Black Jesus, Black Theology (Liberation)   109
6. Geography, Genealogy and [g]ods   133
7. Message to the Mainstream   163

Bibliography   182

Foreword

Professor Robert Beckford

The book you hold in your hands, *Black British and De-churched* by E. P. Louis, is as urgent as it is enlightening. It recounts the faith journeys of Black people in Britain who have left or are on the brink of leaving mainstream Christian churches. It also examines how many have discovered new spiritual homes within alternative Black religious traditions, which, while rooted in the Bible, are critically engaged with Black identity and the socio-political and cultural issues faced by Black communities in Britain. Louis provides an ethnographic insight into the faith journeys of these individuals and communities, lifting a veil to reveal what is at stake for Black Christianity in Britain.

This study emphasizes a fundamental point: Black Christianity must address the cultural, spiritual and social needs of second- and third-generation Black British youth, not as an afterthought or token gesture, but as the heart of its ecclesiology, theology and mission. For too long, Black British churches have depended on inherited models of worship and leadership shaped in colonial Christian contexts, which still resonated with first-generation migrants arriving from the Caribbean and Africa. However, the same practices of faith hold little relevance to the concrete realities of younger generations born and raised in Britain, whose complex post-diaspora identity is formed in the tension of a society that questions their belonging while commodifying their culture. Louis's work recognizes this disjunction and advocates for a more holistic and culturally embedded response that does not shy away from addressing the urgent concerns of Black youth: questions of racism, slavery, colonialism and anti-Blackness, all of which point towards a demand for justice and liberation – not in the distant future, but here and now.

However, as E. P. Louis reminds us, Black Christianity is not the only religious tradition within the Black community. To assume so would ignore the rich diversity of Black religious experiences. In the African diaspora, faith has manifested in many ways, from the Orisha traditions of Yoruba religion to Rastafarianism and the Nation of Islam. The religions of the post-diaspora in Britain are not monolithic but resemble a kaleidoscope, each emerging from the aftermath of slavery and bearing witness to the creative resilience and moral courage of African and Caribbean peoples.

Within this layered spiritual landscape, the 'de-churched' are forging their own spaces of belonging. Their engagement with alternative Black religious communities is not merely a challenge to tradition but a pursuit of authenticity, agency and theological frameworks that mirror their realities.

However, Black British and de-churched communities also serve as a warning. If the historic Black British churches, those founded by the so-called 'Windrush Generation' and maintained through their children and grandchildren, struggle to keep their youth, what will happen to the newer West African British congregations, which are now growing rapidly in size and influence? Yet they face the same challenge of decolonial relevance. If they cannot incorporate the histories, questions and cultural identities of the British-born generations into their theology and practice, they may fall into the same errors as their Caribbean predecessors. The warning is clear: current numbers do not guarantee a secure future.

Black history and Black culture, in particular, are profoundly important for Black Christianity in Britain. Effective ministry cannot succeed without understanding Africa's history, the ongoing struggles of its diaspora, and the complex history of Christian mission to Black peoples – often entangled in colonialism, slavery and the racialization of Black individuals as inferior. Evangelizing or discipling without recognizing this history is not only naïve but also alienating. The young people Louis mentions are aware of this; they carry the burden of a heritage that is both glorious and painful. For the Church to remain relevant, it must take this seriously.

This book is therefore more than just a study; it acts as a catalyst for a new direction in Black theology in Britain. It signifies the emergence of a third generation of Black British and womanist theologians, who continue to prioritize lived experience over abstract theorizing and listen carefully to the concerns of Black Churches and the communities they serve.

Although Louis writes from within the mainstream Baptist tradition in the UK, the questions raised here resonate across different denominational boundaries. Pentecostal, Methodist, Anglican, Apostolic and New Church movements alike will see themselves reflected in these pages. This is not solely a Baptist matter, nor even a narrowly defined

Christian concern. It relates to how Black communities throughout the UK pass down faith, hope and resilience to future generations in a society that continues to racialize and marginalize them.

Ministers, pastors and practitioners who approach this work with honesty may uncover a path to transformation. Although Louis does not offer a complete set of answers, she makes it clear that halting the tide of disengagement with Christianity will require decolonization. Louis indicates a new practice that dismantles colonial theological frameworks, the erasure of Black histories, and the diminishment of Black cultural expression, and instead advocates for a Christianity that is embodied, culturally relevant and unapologetically committed to Blackness in all its forms.

This book is based on the idea that the 'de-churched' should be recognized as conversation partners. They point out what the church needs to do next: this is a *kairos* moment – an invitation to a church that truly embraces historical knowledge, belonging and emancipation. Yet the warning remains. If the insights of the de-churched are ignored, and if Black Christian faith is not decolonized, then the decline of Black British Christianity will persist. Congregations will diminish, young people will walk away, and Christian communities will lose one of their most vital resources for survival and growth. However, if the challenge is taken up, the Church may still discover a renewal as profound as any revivalemerging from the lived realities and creative genius of Black people.

Black British and De-churched calls on all of us: to listen, to reflect, to be transformed. The book acts as both a critique and a message of hope, a lament and a song of optimism. It adds to the growing tradition of prophetic Black British theology that insists faith must be accountable to justice, to history, and to the real lives of those it touches. As you read these pages, I encourage you to engage not only with your mind but also with your heart open. Listen to the Black voices Louis has so thoughtfully curated. Hear in their stories both the pain of alienation and the yearning for a faith that honours their lives and those who came before. And ask yourself, as we all must: What kind of Black Christianity will we pass on to the next generation?

Dr Robert Beckford, August 2025

I

Black Consciousness and Christian Faith

The pursuit of justice for Black and Brown peoples has been a mission for centuries. In recent years, however, these conversations and efforts have been brought to centre stage with the help of social media, and its ability to connect people worldwide has been the mechanism through which recent successes and efforts towards anti-racism have been constructed. The birth of the Black Lives Matter movement is but one example of how a hashtag transformed into a movement, inspired changes to institutional policy amendments and brought international attention to the policing of people of colour in North America and, in turn, the UK, provoking the silent majority into participation in a global debate on racism.

In the background of my research for this book is the ever-growing polarization between those on the 'left' and those on the 'right'. The research process has revealed to me that it is, in fact, unlikely that the majority of people are wholly committed to either 'side', but that these political and philosophical dichotomies undergird much of the unrest around social movements such as Black Lives Matter and the challenge it brings to the churches in Britain. Inspired as I am by its basic concepts and successful commitment to activism, which undeniably has brought racial discourse and social justice to the fore of society, I felt that what was lacking is a deeper consideration at the congregational level of its political and theological implications.

In the British context, the 'Windrush Scandal' and Brexit[1] have been reminders that, although it appears the wider public's attitudes towards people of colour are shifting, on a systemic and social level, there is still a resistance to recognizing the equal value of Black life, Black-Britishness as British and the significant contribution that Black and Brown peoples have made to the building of British society. As well as the wider social implications, this has led some Black and Brown people to look outside the Church for their spiritual support.

Alongside governments, policing institutions and large corporations,

Christian churches have not escaped the scathing criticism of social justice movements. Recognizing the discrimination and exclusion of Black and Brown people as a legacy of European colonialism, many scholars and activists have charged European historical Churches (such as the Roman Catholic Church, the Church of England, and the Baptists) with complicity and silence for decades; and now, with the open conversations, provocative audio/visual bytes on Instagram or TikTok, accessible lectures and courses on mainstream online platforms, the everyday person can be easily equipped with the language and statistical data to join the conversation. Leaders and congregations alike have been challenged to engage with racial justice and injustice, often so heavily wrapped in other topical social-political discussions that it has caused severe divisions within the wider church body.

This book explores how some Black-British peoples are navigating the social, religious and political paradigm of racial justice in the twenty-first century, with specific reference to the alternative Black Bible-reading religious groups that feature little in twenty-first-century racial discourse but have had a significant presence in the past and continue to do so in the margins of the Black-British Christian body. The Nation of Islam, Rastafari, the (Black) Hebrew Israelites and the Holy Qubtic Church are religious groups that have consistently appealed to Black churchgoers who find themselves in passive, ambivalent or resistant spaces about the issue of racism. Although these religions are no longer topical and are arguably overshadowed by hashtag movements, Black celebrity activists and growing Black, progressive and humanist scholarship, I conducted research to better understand how these Afroasiatic Diasporic Religions maintain influence within the Black-British Christian community.

To put this conversation into the context where it was birthed, let me introduce myself. I am a church kid: every week, mid-week, speaking in tongues, casting out demons, the end times – that was my upbringing. Beginning in a signs-and-wonders 'Word of Faith' type community (of perhaps 20 members), moving on to an independent Ghanaian Pentecostal church (maybe 80 members) and finally a local, Black-majority Baptist church (of 150 members which later fell to 40), I have always been in church, and I have always felt deeply shaped by my religion. This is relevant for those reading this book to know because, as so many theologians keep saying – and sometimes still not really believing or writing as such – we all do theology contextually. How we view the world, our experiences, our imagination, and our social interactions, all affect how and what we believe and how far we are willing to be influenced by other ideas. I have personally found my religious experiences to be both spiritually satisfying and emotionally and mentally grounding.

There are a few memories that I feel have led me to this research, the first of which is my earliest dreams from my childhood, which featured me walking around and performing regular day-to-day activities. In the background was this cut-out comic-style image of Jesus standing and watching. It was the typical image of a White man with long brown hair, a white tunic, and a red sash. When I asked my mother what it meant, she suggested, 'It may mean that Jesus is always with you', but it is only in recent years that I realized the significance of dreaming of a White Jesus. I never attended churches with images of Christ up on the walls, yet White Jesus was the Jesus image in my subconscious. As a child, I would often laugh at White (European) men with long hair, beards and sandals as 'trying to look like Jesus'. Although I considered my initial church experience as colourblind, somewhere and somehow, coupled with the broader Euro-American cultural influence from television, here was evidence of a default to whiteness. God, in my imagination, was a White man. Interestingly, as I moved between churches, joined a gospel choir, and danced with a Black-majority Hip Hop Christian company, the colour of Jesus never surfaced as a point for consideration. Each environment prioritized the spiritual aspects of God/Christ over his humanity – his risen-ness, his kingliness, his holiness.

The second memory is from my undergraduate studies, when I also worked as a teaching assistant. I managed to secure a workshop leader position with teenage girls on the brink of being expelled from a school in south London (which had also been my own experience earlier in my life). I put together a short documentary-style learning resource featuring people in their twenties talking about what they would change about their choices as teenagers. So I invited many friends and family (mainly Christians) to feature in the filming. One of the contributors I had previously known as a Christian rapper had, by the time of the filming, become (I would have said) radicalized. He appeared to have undergone a personal religious transformation: no longer evangelizing the gospel as I had known him to, he was clutching a book while telling me about a conspiracy against Black people – some apparent evidence that suggested AIDS and HIV were created to destroy Black people through viral genocide. Admittedly, I brushed off his accusations as nonsense. I had developed a low tolerance for this type of conversation – as far as I was concerned at the time, slavery was 400 years ago, and Black people just needed to get over it. Upon reflection, I consider this an outcome of my 'colourblind' Christian upbringing.

Black identity, culture and history had not featured overtly and intentionally in my religious upbringing; I understood the culture in my home to be spiritual and colourblind despite my Jamaican and Northern-Irish roots. We did not have reggae in the house growing up like other Jamaican friends and family; we had some gospel music (which I failed to link to Blackness), Christian rock, and contemporary Christian music (which in the nineties seemed to be full of what I understood to be Orthodox Jewish references). If we felt like something 'secular', it was Whitney Houston or Kenny G, the saxophonist. We didn't discuss issues within the Black community, or participate in justice initiatives nor cultural activities such as carnival. I therefore completely disregarded the encounter with this former Christian rapper. I considered him delusional and his views offensive, and I put it to the back of my mind. If I ever spoke of this incident, it was only to mock the person I knew who had been radicalized by that 'Black stuff'.

A few years later, a conversation with close friends took an unexpected turn. A friend I prayed with and went to church events with, whom I considered a 'sister in Christ', announced she was no longer sure about this 'Jesus stuff'. Her brother shared videos on the internet that claimed to uncover contradictions in the biblical text and the pagan rituals that the Roman Catholic Church and the Church of England had incorporated into Christianity. As a response, my friend had concluded that Jesus was a 'White Man's Religion' which was not for Black people – that both Christianity and the Bible were tools that had controlled Black people since the time of slavery. As an alternative, my friend had begun reading about Rastafari and occult spirituality rooted in New Age and ancient African traditions that would lead one to discover the 'divinity within'. Admittedly, she had approached her pastor with some questions about the Bible and practices within her African Pentecostal church and was told not to worry about that 'stuff' but to follow their teachings. What eventually pushed her out of the Church was the alienation she experienced within the same congregation. Friends and leaders had begun to pull away from and shun the girl who 'dabbled in Rastafari'. She wanted to be free from control, free from lies, and free from anti-blackness. I was unsure about responding to this announcement, but I felt somehow responsible; as if, as a Christian, I should have the words that would change her mind. I was aware that it would be unhelpful to say that it was the 'plan of Satan' (as was my typical churchy response to this sort of thing), not only because it seemed insensitive but also because some of the concerns she had conveyed piqued my curiosity. I began reading the books and watching the videos my friends discussed, intending to develop an apologetic defence against these racialized lies, but I had not counted on a rude awakening.

It was not until I began my formal theological studies at a London college that I myself experienced significant disillusion with the Church.

God at college seemed different from the God I had come to know growing up, and the difference had startling implications on how I felt about my identity. The college primarily consisted of middle-aged, warm and friendly middle-class people of European descent – until we had God-talk. It was my own mistake to think that studying theology would be like an intense Bible study, so when I arrived I was drowning in history, theory and convoluted literature, and I could not link all this information to our purpose as Christians. I also began to feel like Black charismatic/Pentecostal Christianity was the butt of every joke – the way we prayed, exorcised, 'proof-texted', gave into emotionalism and took the Bible literally. I could never understand the God my peers spoke about or connect with their interpretations in class. So whenever I gathered the courage to contribute 'on behalf of my God', I was often met with silence or politely followed up by the tutor with, 'What she means is … '. Coupled with these other experiences in my sheltered life, the penny finally dropped – I was a Black Christian in a White Christian space that was both theologically and critically underdeveloped.

The rude awakening of my racial–social standing among those I had assumed to be brothers and sisters without condition presented an opportunity for me to 'come correct'; I needed to make sense of the intersections of my identity and my faith, why I felt so different in a place I considered a natural home, and to figure out answers to the questions that had turned my friends away. Because of my learning experiences at Bible college, I was able to view my church experiences as if from the wings of a stage show, seeing all the mechanics working behind the scenes to secure a particular outcome. Outcomes that made me feel uncomfortable, conflicted and unsure. My faith in God and the Bible was unshaken, but my understanding of my religion and the week-to-week experiences I had been having was shattered, and now I could identify with those who had already transitioned from being 'zombified' religious soldiers to Black, British and de-churched.

This book, *Black, British and De-churched*, describes Black people who have left the Church, or are on the verge of leaving mainstream Christian congregations in Britain, and are engaging with alternative Black religious spaces that centre their beliefs on the biblical texts and engage with issues surrounding Black life. For my doctoral thesis, I conducted ethnographic research surveying a variety of influential religious ideas, their implications and the methods employed by these Black religious groups to resist racism and create a seemingly safe place for Black religious flourishing. What I hope this book achieves is a retelling of this journey, and a sensitive exploration of Black Bible Religions and the experiences of those struggling at the fringes of church life in Britain.

The aim is to shed light on this phenomenon for the mainstream Church that leads to a path of adequate response, meaningful action and, where necessary, course correction.

Although answers to difficult questions about and challenges to Christianity can now be easily accessed online, the local church still has a part to play in the discipleship, growth, support and shepherding of the believer who carries with them the cares of this world and seeks to make sense of God in light of their experiences. This, of course, includes a clear biblical response to racism, the legacy of the enslavement and colonizing of Black and Brown bodies and spaces and the whitewashing of Christianity that has been the scales on the eyes of many in Christendom around the world. The Black de-churched population in Britain and around the world is a phenomenon that signifies the broken bridge that should link the Christian body with the experiences of Black people. I do not mean to exceptionalize the phenomenon, nor assert that it is the only worthy bridge to be repaired, nor to champion Black suffering over other sufferings. I simply mean that building this bridge of love, learning, understanding and repentance is the work the Church has been called and equipped to do.

Throughout the course of my fieldwork, I often thought of the parable of the lost sheep:

> Now the tax collectors and sinners were all drawing near to hear him. And the Pharisees and the scribes grumbled, saying, 'This man receives sinners and eats with them.'
>
> So he told them this parable: What man of you, having a hundred sheep, if he has lost one of them, does not leave the ninety-nine in the open country, and go after the one that is lost, until he finds it? And when he has found it, he lays it on his shoulders, rejoicing. And when he comes home, he calls together his friends and his neighbors, saying to them, Rejoice with me, for I have found my sheep that was lost. Just so, I tell you, there will be more joy in heaven over one sinner who repents than over ninety-nine righteous persons who need no repentance. (Luke 15.1–7)

It must be acknowledged from the outset that Black Caribbean and African churches are fast-growing religious communities in the UK, unlike the dwindling attendance and engagement of the White British population. So this is not an appeal to the crisis of a mass exodus of Black people leaving the Church behind, but about those who are slipping away under the radar, in small numbers, perhaps even to the relief of some church leaders – but not to God. My research is concerned with the *why* – why did they wander off? What did they encounter? What can this tell us about the mainstream? From the outset, this scripture presents one of the central conundrums of this study: alternative Black Bible Religions would argue that mainstream Christianity is a farce and that their group, nation or race are the true sheep. And so, while many who read this book will be people from the mainstream wanting to be used to find or build a connection with the lost sheep, there will be many other readers who have re-read this scripture through a Black diasporic lens – seeking out the lost sheep, from within the mainstream Church.

A note about methodology here. Within this ethnographic research, written observationally rather than reactively, mainstream readings or ideals are not given; they are not proffered or afforded precedence. It is crucial to reiterate my interest and background because this research has been inspired by my lived experience and evolving journey as a confessional Christian. I was born into a religiously observant Christian family that can be best described as combining Evangelical, Word of Faith and Pentecostal traditions, so in every sense we have always held a high view of Scripture; yet it has only been in recent years that I have engaged with the academic nature of these views, which has provoked a certain level of deconstruction. My passion for this project is fuelled by my love and respect for, and religious submission to, God revealed through Christ and translated through biblical Scripture, but I have managed this potential bias by taking a methodologically agnostic approach. Bruce suggests that methodological agnosticism in sociological studies is a valuable way of answering our questions:

> If we wish to explain why people act as they do, the explanation will take the form of identifying which of their beliefs (not ours) were brought into play in interpreting their perceptions (not ours) of the circumstances in which they acted or reacted. (Bruce, 2011, p. 109)

This marries well with my intention to privilege their beliefs as religious instead of reducing them to a coping mechanism, which often hides the richness and integrity of people's religious imagination. I do not deny the connection between suffering and new religious expression, but as we shall see, what develops within the Black de-churched cohort is often a longing to be connected to what came before the suffering of colonization, enslavement and legal discrimination.

There are interpretation issues to be considered when the religion(s) is not the researcher's own, and this should always be taken into account as an inevitable limitation in the analysis. This research aims not to legitimize or authenticate truth claims of the various religious teachings but to analyse what Afrocentric Diasporic Religion adherents believe and how those beliefs influence the fringes of the Black-British Church. Although there may be similarities between how these religions and I approach Scripture, there are numerous grounds upon which I reject their religious views. My personal rejection (or embrace) of these Afroasiatic Diasporic Religious teachings is of no consequence to how I conducted my research.

Colonial Christianity

Cornel West, a prominent African American scholar, postulates in *Prophetic Fragments: The Crisis of Theological Education* (West, 1988) a challenging critique of the nature and value of theological academia. Describing academic theology as disorientated and in intellectual disarray, West challenges theologians to consider how theology is still relevant to the everyday Christian; while theologians dialogue, or perhaps legitimize their discipline through interaction with various other academic theories (Yancy, 2001), one must ask what it is about theology as a discourse or subject that holds distinctive value in this secular age. West challenges seminaries to build a sense of vocation, working in the service of the people of God rather than being driven by career and narcissism (self-service). The challenge in this particular work that is most poignant and relevant to the present study is the idea of working on a love ethic. West says:

> Yet as Christians who recognize our finitude and fallenness, we are aware that we never fully escape our own complicity in ideologies, institutional hierarchy, social subordination, textual conflict, hermeneutical violence and societal legitimation, even in our most prophetic moments. (West, 1988, p. 279)

He goes on to suggest that the task is to transform this awareness into an enabling source, a love ethic that resists our complicity to these idols. With this challenge in mind, the study acknowledges the living power of Colonial Christianity within the theological paradigm of Black Bible Religions.

The appropriation of Christianity by European empires throughout the last two millennia, combining the mission to convert lost souls with the mission to dominate nations to satisfy imperialist ambitions, has resulted in what this study calls Colonial Christianity. The Black theologian and cultural critic Robert Beckford describes this movement as 'a religious pragmatism folded into economic opportunity, uniting church and profit' (Beckford, 2014). Michael Tillotson, in his 2010 article 'A critical location of the contemporary Black church', defines the term Colonial Christianity as 'the specific religion transmitted to enslaved and free Africans in the United States of America between seventeenth and twentieth centuries' (Tillotson, 2010, p. 1018).

These definitions set apart Colonial Christianity as a distinct form of Christianity in that, by the very nature of its campaign and the eventual birth of a racialized structure of supremacy, the European powers collectively defined both intellectual strategies and a colonial theology in which Scriptures were used to legitimize invasion, the transatlantic slave trade, colonizing pre-inhabited nations, buying and selling humans and the indoctrination of foreign minds. Tillotson's definition, however, while succinct, is not complete: it takes the position that Colonial Christianity no longer exists in the twenty-first century, while Black scholarship and Black Bible Religions argue otherwise. Throughout the present text, we'll see that many of the de-churched would argue for Tillotson's definition to be taken further, as Colonial Christianity is the current experience for many British people of the African and Asian diaspora, descendants of Caribbean slaves and migrants from Africa and Asia who either subscribe to or wrestle with a whitewashed, White-dominant religious institution. It is believed by those whom I consider de-churched that, in twenty-first-century Britain, people of colour are still receiving religious transmissions that imply their inferiority. These colonial actions are in the structures of Christendom that develop models, cultures, attitudes and theologies which impose White social norms as fundamental 'kingdom culture', impinging on the freedom of Black Christians. Colonial Christianity is the specific religion transmitted to enslaved and free people of colour in Asia, Africa and the Americas, beginning in the fifteenth century and throughout the world in the present day. It is a Christianity that bears a White man as its mascot.

Black, Black, (Black)

I will at this point clarify my use of the terms 'Black', 'Black-British', 'Black Britain' and '(Black)'. Capitalizing the B in Black has become a recent fixture in public writing, particularly in America's news and media industries; many institutions are seeking to recognize and esteem Black people (Africans and the African diaspora) as a recognized people group that has historical, cultural and experiential ties. This study engages with those who seek an identity that is not a product of the experiences of the enslaved and colonized Africans, but that illuminates their precolonial ethnoreligious heritage. Throughout this study, for example, I will refer to Hebrew Israelites as (Black); the use of the brackets is to convey their rejection of the term Black, as they consider their 'Hebrewness' as the ethnoreligious and national identity of the descendants of the enslaved peoples dislocated from African nations in the sixteenth century. I offer this bracketed Black as a helpful reminder to the reader that the (Black) Hebrew Israelite communities are generally exclusive and do not (for the most part) include Jews from around the world – including the significant representation of Jewish people in Europe, America and Britain. I also do this to make the distinction from British Israelism, a separate movement.

However, despite this trajectory, I have some uses for the term Black and its capitalization for this study. Kwame Appiah considers how capitalizing Black refers to the social constructed-ness of the social group; 'Black', therefore, reminds society of 'what white supremacy has created' – a people who have severed links with their religious, cultural and ethnic heritages as a direct result of enslavement, Christianization and colonization. It recognizes the ontology of blackness that carries the legacy, stories, experiences, hopes and struggles of enslaved and colonized Africans – and their children. Appiah says, 'When we ignore the dialectical relation between the labels "black" and "white," we treat a bloodstained product of history as a neutral, objective fact about the world. We naturalize the workings of racism' (Appiah, 2020). Capitalizing the word Black is to remember and recognize that racism is still a force in our societies. This consideration is helpful for my study as I investigate those who ultimately seek a precolonial identity yet are 'Black' because of this very pursuit.

By framing my participants in the confines of being Black, Black-British and belonging to Black Britain, I hope to adequately account for their ethnocentric agenda that denies the ontological blackness that generally undergirds conversations about racial justice. I also hope to critically assess the sense of 'unbelonging' experienced by my participants living in Britain. Black Britain describes a world of experiences shared only by Black and Brown people within the wider British society. I am cautioned by the essentializing that often occurs when using these broader ontological terms. However, I feel this is remedied by the self-proclaimed trajectory of the participants in this study – to discover one's precolonial ethnic and religious heritage despite the shared experiences, histories and legacies of the enslaved.

This critical investigation acknowledges the presence and product of racism and a sense of unbelonging among many Black people in Britain.

Beyond these sobering realities, capitalizing Black conveys the positive presence of a social group whose points of connection (shared continental ancestry, histories, experiences and resulting cultures) acknowledge a determination to thrive and attain socio-political equality, self-determination and, for some, nationalist independence.

In light of this definition, I present my definition of the Black Consciousness Community, which I refer to often throughout the thesis as the wider community that engages in this discussion but does not qualify as de-churched. Black consciousness refers to the intentional social, cultural, religious and political effort of a person or people to explore and embody 'Blackness' in all its diversity, evolution and complexity. This Black consciousness directly responds to an identity crisis within Black diasporic and African peoples resulting from enslavement, colonization and Christianization (some would also argue Muslimization). It is both connecting with the past (pre-enslavement/colonization) and carving out the future for healthy Black identity/ies across the Black Atlantic, hoping that this process will contribute to the betterment of Black life in all spheres of life. Beyond Afroasiatic Diasporic Religions, Black consciousness may be reflected in Pan-Africanism, Black Nationalism, Afrocentrism and other more nuanced expressions. The Reverend Dr Joe Aldred in *Flourishing in Babylon: Black British Agency and Self Determination* (2024) presents a biblical case for Black flourishing, considering the Hebrews' exile in Babylon in Jeremiah. Countering the normative trope of Black suffering, Aldred uses Scripture to explore how Black people can become self-sufficient, build wealth, pursue excellence, and flourish in 'Babylon'. He expresses sentiments much like those from within the Black Conscious Community:

> Living in Britain, Black people should take ownership of their destiny, not looking to others as though salvific powers to flourish lies elsewhere. They must refuse to be distracted, looking to self and their inherent strength and integrity rooted in their own God-endowed agency and self-determination, never forgetting where they are, what to expect, and where their roots are. (Aldred, 2024, p. 19)

Twenty-first-century conversations about the Black-British church have turned their attention to the growing presence of Christian communities from various countries in Africa and their contribution to the changing face of the British church (Aldred, 2019; Chike, 2007). Previously, the Caribbean presence had captured scholars' sociological, political and theological imagination; with particular waves of the Caribbean migrants came new influences and challenges to British church culture –

a theological resistance, most notably captured in the Rastafari religion. Rastafari continues to have widespread influence throughout Britain and has generally received a more positive reception than other Black religions, such as The Nation of Islam. This success is due mainly to the popularization of Bob Marley and other world-famous Reggae artists who translated the Rastafari belief system and cultures into an accessible format for the masses.

Although African churches and the presence of African peoples are having a significant impact on British church life and culture, this study concerns itself with religions that were birthed in the twentieth-century Caribbean and North America and have, in more recent years, resurfaced and established new roots in Britain. That being said, this study does not consider this to be merely an American or Caribbean diaspora phenomenon but also a Black-British concern – second-, third- and fourth-generation British-African and Caribbean diaspora who have encountered Afroasiatic religions on their quest to locate a Bible-based religion that is socially, politically and culturally conscious.

Afroasiatic, woke and de-churched

'Afroasiatic' is a term used in linguistics; the basic premise is to explore Semitic, Egyptian, Berber, Cushitic and Chadic languages historically and comparatively to analyse their developments and mechanics. A standard image used to demonstrate 'Afroasiatic' is a tree with branches, which show both connection and distinction (Hodge, 1971). Following on with this concept, Martin Bernal, in *Black Athena: The Afroasiatic Roots of Classical Civilization* (1987a, 1987b, 1992, 2006), seeks to demonstrate how Western classical civilization has Afroasiatic roots; he does this through linguistics, archaeology and other forms of historical documentation. He argues that the legacy and influence of African and Semitic peoples have been discarded and decentred by eighteenth- and nineteenth-century European scholars, reflecting the influence of 'race' as a scientific premise according to which non-White peoples are considered subnormal. Bernal explains:

> The name 'Afroasiatic' comes from the fact that the languages of this family are spoken in both Africa and Asia. The 'Afro-' comes before the '-Asiatic' because seven of its eight subfamilies, Chadic, Southern Cushitic, Central Cushitic, East Cushitic, Beja, Berber, and Ancient Egyptian, are or were spoken exclusively in Africa, and the seventh, Semitic is spoken on both continents. (Bernal, 2006, p. 84)

These works are extensive linguistical investigations, beyond the scope of this study. Nonetheless, Bernal's method and his employment of the terms 'Afroasiatic', 'family tree' and 'branches' are helpful and appropriate for two reasons. First, while he makes a case for a root language in Africa, the main work focuses on a broader geographical region (which includes Asia), which more powerfully describes the 'family'. I hope to demonstrate that this can also be conceptualized for my study; as we shall see, the religions I have selected place their roots in the Afroasiatic region. Second, his research is scientific and critical; his use of empirical data to demonstrate social phenomena is mirrored by Black Bible Religions or what we could also call Afroasiatic Diasporic Religions, which make cases to correct religious history by using empirical data to demonstrate social and religious crises. It must be noted that Bernal's work is controversial and received much criticism from scholars who challenged his linguistic proficiency (Lefkowitz et al., 1996). Despite this controversy, the 'family tree' model and the term 'Afroasiatic' employed for the present study are not under threat from any of the more comprehensive criticisms about the mechanisms of his claims. Furthermore, *Black Athena* seems to be a well-respected text within the Black Conscious community and serves well to demonstrate their school of thought.

In the same way that Bernal seeks to uncover the Afroasiatic roots of Western civilization, Afroasiatic Diasporic Religions have a similar agenda for Christianity, as it has become known through colonialism and empire. This pursuit may indicate why many de-churched peoples remain centred on the Bible (and Qur'an) because they are reclaiming them as Afroasiatic religious texts.

Julian Baldick, in *Black God: The Afroasiatic Roots of the Jewish, Christian and Muslim Religions* (1997), concludes, according to his survey of (Indigenous) Afroasiatic religions, that duality or bipolarities are the foundational influences of these religions on Judaism, Christianity and Islam. Although not limiting their modes of thinking, he argues that simple dichotomies such as light/dark and good/evil are at the heart of these modes of religious thinking. From these dualities, more complex modes of meaning are produced or birthed. Of Islam, he says:

> What we must consider here is the Afroasiatic bipolarity of the religion itself. This is most evident in the Qur'an, where there are two worlds, this one and the next, and two main races, humans and genies. Further pairs are paradise and hell, believers and unbelievers, East and West, day and night, male and female, past and future, people of the right hand and people of the left, heaven and earth, sun and moon, and piety and wickedness. These pairs are expressed in antithetical verses

which for the Muslim constitute the ultimate miracle of unsurpassable eloquence. (Baldick, 1997, p. 169)

Duality can be seen throughout diasporic Afroasiatic religious teaching, beginning with them/us, Black/White, oppressor/oppressed, Babylon/Zion – these dichotomies are seen throughout much of 'Black' talk both academically and socially. I have memories of hearing (and saying) the term 'Babylon' as synonymous for the police in teen-hood, hinting at the mistrust of British authority in my community and hopes for Zion: freedom, future good, a home, and not hostility, unbelonging and constant suspicion. Later in this book I discuss how more progressive concepts, such as hybridity, have been introduced to counter these simple dichotomies in Black academic discourse. However, I draw attention to Baldick's claim to a sense of continuity that works at the heart of contemporary Hebraic/Afroasiatic religious imagination at this juncture. This sense of continuity is key to what drives diasporic Afroasiatic identification. For example, Black Bible-based Religion seeks to correct the notion that a Bible religion is a 'White man's religion' and to distinguish itself from Colonial Christianity – the Roman/European/British Bible-based religious institution. Charting an alternative trajectory, arguably retrospectively,[2] diasporic Bible-based Afroasiatic religions seek to recover their religious origins, discounting the dominance of the Roman, European and British epistemologies by reconstructing or rediscovering those sites of continuity.

The final key piece to this Afroasiatic religious concept is the pursuit to prioritize the ethnic identity of the biblical peoples. Kevin Burrell, in *Cushites in the Hebrew Bible: Negotiating Ethnic Identity in the Past and Present* (2020), says:

> Thus, it is worth emphasizing that the Israelite population from the earliest time were an 'Afro-Asiatic' people. According to the Hebrew Bible, Israel became 'a people' within an Egyptian-Cushite, Asiatic social, cultural, and political nexus. And it may also be worth remembering that *Egypt is Africa*, with all the inherent implications. (Burrell, 2020, p. 295)

The concept of 'Afroasiatic', with its connected yet distinct features attached to geography, cultures and movement of communities, is an appropriate way of conceptualizing Black religions in the diaspora collectively. These religions connect through their use of the Bible, their experiences, and their sense of return, but they are also distinct in their interpretation, organization, and route of return. 'Afroasiatic', then, conceptualized, describes genealogically and mythically rooted Bible-centred religious traditions located in the Afroasiatic region. This approach conveys the intentional process of decolonizing biblical religion and recovering its Afroasiatic origin.

The second term, 'woke', has historically been associated with the African-American community; during the civil rights era, it was a vernacular term that concerned Black people's social and political awareness. Many Black people are inspired by the activist, theologian, philosopher and community leader Marcus Garvey, for whom becoming 'woke' required Black people to be mentally engaged and to comprehend White America's tyranny on Black lives. With more recent civil unrest in the diaspora and the birth of the Black Lives Matter movement, 'woke' has become a word that primarily describes left-wing, liberal and progressive ideals and cultures. The evolution of Black anti-racist literature that engages more systematically with socialism, critical race theory and feminist thought can portray the idea that 'woke' is best positioned with the 'left' and progressivism. However, I aim to demonstrate that this is not the case – being 'woke' pertains to any danger to Black people, including the progressive ideologies that threaten the value of traditions, cultures, and religious beliefs central to Black identity formation and preservation.

The term 'woke' concerns not only being aware but also waking up from sleep, slumber, or zombification resulting from centuries of oppression and trauma. It concerns waking up and realizing a true Black self, often through study, knowledge building, and internal decolonization. From a religious perspective, 'woke' extends to the rejection or decolonization of the religion that has dominated Black life in the diaspora since the enslavement of Africans in the sixteenth century. As we shall see throughout the book, Christianity, which in this context includes Roman Catholicism, is the most common target for religious decolonization and rejection. Each of the Afroasiatic Diasporic Religions I have selected for this study calls believers to be 'woke' to the counterfeit form of Christianity that has held the diaspora's loyalty for centuries, or else to reject it altogether as the religion of the White man, opting instead for a Bible-based religion that is most representative of Afroasiatic peoples. This can be seen in Robert A. Hill's collection (2006) of the Marcus Garvey and Universal Negro Improvement Association papers and press releases (1923–45). The papers demonstrate the political and religious call to be 'woke' and to 'organize':

> Now it is time for the white priests to tell other whites that the Kingdom of God is near. And Blacks must preach to other blacks. A white person – he won't become right again. What's good to an African is his

right. Wake up! Wake up!! Wake up!!! Africa is our father's country! It is the most beautiful among all countries, and all its wealth must go back to Africans. (*African World*, 1925, p. 318)

Marcus Garvey and the UNIA's activity connected mainland Africa with the African diaspora and spoke both to continental and personal 'wokeness':

Wherever there is a Negro sleeping on his social, civil and economic rights, we would wake him up. Wherever there is a dead Negro, dead on his social, civil and economic rights, we should wake him up because we believe in the resurrection and the life. So do you. Then, wake up if you are asleep and come to life if you are dead. (*Negro World*, 1924, p. 144)

The enactment of waking up and claiming one's rights towards justice can be perceived as being as much a religious process as it is political. Undergirded by religious belief, drawing upon the resurrection of Christ, for example, demonstrates how themes and events from the biblical Scripture fuel and influence the notion of being woke. Malcolm X (1971) suggested that with the awakening of Black people there would be a change in the world – a signifier of the end of White dominance:

So I pointed these things out to the white students at the University of Pennsylvania so that they could see themselves that their world is shrinking, that their world is coming to an end. And the thing that is bringing about an end to their world is the awakening of the dark world. As the dark world awakens, the dark world is rising. As the dark world rises and increases, the power of the white world decreases. (Malcolm X, 1971)

Malcolm X's reference to the dark world is an example of how Black leaders in the diaspora wanted to change perceptions, teaching Black people to embrace 'darkness' as a positive representation of themselves and not as something synonymous with evil or dirty. Leonard Percival Howell (1933, 2008), in *The Promised Key*, a significant Rastafari text, says:

All the Churches religious systems of today, claims to represent the Lord God of Israel; but the Pope who is satan the devil, a false organization is a hypocritical religious system that has three elements, first commercial political and ecclesiastical to keep people in ignorance of their wicked course. (Howell, 1933, p. 6)

As used in this book, the call to an awakening, waking up, and being woke goes beyond just being aware of social and political issues. It is considered a mental and spiritual transformation of individuals, communities and nations inspired by religious teachings such as the resurrection of Christ and the redemption of the 'chosen' people. Woke, from the Afroasiatic diasporic perspective, is as religious as it is political and social. It connects those of the Afroasiatic diaspora to the Afroasiatic region. Being woke leads to organization and mobilization, which results in the realization of justice – both, it seems, an earthly, legal justice and an eternal justification – which should by no means be monopolized by the left or the right.

Finally, 'de-churched' in this study describes the participants who have left the Church and have sought an alternative Black Bible-based religious community and belief system. Caleb Davis (2018) discusses more broadly those who leave *consciously* due to conflict, pain, or politics and those who leave *unconsciously*, distracted by work responsibility, family commitments, and falling out of the habit of attending services. He considers attendance and participation in the local church's life and new meanings of mission that centre on the local engagement between church and community instead of introducing Christ and the gospel to unbelievers. Thom Schultz (2013) analyses the *relational* aspects of the de-churched phenomena – the effect of large church communities and the inaccessibility of the leadership – as vital components of this unfolding narrative.

Brian Harris (2015) briefly considers 'de-churched' theologically; he asks what theological implications of 'de-churched' speak to a church's belief about *salvation*. He likens the de-churched to the prodigal son and the lost sheep, which mirrors my initial theological response to my friend who left the Church: I desired her to eventually come back, won by persuasion and a spiritual encounter. Despite these initial responses, my research takes 'de-churched' further; to begin with, it has no intention of making a case for the mainstream Church as theologically or religiously preferable. 'De-churched' in this study resonates most closely with decolonization, dismantling an oppressive power, and decolonization, articulating the difference between Colonial Christianity and Black Bible Religion.

Ethnographically, this research considers how people have sought emancipation from a religious system that they consider unempowering, disingenuous and erroneous – not departing from religious conviction inspired by the Bible and parts of the historic church tradition but instead departing from the European/British institutional Church's Colonial Christianity. The unfolding chapters aim to flesh out a definition of the Black, British and de-churched that is beneficial for collating lessons learned, equipping churches to respond and contributing to the existing conversations on this topic for a deeper and more balanced understanding of this community.

Black Urban Apologetics

Several significant works were published during the research process that directly engaged with this phenomenon – Black people who have left the mainstream Church to join these alternative religious communities or 'mystery cults'. African American theologians and pastors, also known as Black Urban Apologists, responded to the challenges that Afrocentrists and Black Bible Religions such as The Nation of Islam and (Black) Hebrew Israelites have brought to the mainstream Church. These publications reflect encounters that have been happening on the streets of American inner cities for decades, now made available for accessible reading and the equipping of Christians who want to engage in Christian apologetics.

I can (retrospectively) locate this work as running parallel to these literary efforts; while these apologists seek to defend Christian ideas, my research seeks to critically analyse the influence of the competing schools of thought as a means of understanding the desires and hopes of those who seek to remain centred on the biblical text, yet liberated from mainstream Christianity.

Eric Mason, founder and pastor of Epiphany Fellowship in Philadelphia, has released two works of interest. The first, *Woke Church: An Urgent Call for Christians in America to Confront Racism and Injustice* (2018) is a text aimed at all Christians in America. Through the framework of 'Woke Church', he says:

> We are called, as the people of God, to wake up. To see what others don't and call it out. The Church in America is not awake to the reality of what is happening in communities across this nation, and we are missing out on our calling to shine the light into these places of darkness for Christ's glory. (Mason, 2018, p. 22)

Mason considers racial justice through a conservative evangelical lens; in this way, he is not outlining new ideas such as the link between justice and the gospel, lament, and what it means to be woke, but is reappropriating these ideas for an evangelical American, predominantly White, audience. Anchoring his arguments in plain readings of the biblical text,

Mason shows a commitment to the centrality of Scripture typical of Evangelicalism and less typical of what one might see in Black Liberation Theology – a leading Black academic theological voice. Mason combines a social and historical survey of the Black American experience from enslavement onwards with the core evangelical tenets of the faith to uncover the less trodden path for evangelical America – to be woke, 'a responsibility as believers in Jesus Christ' (Mason, 2018), and to see the need for justice for Black people as being in line with the gospel. Mason asserts points of action and illuminates this call to action with a vision of reconciliation through the lens of Christ's revelation to John in the Book of Revelation.

Mason has drawn on many points of appeal for the evangelical reader: a crucicentric gospel, deference to absolute biblical authority on faith and Christian living, conventional family-centredness and eschatology. The text sheds light on aspects of American society that affirm the necessity for the type of 'Woke Church' he proposes. Beyond the American evangelical context, this text can appeal to those who hold more conservative leanings in other contexts. Although not the primary focus, it does make mention of the alternative religions under *Lament #9: Not effectively equipping the Church to know how to engage black ideologies* (Mason, 2018, p. 110), where he reflects on the failings of the Church to sufficiently engage with 'black ideologies' and the impact this is having on the theological mind of the Black community, as many come to reject Jesus as Lord and Saviour. In *Urban Apologetics: Restoring Black Dignity with the Gospel* (2021), one can read a more in-depth apologetic inquiry into these alternative religions. Eric Mason has a large collection of online content through his initiative 'Thrive in the City' and in collaboration with Black Urban Apologists who engage with the 'Mystery cults' apologetically. This text is a summation of the years of debate, inquiry and discussion. It aims to equip Christians to defend the Christian faith against these religions, and features various Black Urban Apologists. Consistent with traditional apologetics, the contributors develop theological, historical and archaeological arguments (within the frame of logic and reason) to defend a biblical Christianity that is not whitewashed. Apologetic works are naturally combative, and this text has two grounds of combat, the first being the whitewashing of Christianity and the second the Black anti-Christian and humanist sentiments (also found in Black progressive Christian spaces) that aim to discredit the Christian religion. Jerome Gay in *All White Everything* says:

> The whitewashing of Christianity and its Eurocentric focus has led to a growing sentiment among people of African descent, as well as people across the globe, that Christianity is a Western-created, European-influenced, white-owned religion of oppression ... The main reason for this growing sentiment is historical and cultural whitewashing, as well as the under-emphasized reality that the Gospel took firm root in Africa, the Middle East, and Asia long before it reached the West. (cited in Mason, 2021, p. 15)

Black Urban Apologists such as Mason and Gay recognize the challenge for Black ministers as one that speaks to a fractured community of Bible-believing peoples: White, Black, Brown, mainstream, cult, separatist, nationalist and apostates, all a result of the European colonizing and whitewashing of the Christian faith. In this apologetic paradigm, Mason seeks to debunk what they call mystery cults (which I term in this book Black Bible Religions) and to provide an alternative 'gospel-centred' path for those who have concerns about the whitewashing of Christianity. 'Gospel-centred' in this sense, refers to the salvific work of Jesus Christ at work in people towards full reconcilement with God at the end of days; this is not like a social gospel that seeks to broaden the meaning of the gospel to the healing/redemption of society, rather than a focus on personal, individual transformation. Mason asserts:

> The false teachings of Black religious identity groups will fail to deliver on their promises in the end because the *Gospel* is the power of God unto salvation. Trusting Jesus Christ as savior is the only way a person can experience freedom from these false, demonically driven ideologies and cults. (Mason, 2021, p. 234)

Although framed in language that progressive discourses may deem intolerant, exclusive and 'colonial', Mason and other Black Urban Apologists are speaking the language of those they seek to engage, which is where, as we shall see in this study, the relativist, hyper-contextual or 'cosmopolitan' approaches fail to connect. This common language and the central issues (authoritative interpretation, doctrine, current socio-political affairs in light of eschatology, family and right living) demonstrate these communities' common roots in the African American Black churches and the conservative-evangelical underpinnings of their religious epistemology.

This book is not an apologetic treatise; instead, it looks through an ethnographic lens at the appeal and influence these religions have maintained on the fringes of the Black Christian Church. In the twenty-first century, the Black Urban Apologetic movement is a signifier of the ongoing quest among the Black religious community to determine absolute religious truths, not contextual/local truths, and yet to navigate contemporary Black experiences shaped by colonial religious epistemologies.

Vince Bantu has also made two significant literary contributions to this conversation. The first is *A Multitude of All Peoples: Engaging Ancient Christianity's Global Identity* (2020). In this text, Bantu charts the growth of Christianity and contributions to its development within Africa and the Middle East, providing evidence that counteracts the claims that Christianity is a White man's religion. Evidence is an essential factor in conversations with those I term the de-churched. As I shall demonstrate throughout this book, desk-based historical, archaeological, genealogical, scientific and theological research (also known as 'receipts') is vital in building knowledge and constructing an apologetic for one's belief.

These spaces are occupied by many individuals who read both broadly and deeply to uncover the true origins and meanings of the Scriptures, focusing on the unfolding narrative of Black and Brown peoples in the West. Bantu engages with this need and method by providing a detailed historical and geographical survey that builds a more accurate picture of early church history. What is essential about these recent publications is that they do not shy away from the significance of ethnicity and culture in the Church's history but instead emphasize their significance as vehicles of the gospel. This approach, again, engages directly with the interests of the de-churched. For example, in the chapter 'The First Christians of Africa', Bantu says:

> It is important to note, however, that Muslim sources in Arabic indicate continuing Christian presence in North Africa for centuries after the conquest. Interestingly, one of the most common terms for Christians in Arabic sources is *afariqa* – indicating a significant degree to which 'Christian' and 'African' were synonymous concepts. (Bantu, 2020a, pp. 117–18)

Bantu has a second focus, which speaks primarily to theologians and scholars:

> Christianity is and always has been a global religion. For this reason, it is important never to think of Christianity as *becoming* global ... there has been an implication that global diversity is exclusively a twentieth-century innovation of the Christian movement. (Bantu, 2020a, p. 1)

This focus is critical because it challenges the current missiological scholarship around *global* Christianity; readjusting one's gaze to see Christianity as always having been global seems to reflect the historical evidence better and also better decentres the 'Western, white captivity of the church' (Soong-Chan Rah, 2009, p. 22 in Bantu, 2020a, p. 1).

The second publication to highlight is Bantu's *Gospel Haymanot: A Constructive Theology and Critical Reflection on African and Diasporic Christianity* (2020). Bantu and emerging Black scholars explore the Christianity of the Black Church, one that is theologically orthodox and seeks liberative justice for the oppressed. This is a timely task and connects itself to the earlier publications that fill the void in current Black theological scholarship that voices the majority-Black Christian conservative/orthodox perspective on the Bible and social justice. He provides two important terms for this theological pursuit, the first being 'Gospel Haymanot':

> The name *Gospel Haymanot* is in reference to the living faith tradition of Black descendants of the victims of the Transatlantic Slave Trade, which hold firmly to the authority of the divinely inspired Word of God and its call for justice for all of God's creation. (Bantu, 2020b, p. 8)

The second is 'Gospelist reading':

> A Gospelist reading of scripture is informed by the interdependent relationship between truth and justice. Gospel Haymanot holds firmly to the biblical priorities of orthodoxy and social action without prioritizing one over the other; moreover, Gospel Haymanot rejects any alleged distinction between the two. (Bantu, 2020b, p. 9)

Bantu grounds his framing in ancient Ethiopian theological literature (Ge'ez); upon this, he has built a theology not determined by the Western evangelical standards of orthodoxy but one that is African and holds historical rigour. By reclaiming the gospel as holistic, Bantu has carved out a way for twenty-first-century Black theologians to build bridges between contemporary lived experiences and a gospelist reading of the ancient biblical text without necessarily defaulting to Western theology's input. I unpack this type of decoloniality in my conceptual framework (decolonization) as a standard method for negating the necessity of Western scholarship and theological imagination by the Afroasiatic Diasporic Religions.

The final text I would like to consider is Esau McCaulley's *Reading While Black: African American Biblical Interpretation as an Exercise in Hope* (2020). Here, McCaulley demonstrates the holistic sophistication of everyday African American Bible interpretation, which has often been denounced as simplistic, emotional and uncritical. By combining his lived experience with theological reflection on the Scriptures, McCaulley defines the theological space for conservative Black Bible reading that is socially conscious and faithful to the Bible. McCaulley speaks of his personal struggle to locate himself and African American Bible reading in either White evangelical spaces or White and Black progressive spaces. Between colourblind theologies, deep suspicion of the biblical text, and politics of power in all three spaces, McCaulley rightly concludes that another space must be defined for those concerned for Black lives who yet hold Scripture as the highest authority on faith and Christian living.

> There is a well-worn path of Black affirmation in white conservative spaces if one is willing to denigrate Black Theology (and the Black church) full stop. But the converse also occurs, namely that white progressives have often weaponized Black progressive voices and depicted them as the totality of the Black Christian tradition for reasons that suit their own purposes, which have little to do with the actual concerns of Black Christians. (McCaulley, 2020, pp. 15–16)

In this body of works, we can see an assertion from Black conservative Christians carving out a space that absolves the dichotomy between conservative attitudes towards Scripture and the ability to read and theologize contextually for the betterment of the Black community. Black Urban Apologists engage with alternative Black Bible-reading Religions with common language and topics, demonstrating the strong influence of Black Christian upbringing in America. The contributors also engage in the decolonization process through apologetics, looking to history, archaeology, genealogy, exegesis and contextual theology to detach biblical Christianity from colonialism; and, finally, these scholars defend Black Bible reading (as practised by the majority of Black American Christians) as faithful, meaningful and robust without the need for reducing the authority of the sacred text.

Preservation and liberation

I have innovated a conceptual framework that I believe will best capture the concepts that will emerge from data and interpret the inner workings of Afroasiatic Diasporic Religions from a religious perspective. Often, the literature emphasizes the ADR as a socio-political response to the Black lived reality; however, without negating those aspects, this study considers their religious and theological natures as indicators of their appeal to the de-churched. I intend not to separate them from their socio-political function but to provide a necessary balance, since I perceive religion as it pertains to human understanding and connection to God, a high power or an unknown mystical force to be underestimated and underemphasized as core to the decolonial inspiration of these Black religious groups.

I began by considering the religious nature of Black Bible Religions, specifying the genuine relationship to and belief in a divine God and Holy Scriptures instead of an abstract sense of 'ultimacy' (Neville, 2018, p. 9) that serves as a coping mechanism. Further, I categorized Afroasiatic Diasporic Religions/Black Bible Religions as New Religious Movements, acknowledging both their recent emergence in the nineteenth and twentieth centuries and their relation to more established religions (Judaism, Christianity and Islam) and their claims to recover more ancient religions. New Religious Movements are considered indicators of shifts in society; upon diverging from established religions and establishing resistance in their teachings, they faithfully capture their relationship with the wider society which is integral to their religious formation.

I then considered Ethiopianism as a historical religious foundation that gave rise to these Afroasiatic Diasporic Religions. Merging faith, politics and genealogy, Ethiopianism was a successful framework that allowed oppressed Black peoples to make sense of Black consciousness and their Christian faith. My framework seeks to encapsulate critical concepts developed and tested since the era of Ethiopianism and perhaps to broaden its reach and scope beyond the symbol of Ethiopia. At the same time, I want to make more direct genealogical assertions about cultural, religious and ethnic continuity with the Afroasiatic region, which perhaps serves the various religions within ADR a bit more integrally. I hope that the slightly mechanical terms I rely on, *preservation* and *liberation*, are a more explicit reminder of how the framing works and, thus, how it can be applied beyond the ADRs and the de-churched.

Another critical concept in this framework is decolonization, which I have defined by reflecting on Fanon's decolonial lens: considering decolonization in national terms as well as how it applies to other epistemological sites of colonial occupation I felt worked well with religions many consider as Black Nationalist religions. Chapter 2 maintains a religious focus; however, in Chapter 4, I delve into Black Nationalism, its role in Afroasiatic Diasporic Religions and how they contribute to Black, British and de-churched identity formation.

The final concept that I believe brings the conceptual framework into balance is the underpinning influence of conservatism. Conceptualized, conservatism is understood to speak to the preference for institution, history and religious authority, which I argue are central features of Afroasiatic Diasporic Religions. Conservatism anchors Afroasiatic Diasporic Religions in historic traditional, cultural and religious realities that resist the inevitable relativist and pluralist pursuits found within progressive ideologies. In this way, ADRs can create legacies for Black people and remain anchored in ancient ethnoreligious communities that are safe spaces for identity formation in the diaspora and globalized world. Together, these concepts form the *preservation–liberation* framework, a concept I have created to hold in tension the intuition to preserve a traditional, genealogical and religiously (Afroasiatic/Black) conservative institution and yet to liberate Bible Religion from White supremacy and residual colonial and discriminatory attitudes.

Conclusion

This book aims to investigate the Black, British and de-churched phenomenon critically – why are some Black-British Christians leaving the Church and joining other Bible-based Black Religions that have developed within the Caribbean and American diaspora during enslavement, segregation and the Civil Rights era? Furthermore, how have they continued to be an ongoing influence on the fringes of the Black British Church?

My contribution to this conversation is to provide an ethnographic perspective from the Black-British experience; while the literature above responds to the phenomena by countering the claims made, this study seeks to know, from a 'people watching' perspective, why these religious groups remain so influential and what their teachings reveal about the needs and desires of the de-churched.

This book is based on an ethnographic study that directly engaged participants who have had similar experiences to mine; the aim is to make sense of the driving factors and appeal of what I have come to describe as Afroasiatic Diasporic Religions or Black Bible Religions (I will use these interchangeably). During the research process I developed a five-session programme called Black Consciousness and Christian Faith (BCCF), which served as the vehicle that hosted seminars and open floor discussions. It provided the access and space I needed to engage the de-churched on topics such as the legacy of racism, slavery and colonialism in Christianity, the validity of Scripture, Black religious political theology, the Black presence in the Bible, and – most importantly from the research perspective – the experiences of the de-churched. Throughout this book you will see transcript excerpts from these sessions as well as the methodological pointers that helped me to form genuine relationships with my participants.

Several interlinked dialogues were crucial to identifying the key concepts that supported my analysis. First, Black Liberation Theologies, theologically and philosophically, subvert mainstream Christianity by politicizing the life, ministry, death and resurrection of Christ. They seek new ways of liberating those considered oppressed, inspired by themes within the Christian Bible; however, this method is limited in dealing with ethnoreligious claims for genealogical and divine origins. With all its subdivisions and related critical branches, a postcolonial theology seeks to radically dismantle Western Christianity, applying alternative hermeneutical lenses for Bible reading that are inclusive, empowering and allow for the participation of the marginalized; the limitation of this methodology is that what I recognize to be its core ideals, particularly a postcolonial approach to contextualization, are at odds with the core convictions of Afroasiatic religions.

In light of these, I want to draw two underestimated conversation partners into this discussion. The first is Evangelical Conservatism – conceptualized. My intuition during my research was that the undergirding mechanisms of this perspective would have a significant influence on the de-churched perspective and speak to the gaps that liberationist/postcolonial discussions leave behind when discussing racism, justice, decolonization and theology. Most significantly, I turn to the teachings of the Black Bible Religions I have selected: Rastafari, Nation of Islam, The Holy Qubtic Church, and (Black) Hebrew Israelites, as essential conversation partners to understand their influence on twenty-first-century Black-British de-churched.

Afroasiatic Diasporic Religions are controversially critical of Western Christendom and its connections to slavery and European colonialism. Their apologetic approach to knowledge building is often critiqued for lacking the scholastic rigour needed to support their claims, which, it seems, has been one of many reasons for their underrepresentation in the academic decolonial discourse despite their social advancements.

The challenge, then, is to understand Afroasiatic religious beliefs in light of their influence on the Black, British and de-churched while conversing with the other dominant methodological approaches.

Each chapter of this book is set out to provide multi-dimensional perspectives, so it will read like a manual – framed by the voices of the de-churched, the session outline from the Black Consciousness and Christian Faith programme, a methodological point, a conceptual point, and a discussion with the wider academic contributions with reference to a sample of Black religious teachings. It is not possible to fully represent the complete teachings of the religions in this book, so the learning points have been selected based on how they relate to the data gathered from the perspective of the de-churched. My hope with this approach is that the reader gets more than just information about Black religious teachings, more than merely insight on how ethnography works, and more than a challenge from the various academic contributions that speak into the Black lived experience and the resulting religious expressions. My hope is that by bringing you, the reader, my journey of research, handling, respectfully, the experiences, hopes and ideas of those who directly challenge mainstream Christianity, deep compassion will be birthed for the de-churched. A compassion that breeds action: action for next Sunday, a one-year plan, a ten-year plan, and a generational shift in approaches to preaching, teaching and discipleship that readily listens not only to the content of the challenges but to the heart behind it.

The next chapter is a response to the familiar phrase 'White Man's Religion'. We'll look at several mechanical aspects of Black Bible Religion, grounding the entire study in the religious needs of the everyday person and the ethnographic method. The third chapter, 'Out of Kemet?', looks at decolonization from the ADR perspective by considering their relationship and approach to Scripture, as well as how Participatory Action Research worked to serve both the needs of the community and my research. The fourth chapter, 'The Black Face of the Early Church', considers the importance of the Black/African historical legacy and how being both historically and religiously rooted provides the anchor for forward mobility and flourishing. The fifth chapter, 'Black Jesus, Black Theology', discusses Black Liberation Theology in the face of the teaching of Black Bible Religions and a post-foundationalist hermeneutic required for holding the progressive Black academy and Black Bible Religions in tension. The sixth chapter considers conservatism conceptually and how its principles serve to root the de-churched and followers of Black Bible Religions, not only as a controversial ethnocentric paradigm but in knowledge building that can be verified – an apologetic for Black presence and dignity that is arguably lacking in the mainstream Christian spaces. The final chapter presents all the lessons and actionable points for not only moving forward this conversation but also adequately responding and building bridges with the de-churched through teaching, preaching, discipleship, community engagement, and more.

Notes

1 This is, of course, a complex issue and I would not want to reduce it to simply being about racism or xenophobia. Nonetheless, there is a connection, as Anthony Reddie writes in *Theologizing Brexit*, which explores the neo-colonial racial attitudes within Brexit that helped to make sense of why non-European people were also being told to 'go home'. I also name this because Brexit was mentioned frequently as an example by the people I spoke to in this study.

2 One must not forget that the Coptic and Ethiopian churches, remnants of the Eastern strand after the East/West schism (1054) are thriving ancient African Christian institutions.

White Man's Religion?
(transcript sample)

Participant NM: It's only one thing out of everything; what you call yourself Black? [indicating Eleasah]
Eleasah: Oh wow!
Host M: Can I just say something? Because Black is superimposed on us—
Participant NM: There's no country called Black
Host M: Yeah, I know, and can I just say something after this because on my quest and on my journey of doing all this academic study, as I said, I've been introduced to Professor ------------'s work, and I met Eleasah – I also met another academic by the name of Dr ------------, and she speaks about that very thing about Black. Okay, but it's so deep, yeah, and so ingrained in our society the way we call ourselves Black, and she wants to do away with this word called Black.
Participant NM: Absolutely!
Host M: But we're not ready for it yet ...
Participant NM: Yeah.
Host M: But it's a process ... Eleasah is talking about the theological grounds, what the Bible says, the historical context, but what do we do with it? How do we move forward, how we – I perceive myself, how do I look at the word Black etc., and that's gonna be the next session after, so don't think that after this we're just gonna be left like wagwan?! [Everyone laughs.] ....
Participant NM: So there's no answer for that one today?
Host M: What one?
Eleasah: Well, I can answer from my perspective. So for me personally, um, I was just always brought up saying we're Black, so it's a traditional cultural thing, umm, but after more thought, equally, there's no country called Africa, and I've got no idea.
Participant NM: Africa ...
Eleasah: Yeah, it's a continent, but I don't know where I come from.
Participant NM: You don't?

Eleasah: Not in Africa.
Participant NM: Ohhhh ...
Eleasah: I come from Jamaica, and I know that my mum is Irish – but also, I mean, why I call myself Black is a little bit academic as well, and people have done a lot of work on what Black means, and there are lots of ways to view it [a few participants say 'yessss'], and for me, I'm really drawn to whilst I don't know where I come from, Black symbolizes people that have survived a massive trauma, and I'm proud of that. That's my history. I have survived; my ancestors have survived that particular trauma. We went in Africans and came out actually something very different, because of the trauma, because of the new things that we had to do to survive, um, in many ways, not surviving, kind of a little bit broken, um, in that sense, and Black is also very contextual. It's a resisting force against this terror of White supremacy, and so, for me, it's not necessarily that Black is a genetic thing. It's actually more of a political statement to say that I'm here, I survived, my ancestors survived. I dunno where we came from originally, but we're here, innit, and for me, Black ties that into and in the shadow behind that is Africa, but I just don't know where. So it's a bit more of a political-ideological thing, mainly because I don't know where I come from, if that makes sense – as opposed to Black as a genetic thing, because maybe I should go around saying I'm Jamaican and Irish or something?

Participant N: Yes, see, we're called Black after we're called coloureds; it's everything but your identity and the place where you came from, where you stem from, and many mean West-Indians, funny name [everyone laughs]. Yes, West-Indians and you look like that, I can't work it out? But you know, when you say coloured, and then it went to Black, West-Indian, all these different titles, that is nothing of us. Nothing that I can see in this room anyway. (White Man's Religion?, 2018)

2

Black Man's Religion?

Participant AU: Well, for me personally, the reason why I'm here is my son actually just told me about it this afternoon. What's been bugging me actually, I was privileged to be born into a Christian family, Christian school and everything, I'm still a Christian, but I'm very eclectic. I can go to Roman Catholic church, I can go to Pentecostal, but fundamentally, I'm from the Anglican church. And I've always – I tell my children this, and they don't believe me – I don't see a White Jesus because I always have that verse in the Bible that says that he made me in his own image. And surely, if he made me in his own image, he must be representing me. And my children, very good children, they grew up in the church, went to church, Mondays, Fridays, and when they got older, I said to them, you know what, you don't have to go to church if you want, you've come to a point now where you decide where you want to go. And now I kind of regret it. They didn't go, and now they've started questioning that you know the story in the Bible is not true, Jesus is not White, you know things that happened in Egypt, they just put it somewhere else; and I say to them, you know, surely if that is the case you need to reclaim it. We need to reclaim it. There's no point in running away from it because you can stand outside, criticize and everything, but you've got to be part of it. In most of the Pentecostal churches, they have youth week; you have to be part of it to make an impact. Unless you don't want to practise Christianity any more, anyone can say this is wrong, and that is wrong, but how do we prove true knowledge, true history, and say to our children, you know this is your religion, reclaim it? Because I think this is what is wrong with our race is that we complain and expect other people to fix it.
(White Man's Religion?, 2018)

In this chapter, I explore my findings on the Black religious response to the 'White Man's Religion' problem; I begin with discussing how ethnography serves as a listening tool that bears some important lessons for engaging with the de-churched. This is followed by a description of the 'White Man's Religion' session, the first part of the BCCF course, where I collected my data, which considers the group's starting points and topics of interest. The rest of the chapter is dedicated to exploring the functional, diasporic and formative nature of Black Bible Religions.

Ethnography

Black, British and De-churched is the result of a qualitative ethnographic study where I sought to understand a community of people through observation by being present among them. The community I have identified as de-churched is not a fixed or organized community but is composed of individuals who share similar social and religious experiences and desires or who are interested in the de-churched phenomenon. The following qualifiers identified this community:

- They have left their church community and joined an Afroasiatic Diasporic Religion like Rastafari, The Nation of Islam, The Holy Qubtic Church or the (Black) Hebrew Israelites.
- They can be considered as being on the fringes of their church community and asking questions connected to the beliefs and challenges presented by Afroasiatic Diasporic Religions.
- They are experiencing disillusionment with their faith and understanding of Christianity on account of the legacy of African enslavement, colonialism and neo-colonialism.
- Some of the participants from this study were active confessional Christians interested in the notion of 'woke', Black consciousness and the decolonization of Christianity.

This qualitative ethnographic research aimed to make sense of a broader social phenomenon through a focused investigation. As explained in the previous chapter, I designed and facilitated a five-session programme called Black Consciousness and Christian Faith (BCCF), which took place in local churches in London (2016–18). This five-session programme combined a provocative seminar-style talk with an open discussion forum, which became my data pool. The sessions were designed to focus on the experiences of the de-churched, those who had been influenced by the claims and religious perspectives of Afroasiatic Diasporic Religions.

There are three main functions of ethnographic research I want to emphasize; the first is *contextual*. Martyn Hammersley calls these 'social microcosms'; he says, 'the value of ethnographic work often depends on showing that the particular events described instantiate something of general significance about the social world' (Hammersley, 1992, p. 17). I hypothesized that this social microcosm – the de-churched – speaks of resistance to progressive shifts in society that we see demonstrated clearly in critical discourses and the louder political voices, which perhaps do not necessarily speak for the majority and by causing a severance from tradition destabilize a community's ability to maintain a meaningful identity. Spending time among the de-churched repeatedly, socializing as well as working and discussing together, helped to define the shape of the social microcosm.

Second, this critical research was responsive to the conditions in which the religions were birthed and the general sense of complaint and dissatisfaction of the de-churched rooted in racial discrimination and White hegemony. As a result, this research seeks to raise awareness of injustice and address inequality on an epistemological level that has not considered ADR to be equal conversation partners in twenty-first-century Western theology.

Although, as mentioned before, Afroasiatic Diasporic Religions are often referenced as sites of resistance, it seems their advancement in decolonizing mainstream Christianity is understated and underestimated by both conservative and liberal theologians. In this sense, this critical ethnography does not observe through a single lens such as womanism, socialism or conservatism, if one would permit that it is considered critical, but seeks to convey the criticisms that emerge from the data and apply them more broadly to all positions that have excluded ADR. Hammersley notes this complex issue:

> It is not obvious that there is only one source of oppression. This threatens the coherence of the critical model, unless there are reasonable grounds for believing that a single form of theory-guided practice can lead to the simultaneous abolition of all sources of oppression. Without that assumption, it seems likely that from the point of view of different critical theorists, or even that of a single one, many people may be simultaneously both oppressor and oppressed. (Hammersley, 1992, p. 103)

My intuition is that this social microcosm reflects more broadly an underestimated and undervalued community, the ADR and the de-churched, who are more advanced in the decolonization project than academia has been in praxis. In *Key Concepts in Ethnography* (2008), Karen O'Reilly says that critical ethnographic research 'interpret[s] the data, using image and metaphors that show them in a new way, to reveal the hidden depths of exploitations, power, and disadvantage' (O'Reilly,

2008, p. 54). Critical ethnography seeks change. This study presents itself as a contribution to the decolonization of the British Church. It also challenges the progressive relativization and humanist undertones of postmodern Black religious scholarship (considered the most critical), which cannot facilitate the presence of Afroasiatic Diasporic Religions as they present themselves but instead must repackage or dismiss their validity. Consistent with critical scholarship, this research looks for change from the bottom up.

The final emphasis taken from this method is contact. Campbell and Lassiter (2015) outline the necessity for ethnography to have direct contact with the research subject; it is distinct from other forms of data collection because its very integrity is based on the insights that are gained through direct interaction.

> Doing and writing ethnography itself rests on an analogous idea, that direct participation and genuine engagement in the day to day lives of others can provide unique insights into how various and diverse ideas and activities generate meaning. (Campbell and Lassiter, 2015, p. 55)

Contact was foundational to the research process; the original data was derived from spending time with the de-churched community. Developing relationships with people week by week allowed me to collect qualitative and detailed data that was current and raw. It allowed the participants to course-correct any assumptions I brought to the sessions and develop a hypothesis that was relevant to the time and context from which these participants came. This was particularly necessary as the religions I am also conversing with were birthed in a different generation and context that does not parallel that of the participants. Contact in my ethnographic research allowed me to develop evidence upon which my hypothesis depends to justify what I call the preservation–liberation framework and to share the present mind of the twenty-first-century Black, British de-churched. This unique data set also provides the necessary insights into which various fields of study and praxis can benefit from the knowledge and ideas of those on the margins.

White Man's Religion

'White Man's Religion' is a phrase commonly used among those who hold suspicion against mainstream Christianity from within the Black Conscious Community, which includes those who also observe Black Bible Religions. The term assumes that mainstream Christianity is a religion for White people by White people (people of European descent), undergirded specifically by imperial and colonial ambitions at the expense of Black and Brown flourishing. This is the first topic in the Black Consciousness and Christian Faith programme designed to explore and understand the de-churched phenomenon, and we began by discussing what is meant by 'White Man's Religion', focusing on three central claims:

- The Bible endorses slavery, and therefore Europeans relied on Scripture to endorse the enslavement of Africans.
- The Europeans created, edited or twisted the biblical Scriptures to control and subdue people of colour.
- The image of a White Jesus is representative of the White supremacy that underlies the Christian faith and rejects bodily blackness.

'White Man's Religion?' works as an introductory session that serves as an ice breaker for the group; it begins with a short, provocative lecture in which I aim to outline the issues that have led to my research. The 'White Man's Religion?' session posits a vital question – whose religion is Christianity, and how is that qualified? The complaint that brought my participants together is that the Christianity of the Bible is different from the Christianity they have experienced going to church in Britain. While this may have been influenced by anti-Christian groups, Pan-Africanist literature, and other transmissions within the wider Black Conscious community, many participants came bearing their own stories of rejection, confusion and disturbance.

Each session is shaped to help the group realize they are coming together with a common struggle – the legacy of White supremacy and European colonialism; so that even if people have different perspectives, one hopes there is a general attitude of working together to solve the given issue. One of the challenges that Afroasiatic Diasporic Religions bring to the Black, British and de-churched is to question what they believe Christianity to be and what factors have shaped their understanding of the religion or religious organization. To begin with, I highlighted key arguments against Christianity and offered some apologetic-type responses that sought to provoke a response from the group and help them develop questions for the open floor discussion that followed.

Together, the group addressed the issue of 'White Man's Religion', the notion that White people created Christianity to dominate and control people of colour. Central to this discussion is the role of the Bible within Christianity, often with questions about its validity, historicity, authenticity and inclusivity/exclusivity. In many participants' experiences, the

Bible had been sold to them as the unchanging, infallible 'Word of God', a perfect combination of true historical events and prophetic mysteries of things to come. For those who have left Christianity, it has become a common idea that the Bible is unreliable, contradictory, and the word of men and not God. This shift in theological perspectives seems to be linked to their disillusionment with Christianity and has led them to ponder on how the legacy of slavery within Christendom has shaped or distorted their perspective of Black identities. To challenge the group's understanding of the Scripture, I reintroduced 'how we got the Bible' by merging a variety of perspectives: textual criticism, history of the manuscripts, theo-politics surrounding the translations, the mystery of the prophetic (foresight) Scriptures, and geography (Africa's influence). Although the input is foundational, the aim is to present other perspectives on the Bible as a sacred text to participants who perhaps previously had more one-dimensional views of the document, such as a 'living word', 'erroneous', or 'a conspiracy'. With the added layer of the various English translations and the conflicting theologies that surface, the participants could perhaps appreciate the complexity surrounding Christianity's sacred texts which do not necessarily begin with the mystery of God but with the human transmission of Scriptures.

The very nature of the programme is to challenge the whitewashed, spoon-feeding nature of mainstream church pedagogy, and it couldn't afford to replicate those models with Black face. However, as a researcher who was not a trained apologist and has mainly engaged with evangelical Christian teachings as part of my own formation, this was a challenge I had been aware of from the beginning and in designing the programme. I had to relieve myself of the responsibility of having all the answers – which was typical of the teaching styles I had been exposed to. The participants often came with questions relating to historical eventualities or anti-Christian claims for which I didn't have the answers, and the post-foundationalist approach (covered in Chapter 5) allowed my responses not to be confined to an apologetics-type format but for us as a group to explore together.

During the programme's pilot, adherents of the Atonist/Qubtic religion initiated a conversation about gender equality after the first session. This was a unique contribution among the other religious voices in the room, which were largely Hebraic (Rastafari, Nation of Islam, Hebraic/Asiatic) and from what are generally considered male-led movements often critiqued for their patriarchal models. This conversation created a necessary opportunity to explore gender equality in Christianity, where women can ask themselves about how they see themselves in this broader discussion of Black religious identity, having had some experience with mainstream Christianity. I followed up this challenge with a session on slavery in the Bible, particularly the model of slavery in the Old Testament. I set aside a moment for reflection; first, on how we understand slavery in the Old Testament in comparison to the enslavement of Africans in the sixteenth century, and, second, on the treatment of women in the Old Testament, in particular, where a man can sell his daughter into slavery without the opportunity for freedom after seven years as males would have. Not to mention the guideline for enacting physical discipline upon an enslaved person – these were all difficult caveats within Scripture for which I had no reassuring response. Yet it was important for the group to see that this Hebraic system was not the slavery system of the Old Testament, and so to dispel the notion that the Bible is a manual for enslaving other nations for personal pleasure and gain. It was an internal social mechanism that mitigated poverty and crime, an existing system that we see God speak into in Exodus and Leviticus.

The question that arises from the 'White Man's Religion?' session is: Whose religion is Christianity, and how is that qualified? Of course, the questions that should rightfully precede this are: What is Christianity? How is it qualified, and how does it compare to the Christianity one has come to experience? The following sections consider a definition of Black Bible Religion. In many conversations, I have encountered people who consider themselves to be spiritual and not religious, and it is this framing that I'd like to explore: a religion that has structure and organized boundaries and that necessarily relates to a higher mystery.

Religion

Religion – as it pertains to this study, which considers Rastafari, The Nation of Islam, the Qubtic community and (Black) Hebrew Israelites – speaks of a communal, organized way of living, believing and submitting to a God or gods, or a higher power, and guided by a sacred text or tradition believed to have divine origins. In his 2011 article 'Defining religion: A practical response', Steve Bruce suggests, with Hinduism, Buddhism and gods in mind, 'religion then, consists of beliefs, actions and institutions which assume the existence of supernatural entities with powers of action, or impersonal powers, or processes possessed of moral purpose' (Bruce, 2011, p. 112).

Bruce offers a broad definition that he argues allows for the variety, scaling and scope of religious life for research, which is useful for the religions we will encounter in this book as they are by no means monolithic. An interesting comparative exercise, for example, is analysing the teachings about the ways in which one relates to, connects with or encounters God. From the Nation of Islam perspective, the Black man is god, god is a man, and followers are submitted to Allah (god) in his incarnated forms; but for a Hebrew Israelite, God is The Most High, a spirit, and they are a chosen human community who serve and obey God and depend on his mercy and covenant for redemption. While there is diversity and contradiction among all religious peoples, with the definitions that Bruce and I convey there is no question about the reality of God or a higher power. It is with this framework – which doesn't include ideas like religious humanism – that I explore the de-churched phenomenon, those in or from organized religion transitioning into another, those who believe in something beyond humanity.

Robert Neville, in *Defining Religion: Essays in Philosophy of Religion* (2018), considers the term 'ultimacy'; he is cautious of Europeanizing the term 'religions' by focusing the definition on ways that distort other cultures (Neville, 2018, p. 7). He says:

> Now suppose we define religion as *human engagement of ultimacy expressed in cognitive articulations, existential responses to ultimacy that give ultimate definitions to the individual, and patterns of life and ritual in the face of ultimacy*. (Neville, 2018, p. 9; italics original)

By considering religion as an engagement with ultimacy (and whatever, whoever, finds meaning there) rather than God, Neville generates a concept that has some use for the decolonizing project. Doing any type of theology is subject to the cultures and contours of our personal lives and, I dare to say, will never perfectly express God or 'ultimacy'. However, I would argue that it is only in the last century that a European collective mind on what religion is has been anything other than what they have learned in the East, Africa and Asia. Roman Catholicism, Islam and Christianity – being most influential for centuries in Europe, undermining Paganism, druidism and other religious expressions indigenous to European people groups – have Afroasiatic roots. And so, while ultimacy may resonate with what we might call general revelation (here I think of Psalm 19.1: 'The heavens declare the glory of God, and the sky above proclaims his handiwork' and the resulting rituals that are formed by those yet to encounter the people of God, the sacred texts of the Hebrews and Christians tell us that we engage more specifically with the terms through which God revealed himself to Abraham, to Hagar or to Moses. He revealed himself as a person, a Father, the I AM, God Almighty, and designed rituals, ordinances and defining markers to organize and identify his people. What we encounter with Black Bible Religions is a nuanced perspective on these identifying markers in the face of Colonial Christianity – a racialized expression that gave rise to a racialized response. In this sense, ethnicity, skin colour and bloodlines are at the fore of Black Bible Religion.

New Religious Movements, sometimes considered synonymous with cults, can describe religions that have emerged in recent history, and which, while distinct from ancient or historical institutional religions, take note of the relationship that they have with older religions and traditions. Often, the term 'unorthodox' or, in the words of J. Gordon Melton, 'strangeness', is a reflection of the 'beliefs and practices perpetuated (or altered) from the older religion in which it is rooted' (Melton in Bromley, 2007, p. 30). Black Bible Religions are often called mystery cults or cults among Urban Apologists, pastors, teachers and Christians. Pastor Eric Mason, having discussed in a previous work Afroasiatic Diasporic Religions and the claims they make against the Church, turns in his latest text, *Urban Apologetics: Cults and Cultural Ideologies*, 2023, to the mainstream church and other long-standing Bible reading religions to consider the concept of 'cult'. He provides three useful framings for what people can experience: 'cultish tendencies', 'cultic', and 'cult'. This being an ethnographic study, I was compelled by the critical influence that religions such as the Hebrew Israelites were having on people who struggled with historical slavery and ongoing racism in the mainstream church, and so to have this grading system helps to explore the religions from this angle without buckling at the initial hurdles of the controversy that surrounds them on the internet. Mason says:

> Cultic groups also have doctrines that either contain additions to the gospel, are characterized by heterodoxy (clear deviations from historic orthodox doctrines or belief), or are heretical (a formal rejection of a belief articulated by one of the ecumenical Christian councils). (Mason, 2023, CULTIC section)

This describes what we see of Black Bible Religions in an effort to bring correction to what they consider to be a stolen, modified and corrupted version of their ancient religion. Mason and other apologists for the gospel are clearly mapping out what is right and acceptable and by what measure; and this, in turn, helps us to see how Afroasiatic Diasporic Religions are doing the same, rejecting Christian councils and grounding their beliefs in those who reveal truths claimed to be hidden from Black people by the mainstream yet revealed through prophets who are being raised up to emancipate Black people.

So, knowing that the religions considered in this text have surfaced as a result of great struggle, in violence, in death, in oppression and in hope for salvation, not unlike the first-century Jews of the New Testament, we must consider their relationship with the wider society. John A. Saliba, in *Perspectives on New Religious Movements* (1995), says:

> The new religions can also appropriately be called 'movements' in the sense that they reflect important transitions in people's lives. They are small currents in society that may be pointing to greater upheavals and changes in religious life. They cause shifts in the converts' previous religious allegiance and in the behaviour of people affected by the change. (Saliba, 1995, p. 10)

David Feltmate, in his 2016 article 'Rethinking new religious movements beyond a social problems paradigm', describes the scope of New Religious Movements quite broadly:

> Some religious communities will move from one geographic location to another, being historically old but situationally 'new'. Others will be variations on ancient themes but be considered different enough by larger and more established religions that they are seen as 'new' and significant in their deviance. Still others will be built around novel ideas arising from the mind(s) of charismatic figures, which can lead to the formation of intentional communities, public outreach, or publications. (Feltmate, 2016, p. 83)

The Afroasiatic Diasporic Religions I have selected for this study are grounded by combining these elements, seeing themselves as ancient people who were involuntarily relocated. Afroasiatic Diasporic Religions reject the Christianization of the enslaved and colonized Hebrews/Africans and set about returning to the 'true' religion of the Bible; and they have also been inspired by, centred on or cultivated by a key figure. Feltmate suggests that New Religious Movements are regarded as new when considering the time and context of their emergence but are not dissimilar, in nature, to the dominant religions from which they diverged, which historically would have come to prominence from much the same conditions as outlined above. Feltmate argues in this text that studies on New Religious Movements are often given to problematizing the religious communities by focusing on negative social aspects associated with them:

> What do Scientology, Rastafari and Neopaganism have in common? The answer is that people in social mainstreams have treated them as dangerous and problematic groups. The reasons why they are deemed dangerous varies and may not be comparable, but that they are seen as dangerous is all that is required for comparison within our field. Hence, the social problems paradigm is an underlying organizing force in new religious studies. (Feltmate, 2016, p. 84)

Feltmate argues that what is considered successful research is the work that identifies why new religions are problematic – such as new norms, violence or deviance. Most of these movements have little in common but are brought together because of the problems they create. He demonstrates the prejudice towards New Religious Movements by evaluating the contents of standard teaching handbooks, identifying themes that continue to 'orient the field: definitions of religion, Satanism scares, sex, violence, and leading people astray. Social problems – especially ones that lead to legal intervention – are dominant frames' (Feltmate, 2016, p. 88).

Feltmate suggests three ways of moving beyond the social problems paradigm in the classroom when teaching NRMs:

> First, we need to stress that new religious movements are a constant feature of history and that understanding new religious movements is part of understanding a basic human quest to find meaning in this world in the company of others. (Feltmate, 2016, p. 93)

Although venturing into a reductionist territory, there is much value in stressing the reality of the ongoing emergence of religions as normative; it humanizes the phenomena instead of perpetuating sensationalist cult tropes and speaks to the human preference for a religious institution.

Second, rather than be subject to categories that support the social problems paradigms like 'suicide cult' or 'sex cults':

> [w]e want to ask who determines significance when creating comparative categories ... (and to) diffuse the power of categorization from the hands of those who have created analytically restrictive comparative categories and create stronger grounds for comparison based on better empirical evidence. (Feltmate, 2016, p. 94)

This is a decolonial pursuit; by resisting the conventional categorization processes that demonize new religions, studies on new religious phenomena can engage with a more integral critical analysis and ethnographic study.

> Third, we have to acknowledge the sources of power that give significance to the social problems paradigm and find ways to challenge them. Money, political and legal power, and a sense of moral superiority all contribute to the importance vested in the social problems paradigm. (Feltmate, 2016, p. 94)

The social problems paradigm is appropriate for this study as Afroasiatic Diasporic Religions have been largely perceived as problematic and socially unsettling. Admittedly, among the diverse groups, leaders and teachings, there are undoubtedly notions of Black supremacy and racial discrimination against non-Afroasiatic diasporic peoples. While I contend that these notions should be challenged and condemned, a biased categorization system often overlooks its own complicity in racial discrimination and notions of superiority. It negates NRM's more common everyday beliefs and practices that do not concede to extreme racist ideologies.

Using the term New Religious Movement to describe Afroasiatic Diasporic Religions in the twenty-first century acknowledges their recent emergence and relationship to larger religious institutions – Christianity, Judaism and Islam. Yet, despite the term 'new', the focus is less on the age of a religion's existence and more on its stage of development. Rational Choice Theory (see Chapter 7) engages with the realities of globalization and the global market. High levels of accessibility through the internet allow people to engage with religions that speak to their needs; it allows one to consider the religion's attractive features that compete with longstanding, mainstream religious institutions.

Considering Black Bible Religions, therefore, as New Religious Movements helps to manage the expectations within this study for the religions to bear the heavy load of legitimizing their validity through the normalized methods – a canon of ancient texts and manuscripts, longevity of traceable practice in history, councils and an extensive amount of adherents who have engaged in a religious transformation that also shapes a new type of engagement with society.

While Black Bible Religions can at least build upon the latter point as controversial religious and political participants on the topic of racial oppression in the last century, in the words of Andre E. Key:

> The central tenet of black religion is that racial oppression can be combatted on divine terms with theologically based anthropologies. Black religion operates not as a single religious tradition but rather as a *plurifaith*, a collection of religious traditions undergirded by the concern with protecting, defending, and advocating for the full humanity and spirituality of African people. (Key, 2014, p. 37)

The (Black) Hebrew Israelites present a good sample of teachings that exemplify how Black religion intentionally tries to rebuild Black identity in a way that decentres the European power of colonialism, attributing their suffering to their national disobedience against God. Here, Key considers (Black) Hebrew Israelites in more broad terms, not restricted to the 'camps' such as Israel United in Christ (IUIC) or Gathering of Christ Church (GOCC); he instead defines them under the umbrella of Black religion.

> I define Black Judaism as a denomination of the African American spiritual orientation known as Black religion. It is primarily a Bible-based religious tradition that is informed by a belief in redemptive ethnic suffering and Black messianism, and it asserts that individuals of African descent in the Western hemisphere are the 'true Jews,' a claim that rests on a belief that African Americans are the descendants of West African exilic Hebrew communities. (Key, 2014, p. 39)

Despite the view that Black Bible Religions exist simply as a result of social and political formation in recent centuries, they emphasize a rediscovery and return to ancient ancestral religion rather than a productive or generative process. This position lends itself to growing hostility towards the Black Church from groups like the Hebrew Israelites, despite their being connected in experience and sacred texts. Key's analysis demonstrates not only the theological diversity and doctrinal conflicts underplayed in the scholastic terrain but also the overlap between different Black religious movements/denominations that are less common in mainstream Bible religion.

> Torah-only sects are equally opposed to the Black church as a source for theological content. The Black Church is rejected as the religion of slavery and for its acceptance of Jesus as the Messiah and/or the son of God. Torah-only sects maintain a strict monotheism that may be attributed to the cultural and theological influence of Black Islam and perhaps Sunni Islam within the African-American community. This demonstrates the necessity in view of Black Hebrew Torah observance as a part of a larger plurifaith in which the boundaries between Black Judaism and Black Islam converge culturally and theologically. (Key, 2014, pp. 58–9)

These points of convergence help us to see how Black Bible Religions focus on the elements that help to define the contour of one's identity, both ethnic and religious – which means, as I witnessed among my participants, that those de-churched members who have yet to make a firm religious commitment collect an array of information and perspectives that fill the gaps in their own identity matrix. For those so offended by the image of a White Christ, for example, to consider him now merely a prophet maintains the continuity of being a Bible-reading person while resisting the shaping of the White Messiah in their theological imagination. To drop the New Testament and focus only on the unseen God and his chosen people allows many to drop the terror of the blue-eyed, blond-haired bogeyman and build on the identification marker of being Hebrew, chosen and gathered.

Functional religion

In 1944, Arthur Huff Fauset's influential study *Black Gods of the Metropolis* (1944) (2002) sets out to observe some of the 'practices prevailing among several representative groups of cult worshippers' (Fauset, 1944) to generate a deep and meaningful understanding of how they have been developing their religious concepts as Black Religions in America. By visiting homes and places of worship and conducting interviews, Fauset made observations and attempted to outline and describe the distinct religious features of various Black religious cults: Mt. Sinai Holy Church of America, United House of Prayer for All People, Church of God (Black Jews), Moorish Science Temple of America and the Father Divine Peace Mission Movement. Ultimately, Fauset sought to predict the trajectory of Black religious life in America as it pertained to the social and political needs of the Church. The work begins by addressing the controversial intellectual discussion about the 'Negro' religious disposition, which asks the question, 'Does contemporary religious practice among Negros in the United States disclose definite African survivals?' Fauset examines the data for indications of functional expression as against 'pure' African survivals, destined to transform specific social needs of the American Negro folk and concludes that there is little evidence to suggest such an innate *bent*. Fauset centres his research field on the northern metropolitan cities – 'Negro city within a city' (Fauset, 1944, Chapter I).

Fauset suggests that the main attraction of these cults has been 'the desire to get closer to some supernatural power, be it God, the Holy Spirit, or Allah ... relief from physical or mental illness, race consciousness or nationalism [and] the compelling personality of the leader' (Fauset, 1944, Chapter VIII). Many of Fauset's participants were former members of mainstream Christian congregations. Fauset concludes that the attractions of cults need not be considered exclusive to Black cults; orthodox-evangelical churches do not explicitly state their appeals in such terms as these, but it can be argued that there is overlap between the two in their points of appeal. Fauset also suggests that the appeal to cult life is a response to the movement of Black people from the South, where legal segregation was still at play, to the North, where huge psychological adjustments to desegregated society would have made the transition difficult and unsettling. The cults would have provided the religious framework with which to manage the transition:

> Certain religious cults in northern urban communities assist the transplanted southern worshipper, accustomed to the fixed racial mores and caste requirements of the south, to adjust his psychological and emotional reactions to conditions in the North, where all life and living are more fluid and intermingling of the races is inevitable. (Fauset, 1944, Chapter VIII)

Fauset indicates that joining the cult was also seen as an elevation or graduation to something higher than the mainstream church. In these cases, it was not necessarily a rejection of the church, but the belief that it only operated at an entry-level, and many of the participants felt that the cults assured them that, through their religious demands, they would be truly saved. This notion is also supported by the esoteric nature of these cults that distinguished them from one another and mainstream Black church denominations. Fauset acknowledges, although to no extreme extent, that it is possible to make tangible religious links between African traditional religions and survivalist religious functions found in both mainstream Black Christian communities and the Black cults.

> Negroes are attracted to the cults for the obvious reason that with few normal outlets of expression for Negroes in America due to the prevailing custom of racial dichotomy the cults offer on the one hand the boon of religion with all its attendant promise of heaven either here or above or both; and on the other hand, they provide for certain Negroes with imagination and other dynamic qualities, in an atmosphere free from embarrassment or apology, a place where they may experiment in activities such as business, politics, social reform, and social expression. (Fauset, 1944, Chapter XI)

Another interesting finding from Fauset's research was that the cults that have the 'most rigid adherence to the bible' (Fauset, 1944, Chapter XI) also have the least engagement in social, economic and political programmes, whereas the cults that set their own rules or take the

Bible less seriously are most engaged in the programmes of community betterment. Fauset suggests that the Black Church is 'likely to witness a transformation from its purely religious function to functions which will accommodate the urgent social needs of the Negro masses under modern stresses of politics and economics' (Fauset, 1944, Chapter XI).

With the benefit of doing my research nearly a century after he was writing, it can be noted that Fauset was correct to an extent: the Black Church has had significant moments of transformation where its religious function was extended to significant effect to the betterment of Black lives socially, politically and economically. There is also something to be said about the obvious link between the continual growth of the prosperity gospel powerhouses, the growth of the Black professional and middle classes, and the motivational coaching we now see on many Christian platforms across Black Britain and the United States. Are these evidence of the functions of Black Religion in the twenty-first century, motivating and developing high flyers in the face of historically systemic discrimination?

On the topic of Black cults, it can be said that they continue to operate on the fringes of Black religious (Christian) society. Thus, these movements are still 'suggestive evidence of the continuing dynamic character of the American [and British] Negro's religious experience in a milieu which has made the unique unfolding of that experience compulsory and inevitable' (Fauset, 1944, Chapter XI).

Fauset's ethnographic work discusses twentieth-century Black religion's social and religious function in North American urban contexts. He demonstrates the interconnectedness of Black Religion, experience and social progress among the religious communities, and predicts a trajectory that sees the Black Church as more socially and politically engaged and active, distributing its function in society between this activism and its religious nature.

Carol White's interdisciplinary approach, in *Black Lives and Sacred Humanity: Toward an African American Religious Naturalism* (2016), presents an alternative perspective in which she reduces African America's religiosity to a set of functions that 'distinguish this humanistic bent as one of the highest aspirations of African American character, namely, its claim on life' (White, 2016, Chapter 1). Here she explores, through radical humanism or humanism with 'religious sensibilities' (White, 2016, Chapter 2), the new meanings of 'human'. White refers to very broad and general conceptual frameworks such as functionalism:

> Through the lens of functionalism, I see the religious pattern as affirming blacks' humanity and advocating a fuller, richer life for African

Americans as part of an ongoing existential exercise undertaken by humans in every generation. (White, 2016, Chapter 1)

White's method is valid in the sense that Afroasiatic religions search for answers that affirm their humanity; however, as per its nature, humanism centres on the human, whereas in much of Black Religion, although it centres itself in the religious narrative, the teachings maintain subjectivity to the will, designs and desires of the 'most high', 'supreme being' or God.

An example of this can be seen in an excerpt from my own research where the group of participants were trying to make sense of the African diasporic identity crisis through Scripture. Participant P says:

> *Deuteronomy 28.27 it says, and you shall become strangers ... and a byword among all nations where the Lord will drive you. So when you're saying I'm ting I'm that and we're looking and we're searching down the ages, through everything that we've gone through as a nation of people, we're not Africans, we're not West-Indians, we're not this, that and the other – we belong to God. But because God knew that we were going to be disobedient to him, he told us what we would become, a proverb, a byword of our disobedience to him.*
> *Someone says: So what do we do then?*
> *Participant P: We need to be obedient.* (White Man's Religion?, 2018)

Much in line with Hebrew Israelite teachings, Participant P believes that the enslavement of those then known as negroes was a direct result of disobedience. Although some may consider this to be a problematic view of God, what can be seen here is the decentralizing of the European players. Through this perspective, the European slavers were no longer powerful players in their own narrative but merely a tool in the unfolding divine narrative of the Hebrew people.

Participant P attends to the conversation theologically; she interprets Deuteronomy 28, the warning from God to Israel, as the answer and reason for the dislocation of 'Black' peoples in a fashion consistent with (Black) Hebrew Israelite teachings. The interpretation follows that, because of Israel's disobedience towards God, God allowed his chosen nation to be overcome, enslaved and scattered. So, while conceptually intriguing and progressive, White's method deviates drastically from the intentions of the religious groups themselves. It re-writes their legacy and nullifies their influential core contribution to the struggle.

The religious naturalism that White envisages (which ultimately roots religion and spirituality in the natural world rather than a supernatural world) examines the 'philosophical and humanistic assumptions embedded in contemporary African American religiosity' (White, 2014, preface). Moving away from a religious premise, White brings Black religion into the purely scientific domain. She is charting non-traditional paths that, as a result, and with great intention, seem to move the Bible-based Black religious framework beyond fundamentalist epistemologies. White says:

> As an alternative to theistic models of African American religiosity and spirituality, this study is an unabashed celebration of religious humanism. I am hoping that its perspectives and main argument will inspire a generation of scientifically oriented African Americans in search of newer, conceptually compelling views of religiosity that address a classic, perennial religious question: what does it mean to be fully human and fully alive? (White, 2016, Preface)

Much in line with progressive scholarship, White is keen to reject what is considered modernism, fixed and absolute truths, for a view that shifts and changes as human thinking changes:

> This type of religious valuing, then, becomes one dimension of cultural transformation that evolves as our thinking evolves. More importantly, with this orientation, we are led away from a modernist view that demands an 'all or nothing' epistemological framework and toward one that takes into account our complex historicity and our radical relatedness as sacred humans, and all the possible nuances associated with that phrase. (White, 2016, Chapter 6)

In this sense, God, Yah, Jah or Allah has no significant religious contribution to one's understanding of sacred humanity and what it means to be human. Instead, White draws upon the intellectual works of iconic thinkers Anna Julia Copper, W. E. B. Du Bois and James Baldwin to build her concept. By taking their lead in resisting the exclusive, discriminatory and universal approach to defining humanity, White aims to produce a framework that illuminates the drive and capacity of Black individuals and communities to redefine what it means to be human, using religious imagery to attain dignity and freedom from the epistemological constraints of Enlightenment and modernism. This work speaks to the possible futures of Black Religions, driving a distance between Black people and millennia of religious grounding. My work resists such a radical approach, giving preference to how the Afroasiatic diasporic religious teachings look backwards into their origins to find redemption.

Diasporic religion

We can also look at Black Bible Religions from the diasporic perspective – those in transition, or journeying, living or existing in a new space. It was among the African diaspora, in the Caribbean and in the United States, that we witnessed the emergence of religions whose immediate claim is a religious home elsewhere. Edward E. Curtis, in *The Call of Bilal: Islam in the African Diaspora* (2014), brings Islam and slavery into conversation and anchors his focus on the experience of African Muslims or Muslims of African descent. Curtis asserts that the story of Bilal, an African who was enslaved and then elevated to the role of prayer-caller at the genesis of Islam with the Prophet Muhammad, is a symbol of belonging and heritage for African Muslims around the world who continue to experience discrimination based on ethnicity and skin colour. Curtis's work explores the impact of travel and dispersion on diasporic communities rather than the religious interpretation and metaphysical perceptions of being diasporic – the Africana Muslim diaspora.

An integral part of his work is to understand how practices of Islam are influenced by the experience and meaning of diaspora; among Black Muslims who explicitly claim an African Islamic ancestry or origin, some will name certain Islamic traditions as having African influences. Some African Muslims establish a religious genealogical connection and a claim to Islam through the African Saint Bilal – an African who was close to the Prophet Muhammad. The Nation of Islam absorbed Bilal into their identity formation process under W. D. Mohammed's leadership, broadening and bringing more dimension to how African-American Muslims negotiated diasporic Muslim identity. ADRs are concerned with correcting the perception of the origin of their religions; most scholars see their beginnings as fairly recent, a product of religious resistance in the eighteenth, nineteenth and twentieth centuries. The NOI attribute their resurgence to these eras, awakening to their true religious origins, ancient religions revived through revelation to prophets and elders. The NOI leader Leo Muhammad teaches that Islam predated the Prophet Muhammad:

> But beloved Islam is a pure system of freedom, justice and equality which didn't begin 1400 years ago; it didn't come with Prophet Muhammad, peace be upon you, that was the latest revelation to the Arabs. But prior to that, Islam was the system that governed the universe. It's called peace and Black people, that's our very nature from the beginning; that's why at the time of the Prophet in the Arabian Peninsula, when he began teaching an Ethiopian Black man by the

name of Bilal who was being enslaved by Arabs, he heard about this Arab in the Arabian Peninsula teaching this, what they said was a new religion, but to Bilal, the man was teaching the old-time religion – Bilal already knew the religion. It was Bilal who climbed up onto the Kaaba, that house built by Abraham and Ishmael from a longer time before, it was Bilal who climbed up on the top of it and said for the first time 'Allahu Akbar'. Prophet Muhammad didn't teach him how to do that. When the Prophet saw Bilal doing that he probably said, wow that's a call, but Bilal already knew that call, he already knew the name of Allah, it wasn't new to us as a people. (Leo Muhammad, The Beginning, 10:18–12:23)

These teachings aim to correct the perception of Islam beginning in AD 610 through the Prophet Muhammad, saying instead that it has always been the religion of the original man, to which the Arabs have received access through revelation. Muhammad considers how Bilal, an Ethiopian slave and adherent to the 'old-time religion', recognized his own religious teachings taught in other nations. Bilal is a crucial African Islamic figure because his prominence affirms Black and African Muslims in what is considered an 'Arab' religion. There is a sense of continuity tracked through Bilal; he is a connecting figure between Ancient Islam, mainstream Islam, and the Nation of Islam as we know it today.

In this case ... the linking of African American Muslim ethnic and religious identity to a close companion of the Prophet Mohammed signalled a shift in Muslims' notions of 'thick blackness' – that is the black identities that Muslims themselves constructed. Rather than imagining a primordial and mythological origin for black/Muslims as the 'original man' as Elijah Mohammed had done, celebrating Bilal was a way to link black people to the earthly history of the religion of Islam while also carving out a particular ethnic identity inside that larger story. It was a theme that would continue to echo across the black Atlantic over three decades later among some British- and Caribbean-born Muslims in the United Kingdom. (Curtis, 2014, Chapter 6)

This text embodies a deep sense of return for all Muslims, whether literal or religious. Caribbean migrants and Black-British Muslims, both those born into Muslim families and those converted from Christianity as teens and adults, struggled with the socializing forces in Britain. The NOI presents the resistance and critique of European/British imperial and colonial legacies in their religious thought and practice and defines a distinct Muslim practice that would reflect both a Black identity and an Islamic conviction. Black diasporic Muslims in Britain are the minority among Somalis, Arabs and those from Southeast Asia, all of whom would have distinct ethnoreligious qualities. The Nation of Islam and their consideration of Bilal, then, works uniquely as a socializing force for Black-British Muslims.

As an ethnic symbol, Bilal often also has an important political meaning. Whether among Black North Africans, African-descended South Asians, Afro-Europeans, or African Americans, the figure of Bilal has become a symbol in the struggle for self-determination and political autonomy (Curtis, 2014, Conclusion). Through Bilal, a more complex view of Islam emerges beyond simple groupings; African Muslims and Muslims in the African diaspora specifically illuminate a diversity marked by ethnicity, movements and migration, leadership, experiences, and hermeneutics. This approach is helpful because it details the effects that movement has on religious features within the faith; for the present study, movement, travel and migration in light of Afroasiatic interpretation of the sacred texts focuses mainly on the involuntary movement of those enslaved and translocated in the sixteenth century (and into the nineteenth century). Although, through the mixing and separation of families and people groups during this time, 'niggerization' (through brutalization) aimed to stamp out the bonds formed by Indigenous identity markers such as language, dress and ritual – aiming to turn one from an African to a nigger – the movement caused the diaspora to *remember*, religiously and mythically.

Formative religion

The formative aspect of religion simply describes the ways in which religion plays a part in building the blocks of one's identity – individual and collective. As we shall consider in more depth later in the book, Black identity is usually understood in light of the experience of slavery and colonialism that Black and Brown ancestors underwent in modern history. There is no country named Black; it is not an ethnic category proper. Instead, it is a political term that categorizes those of African descent in non-African nations. And with that categorization comes the load of historical suffering, subjugation, dehumanization and being 'other'.

Andrea C. Abrams in *God and Blackness* (2014) focuses on the First Afrikan Presbyterian Church in Atlanta, an American Afrocentric Christian church, which essentially combines or fuses Afrocentric notions of blackness with the Protestant, more specifically Presbyterian, Christian religious tradition. At the heart of their teachings is Christ as an African Messiah. The aesthetic outworkings fashion themselves in a combination of traditional gospel hymns, traditional Afrikan dances, terminology from various African languages, and a cross-section of classes. Abrams here focuses on the identity formation of the middle-class members of the congregation, particularly on how their idea of blackness may be somewhat different from that of those who are less affluent. She frames her analysis conceptually by combining Du Bois's double consciousness, cultural and ontological blackness, Black and womanist theologies on account of gender politics and Afrocentricity. Abrams says:

> On the one hand, discourses of racial essentialism contribute to a powerful sense of shared identity; on the other hand, heterogeneous constructions of blackness simultaneously contribute to a sense of ambivalence. A core contention of this book is that this tension between essentialism and heterogeneity is not a problem to be solved; rather, it is a fundamental and necessary part of racial identity. (Abrams, 2014, Introduction)

Abrams identifies Black identity formation as a space of contradictions and, within this tension, describes the ways in which middle-class members of the church 'determine what authentic blackness is and how it should be practised, how biblical narratives are employed to prove the value and essential nature of blackness, and how middle-class status and womanist theology promote counternarratives of heterogeneity' (Abrams, 2014, Introduction). By examining the members of the church who employ Afrocentricity in their behaviour, changing names, appearance, and the relationships they have to the continent of Africa, Abrams finds that the members had a more true sense of self than the false identity that had been operating pre-Afrocentric conversion. She further demonstrates how the teaching of the Bible contributes to the Afrocentric formation by 'the reading of the Bible as an African text' (Abrams, 2014, Chapter 3). The study describes this Afrocentric re-reading as a critical factor of appeal to those looking for something more than what they experience in mainstream Christianity. This research uses observations and interviews to generate data material that she refers to throughout the text to support and demonstrate the complex identity formation within this unique Afrocentric Christian setting. The conceptual framework that she has innovated allows her to comprehend the participants' contributions as intersectional.

Abrams makes an interesting analysis of the 'anxiety and guilt' associated with being Black and middle class. She says:

I contend that members of the First Afrikan Church have added another tool to their Black middle-class tool kit – Afrocentrism. I suggest that, for many of the congregants, belonging to an Afrocentric church is, to some degree, an attempt to assuage the guilt and anxiety by, at times, emphasizing Black identity over middle-class status. However, the emphasis is not just on any black identity but on an authentic Black *African* identity that can hold its own when compared to the Black cultural capital associated with poorer African Americans. (Abrams, 2014, Chapter 4)

Ultimately, the most authentic blackness is situated among the poor, and, when understood through the lens of class, the conclusion is that blackness is most found at sites of poverty, which is an ontological perspective, not a cultural or ethnic stance. Afrocentric scholarship often focuses on the greatness of ancient African kingdoms, cultures, and intellectual prowess. Although one could consider that an inconsistent notion of blackness, Abrams emphasizes the enhanced possibility of assimilation to Euro-American culture due to the participants' education and work environments. This, according to Abrams, is appeased because First Afrikan provides the opportunity to 'perform blackness' – Black or African-inspired attitudes, values and 'cultural ways'. Acknowledging the problem of locating 'blackness' most strongly with poor people, who would then be assumed to all think and live the same, Abrams suggests Afrocentricity provides a sense of blackness that is not class-based but is centred on culture.

Abrams concludes that middle-class African Americans are drawn to this Afrocentric congregation because it celebrates their ethnic/racial identity in ways that their European work and church environments celebrate 'neither their phenotype nor ethnicity' (Abrams, 2014, p. 172). In this environment, not only do congregants celebrate and embrace blackness through an Afrocentric framework, but this Afrocentric framework supports community work and the use of resources from within the affluent community to aid improvement in the local poorer Black communities. Abrams says:

Marginalized within the larger community, the Afrocentric community provides a space in which there are shared notions of what it means to be a good Christian, a loyal member of the nation, and a spouse with appropriate family values based on shared notions of blackness and Africanness rather than whiteness and Europeanness. (Abrams, 2014, Conclusion)

Abrams has highlighted the appeal to Black religious peoples of Black culture and Afroasiatic readings of the biblical text, and she interrogates the intersection of class, 'race' and gender, and the implications of this Afrocentric Christian church space. However, while Abrams' congregation celebrates African histories and cultures and marries them with their Christology and ritual meeting space, Afroasiatic Diasporic Religions define themselves as distinct from Christianity. It is not the celebration and honouring of Afrocentric Christianity that is desired but the uncovering of a true religious identity that is not Christian.

In contrast to the Afrocentrizing of Presbyterian Euro-American Christianity, the adherents of the Moorish Science Temple have a unique claim to American identity. In *The Aliites* (2019), Spencer Dew explores the teachings of Noble Drew Ali, Leader of the Moorish Science Temple of America, and analyses their religious understanding of citizenship and their drive to both resist and reform the American legal system, moving towards realities reflecting their ideals for society. Noble Drew Ali claims that the Moors (which he identifies as Black people) are the original inhabitants of the Americas, even predating the various ethnic groups known as 'Indigenous Americans' or First Nation peoples. With this view, Ali leads a community of people through a legal project to establish citizenship that recognizes their historical habitation and presence in America and enables them to be seen no more as the descendants of enslaved Africans.

The Moorish Science Temple of America draws upon various religious concepts and symbols as points of knowledge but focuses on the religious symbols that they believe to be deliberately and secretly woven into the national symbolism of the United States of America as constructed by European invaders. Moorish, Egyptian, Judeo-Christian, freemason and Islamic themes are at the heart of this religious knowledge system and are used as the framework through which these Moors define their historical presence and religious sense of citizenship. This counternarrative drove Aliites towards survival and self-determination (Dew, 2019). Dew's work is significant because of his focus on the claims to citizenship that are often conceptualized abstractly within Black religious/theological God-talk. He also explores the nature and beliefs of the religious community from the perspective of the individuals who are a part of the Moorish Science Temple of America instead of centralizing their controversial leader, Noble Drew Ali. In this way, Dew hopes to look behind the charismatic figure and draw attention to

> [t]he mass of seemingly everyday people who are exceptional in their thoughts and practices, like those Washitaw contributing to

the 'nation-building' Sunday-night conference call, the Nuwaubian Yamassee posting their ideas in response to memorial videos of the movement's achievement at Tama-Re, or the Moorish American spending the evening crocheting a giant U.S. flag. (Dew, 2019, Introduction)

Dew opted for the term 'religious community' instead of 'cult', which he considered derogatory. The study explores the religious motivation of a Black religious community, which is to realize sacred citizenship in America and is thus embedded in concepts of law and 'race', religion and identity.

> Aliites exist in tenuous relation to state power. Citizenship, that status which serves as predication for any political negotiation within the state, does not exist without state recognition. While understanding the sovereignty of the people in a democracy to be real, Aliites also take it to be – like all forms of sovereignty short of the ultimate authority of true law – always situational, fleeting and dependent upon recognition by the sovereign state. (Dew, 2019, Chapter 3)

Dew considered the postcolonial efforts of the Aliites and their quest for recognition, in that the Aliites sought to work with the existing system rather than radicalize it and dismantle the oppressive European system. The Aliite religious conviction, as Dew describes it, seeks eventual reform towards what satisfied their religious perspectives, but designed a strategy that would acquire the type of recognition necessary to then participate in those reforms. Unlike the most separatist approaches, such as we see among the Rastafari, Nation of Islam, and the Hebrew Israelites, the Moorish Science Temple community makes a unique claim to the land of their oppressors and has been pursuing participation and reform, which is uncommon in the broader Black consciousness movement. However, they undeniably provide building blocks for identity formation that revise what have become widely acknowledged social and historical facts in America.

Conclusion

The objectives of this chapter were to explore the Black religious response to Colonial Christianity or the White Man's Religion, which I maintain is part of the European genealogy of Christianity and not the entirety of the religion's historicity and expression. The method of ethnography is a useful listening tool; it's an observational mechanism that requires the researcher or, in the reader's case, the listener to go among those they are trying to understand. The internet is full of reactive apologetic videos against the Black Bible Religions, but few stop to consider what the strength of their influence has to say about issues, gaps and disappointments in the mainstream. The first session of the Black Consciousness and Christian Faith programme explores claims made against Christianity as a religion of slavery, racism and white supremacy – a dangerous religion for Black people who had been victimized and Christianized in the name of Jesus.

Black Bible Religions make distinctions between European Christianity and the religion of the Bible. To make these distinctions, religions such as the (Black) Hebrew Israelites separate themselves from the mainstream, dissolving the supposed inclusive ethic of the mainstream and adapting their religious parameters. The key solutions discovered in this session were knowing the truth, obedience to God as described in the Scriptures, and participation in correcting and challenging the false religion. The broader conversations about Black Bible Religions and the teachings themselves highlighted functional, diasporic and formative religious elements that provided shape to how these new religious movements served the de-churched.

From a functional perspective, it is believed that engaging in these alternative religious spaces would help one to excel both spiritually and socially; an ethnoreligious framework provided a more fulfilling religious life that readily accommodated the experiences, needs and hopes of the Black community as discriminated or marginalized peoples in the West. The diasporic nature of the religions and the movements (both voluntary and involuntary) causes the adherents of Black Bible Religions to remember to look back to their ancient religions as sources of life and flourishing. This type of remembering positions Afroasiatic peoples, particularly the Hebrew/African/Asiatic ancestors of the de-churched, as gatekeepers to the origins of truth and spiritual enlightenment, the pathway to the Most High, to divinity.

The aspect of religion that deals with identity formation helps to provide roots for the de-churched, eliminating the need to default to the genealogy that takes precedence in seminary education, that which stretches from the Early Church to the split from the Roman Catholic Church at the time of the Reformation. Forming other pathways back to the inception of Christ's Church through Ethiopian, Coptic and/or West African genealogies resists the whitewashing of Christianity and gives the Black and African community a future blueprint and more centred role in the unfolding plan of God. A plan that includes the restoring of dignity to those who have been denied it, the flourishing of the diaspora and the return(s) of a 'not white' Messiah.

Out of Kemet? (transcript samples)

People who advocate the ancient Egyptian way of life ... the Bible stole from it ... is that when you compare the core of the teachings, the two different teachings, and you say way of life and the Christian way of life, they're like completely different. When you find a lot of West African or ancient Egyptian, it may be centred around some sort of ancestral worship or being a god yourself ... and the Christian doctrine is completely opposite, saying not to do those things. So when I personally, when I come across comparisons like that, that's when I say no – it becomes chalk and cheese, but I can sympathize when people say that you know how Christ has been presented to them from Sunday school, from pastors, what have you, has been very kind of sort of European focused to make them feel like they're not accepted, whereas with Egyptian way of life because you know they're historically Black they're more ... into that. (Participant A, 2017, Out of Kemet)

.... And also I find, um, that the African journey in the Bible, I try to make that connection and, uhh, from the [research] that I did, I did a tour of the British Museum and it's the separation of Egypt from Africa and it's like no, Egypt is in Africa, you know, and they were Black kings who were proved within Egypt; and I want myself to explore the Bible journey as it's told, and in a truthful way, because there's a lot more in the Bible, umm, regarding Africa itself and the whole continent, not just Egypt separately, because we shouldn't speak of Egypt separately to Africa, it's a country within Africa, you know, as with some of the other northern and southern African countries. So just to put that as well, oh, we're talking about Egypt; we're talking about Africa. So I think that's really important as Black people that we, you know, we're the first man Black people come across, and the more that we deepen our knowledge and understand, you know, hopefully we become less afraid just to say that openly, you know, because it's, you know, the evidence – the canons etc. But, you know, that is that – that's important, we should feel safe and just, you know, be happy to explore that in our history and the

critical role that we play in Christianity. (Participant EO, Out of Kemet, 2018)

From my experience, I feel like a lot of the reason why discussions like this or the reason why people have searched for these stories in the first place is because of the whitewashing in Christianity to start with, and people don't feel that they're included as Black people in Christianity. So every time we've been removed from the narrative and cause, like I grew up in Catholic Church, so I grew up White Jesus all over my home, and that's what I saw Jesus to be just because that's what I was told, I didn't know any better, but, umm, I can see where somebody growing up with an issue of that and not seeing themselves fitting into the story of Christianity, that they would maybe more entertain some of these stories what's out there. And me, I've looked into what's out there; I don't shy away from them, and I like to. I'm more concerned with the truth, even as Christians were taught that, even by Paul – that we should be noble in that sense that we should seek the truth in all things, and I think that it's just helped me to actually see the truth and where we as African are actually in the Scripture, which has actually strengthened my faith and what I believe, more so [than] pushing me away, because I've never in my life studied the Bible yet and seen the whiteness in the Bible. The more I've studied the Bible, the less White it seems to be; there's just no White narrative no matter where if you actually study it, there's no White narrative, there's no White narrative, um, so it's something that's probably pushed me to feel more inclusive of the Scriptures as a Black person, so I think that it's a good thing to not shy away or be afraid of it because it can work out in your favour as a Black people. (Participant DA, Out of Kemet, 2018)

3

Out of Kemet?

Yeah, I agree with most of what you said; we had a brief discussion last week saying that, um, the idea of infinite knowledge, especially without action, is largely a Western ideal in terms of wanting to conquer everything and to know everything, all of that, so ... but I think, umm, I don't think everyone wants all the knowledge before they go out in action. My favourite Bible verse is 'faith without works is dead', which you can do ... but I think it's the fact that a lot of the time the church rejects the questions or does not want to own up to answering is the off-putting part for some; it's not the fact that questions are being asked, but it's the kind of response that people sometimes get to the asked questions that then leaves that disparity and anger. (Participant MI, Out of Kemet, 2018)

Part of the decolonizing project of the Afrocentric movements has been to challenge the integrity of the Bible as we know it today. Afro-Kemetic teachings, such as those taught by the Holy Qubtic Church, suggest the Bible to be a plagiarized work of ancient Kemetic (Egyptian) religious writings. As a result, adherents to this belief system dismiss the credibility of the Bible as used by mainstream Christian and Roman Catholic churches as a way of subverting the historical whitewashing of ancient Black religious sophistication and the reappropriation of African esoteric spiritual truths. Those among the de-churched who are influenced by these challenges are struggling for true, correct and authoritative epistemological foundations to live out the right Bible religion.

The second session of the BCCF programme, which I named 'Out of Kemet?', unpacks mythologists' claims that the Jesus account in the New Testament is a repackaged revision of ancient Egyptian mythology – specifically the Horus myth. By comparing the accounts and reviewing the arguments for and against this claim and others of this ilk, as a group we considered why this claim matters on account of Black identity. Although my own research in preparation for the seminary style input for session two concluded that arguments lacked the cohesive material to support these claims, and even the basic paralleling of accounts did not fulfil the claims of the mythologists, there was, in fact, value in this type of work and the development of thought as seen within the neo-Kemetic movement. To move this forward in a way that captured the competing voices on this topic, I drew upon the account of Akhenaten, a Pharaoh in ancient Egypt who established monotheism during his reign. I chose this example because it can help to illuminate some shared spaces among differing world views: first, that of time and space, the interaction of Old Testament Hebrews with Egyptians – in Africa; second, the possibilities of the exchange/interaction of religious beliefs, monotheism or the development of the Ma'at and the Ten Commandments (thinking more specifically of Abraham, Joseph and Moses, who had all spent considerable time among Egyptian leaders in Egypt); and third, religious practice such as circumcision.

It must be said at this juncture that Black Bible Religions cannot take all the credit for the alternative or revised histories that have been put in place of the normative; in many cases, mythologies such as the Jesus//Horus parallel actually originate among European New Age and Occult communities (and mythicists such as D. M. Murdock), and, as mentioned before, often lack scholastic rigour. It is from the ethnographic 'people watching' perspective that we can draw some lessons for consideration because, quite apart from the outcome of the research, the phenomenon alone reveals gaps in mainstream Christian teaching and preaching, at least in recent decades. Why do Christians have to go to seminary or university, or be challenged by anti-Christian apologists, to discover the historical origins of their faith, the doctrinal teaching of the Church or the multicultural contributions to what we know now as Christianity? Why have so many people known the Scriptures but not known how they were canonized and verified as credible?

In the wider context of the whitewashing of the religion and the subjugation of Black peoples, the emancipatory project often requires pushing and prodding at all the systems, boundaries and norms, which include what is taught in seminary and on the pulpit. If Black people are to consider Christianity seriously and truly participate in 'faith seeking understanding', Black Bible Religions are an example of resisting the norms.

In this chapter, I explore elements of ADR's decolonization process with a focus on their use and interaction with the Bible and how the de-churched wrestle with the tensions of having faith while pursuing knowledge that might free them from the mainstream. I'll begin by providing an overview of how Participatory Action Research works applied to the fieldwork, as it provides useful lessons for building relationships with the de-churched. I move on to consider existing paradigms of decolonization with the aim of then illuminating the nuanced method presented by the de-churched and Black Bible Religions, which relies on more conventional or conservative theological methods for dismantling the appropriating powers such as *Sola Scriptura* and *Sensus Plenior*.

Participatory Action Research

I chose to combine my ethnographic research with Participatory Action Research (PAR) because of its democratic and critical approach to data collection and solution production. In 'The Entanglements of Ethnography and Participatory Action Research (PAR) in Educational Research in North America' (2019), Margaret Eisenhart considers how, although they are seemingly compatible and often conflated, the roots of these methodologies present weighty tensions that the researcher must consider seriously when bringing the two together. The issues of concern for this study are the power relationships and the development of the research plan. This section demonstrates how I used Participatory Action Research in my research field and my intention to privilege the participants' voices and religions as key actors in creating solutions.

Participatory Action Research is when the researcher enters a community space and works with the community to solve an issue through research and dialogue. This process requires democratic, safe spaces where all the participants can flourish and feel heard. In this space, everyone should feel equal, empowered, and valued within the group. What is unique about this approach is that it allows the participants to dictate the research direction and decide what outcome they would like to work toward. According to Peter Reason and Hilary Bradbury, action research is:

> A participatory, democratic process concerned with developing practical knowing in the pursuit of worthwhile human purposes, grounded in a participatory worldview which we believe is emerging at this historical moment. It seeks to bring together action and reflection, theory and practice, in participation with others, in the pursuit of practical solutions to issues of pressing concern to people, and more generally, the flourishing of individual persons and their communities. (Reason and Bradbury, 2001, p. 1)

This was a necessary part of the investigation, for to truly define the de-churched and the Black religious paradigm they considered ideal, I needed them to lead me to their interests rather than relying on my own assumptions, no matter how much of an insider I considered myself. Although I gave a seminary-style talk for each session, the main function of this was to provoke the participants to engage, respond and, if necessary, correct the researcher. Rather than assuming the authoritative stance they may experience with religious leadership (in both mainstream and Black Bible Religions), acting as a facilitator allows the participants to steer the conversation.

Participatory Action Research creates a safe space that aims to be inclusive of multiple voices – in the case of this study, religious and political voices concerning identity. 'The respect action researchers have for the complexity of local situations and for the knowledge people gain in the process of everyday life makes it impossible for us to ignore what the "people" think and want' (Brydon-Miller et al., 2015, p. 25). This is the type of data I committed myself to collecting: the ideals and ideologies that cause someone to reject the mainstream Church or to take offence at it. Discussing what people want rather than what they know, have learned or researched provided better insights into what they wanted and their disappointment with the mainstream Church. Allowing people to share their stories would serve as the foundation for solution-making and help to build and solidify a sense of camaraderie between the facilitator and each participant, and among the participants as well.

Relationships are essential in PAR; the researcher facilitates the sessions and engages directly with the participants rather than observing from the sidelines. This method benefits from reflections of the researcher, who can describe atmospheres, tensions and moments of group consciousness that might not be so easy to decipher or conjure up with one-on-one interviews, written testimonies and quantitative data.

Those undertaking Participation Action Research take seriously the issues affecting the community they are working with. Brydon-Miller et al. suggest that '[a] key value shared by action researchers, then, is this abiding respect for people's knowledge and for their ability to understand and address the issues confronting them and their communities' (Brydon-Miller, 2015, p. 14). Ultimately, PAR seeks to let the participants speak for themselves and empower them to move toward a solution for their circumstances.

Decolonization

Frantz Fanon (1925–61), a Caribbean psychiatrist, spoke much of decolonization regarding nationhood and the emancipation of occupied states. However, his work was produced in ways that often translated to more abstract sites of occupation, such as religious epistemology, and thus it was a valuable frame for decolonization in this study. In *The Wretched of The Earth* (1961), he speaks of decolonization in national terms, which mirrors nationalist stances present in Afroasiatic diasporic religions (more on this in Chapter 4).

> National Liberation, national renaissance, the restoration of nationhood to the people, commonwealth: whatever may be the headings used or the new formulas introduced, decolonization is always a violent phenomenon ... decolonization is quite simply the replacing of a certain 'species' of men by another 'species' of men. (Fanon, 1961, p. 35)

It is important to emphasize the notion of recovery and return when thinking of the ideals of the de-churched and those belonging to Afroasiatic diasporic religions; however, Fanon's decolonization also considers the inevitable changes during both the colonization and decolonization processes. While recovery and return are ideals, how we conceptualize the de-churched phenomenon must account for how the diasporic journey has brought about change and activity towards emancipation, negotiated in contemporary contexts and not the context in which the Bible was written and in which the precolonial Afroasiatic communities existed.

> Decolonization never takes place unnoticed, for it influences individuals and modifies them fundamentally ... It brings a natural rhythm into existence, introduced by new men, and with it, a new language and new humanity. Decolonization is the veritable creation of new men. (Fanon, 1961, p. 36)

Fanon talks about decolonization as an inevitably violent struggle between the colonizer and the colonized, a process that dismantles the systems that colonizers have put in place to organize their new property profitably. Fanon's text is focused on the political struggle of colonized nations, but as is evident in the masses of literature inspired by this seminal work, his decolonization treatise can be applied to various aspects of social life, including religion.

Efforts to decolonize theology are concerned with the colonial values and premises that have underpinned the interpretation of Scriptures and the structures of the organized European Church, in which Black people or the 'other' have little power, participation or presence. Fanon says:

> In the colonial context, the settler only ends his work of breaking in the native when the latter admits loudly and intelligibly the supremacy of the white man's values. In the period of decolonization, the colonized masses mock at these very values, insult them, and vomit them up. (Fanon, 1961, p. 44)

ADR's controversial teaching displays the type of rejection and distaste that Fanon alludes to here, demonstrating how intentional they are about the decolonization process. The distinct separation that ADR religions make, shown in terms such as 'the White Man's Religion', is evidence of this raw and unwavering rejection.

Decolonization, in more academic spheres, is concerned with dismantling the power of White Supremacy, White hegemony, patriarchy and other named modes of oppression by designing ways in which the power can be equally disseminated among those who are considered the victims and the oppressed under the powers of colonialism and neo-colonialism. Robert Beckford, in *Documentary as Exorcism: Resisting the Bewitchment of Colonial Christianity* (2014), presents a compelling argument for 'exorcism' in the Gospel of Mark (1.25–28, 34; 4.39, 5.1–10) to be seen as an anti-colonial sentiment:

> As part of the emancipatory framework, these postcolonial readings of Jesus' exorcisms define the meaning of cast out. To cast out is to remove an occupying or harassing malevolent spiritual force from the physical body and also social world. (Beckford, 2014, p. 70)

In this text, Beckford's focus is on the bewitchment of Black-British Pentecostalism, defining witchcraft as a structural evil which is ultimately understood as Colonial Christianity, but this can also be translated for Black Religion as it has been outlined for this study. While holding a high view of ancient Scripture, Afroasiatic Diasporic Religions question its current form and the versions produced by European scholarship. ADR falls out of favour with current decolonial trends in mainstream theology because of its exclusive nature; decolonization is typically such that all peoples are welcome to participate in God talk. Bo Sanders and Randy Woodley in *Decolonising Evangelicalism* say:

> Applying critical theory (such as decolonization) has an amazing capacity to level the playing field and expose what have been historical privileges and examined advantages. Each school of thought and tradition comes to the arena and puts its best foot forward. It explains its priorities, its goals, its big question and major concern, each one

gets to frame its project with its own categories, vocabulary and concepts. This way, no one has a home-field advantage (to use a sports analogy). Then the examination begins. The question then becomes, what is your relationship to the powers and authorities? (Sanders and Woodley, 2020, Chapter 2)

However, the ADR nuance of 'chosenness' or 'original people' suggests a decolonization that consists of removing the captors and regaining control over one's cultural assets. This exclusive quest presents questions about ADR's epistemological challenge: much of what we see in academic decolonization discourse makes assumptions about what qualifies as the 'colonial' or 'neo' that Afroasiatic diasporic religions and those they influence on the fringes seem to contest. For example, justice through the decolonization process is not realized through sharing power equally among communities but by regaining power as those chosen by God; as noted by Fanon earlier, it replaces one 'species' of men by another (Fanon, 1961, p. 35). Herein lies the nuance of Black Bible Religions and their process of decolonization.

Lewis Gordon, an Africana philosopher, has this to say about colonialism in *Freedom, Justice and Decolonisation* (2021):

That which aims at the conquest of all reality, colonialism becomes a system whose goal is not only conquest but also the offering of the domination of life and the assertion of itself as ontological and the primacy of ontology. Thus knowledge is, as nearly all decolonial theorists have argued, implicated here in the form of epistemic colonization. (Gordon, 2021, Chapter 3)

Gordon and Jane Anna Gordon, in *Not Only the Master's Tools* (2006), in response to Audre Lorde's sentiment, 'The Master's tools will never dismantle the master's house', talk about the method of dismantling. They posit that a more beneficial approach is to focus efforts not on dismantling but instead on creating new spaces, in the same way that oppressed people built houses of their own: 'It is our view that the proper response is to follow their lead, transcending rather than dismantling Western ideas through building our own houses of thought' (Gordon and Gordon, 2006, Introduction). This captures, in part, the ADR project, but with nuance – ADR decolonization essentially comprises rebuilding their homes and reclaiming their tools. The image of building one's own house, study, philosophy or religion resonates with how Lewis Gordon, reflecting on Fanon's ideas, also interrogates theorists' struggles when engaging with morality and ethics related to power and authority. Morals must depend on a set of rules, but this presents the conundrum of having to submit to the rules, set, for example, by a European epistemology, to realize new or improved ethical norms:

> Reflection radicalizes the problem. If they attempt to establish an ethical relationship, they must do so by the rules (morals) of a society premised in their exclusion. Thus, if they attempt to enter the ethical sphere of that society, the already included people treat the excluded ones as *violating the ethical space by virtue of doing the same to the avowedly moral rules.* Fanon's name for this was controversial. He called it 'violence'. (Gordon, 2021, Chapter 3)

Gordon says that morality creates the inclusion–exclusion paradigm by its very nature. Therefore, Black people participating in the European colonial moral space are considered violent because they are the 'excluded' operating (or appearing, as he puts it) in the space of the 'included'. The presence of ADRs presents the same difficulties because one could argue that they purport to offer a strictly religious, moral epistemology for Black people. Nevertheless, it appears to have structures similar to those we see in European colonial epistemological structures. It has already been noted that the resulting critique is often that these religions are colonially minded after centuries of subjugation to modernist, conservative reading conventions. However, because ADR religions are on a recovery project rather than a progressive or academically radical one, considering a 'strict moral code' as colonial (as it pertains to European colonialism) is an error. I will return to this point later in the book. The nuance of 'chosenness' provides the internal or exclusive remedy – much to the dissatisfaction of progressive decolonial theorists and also of Christians around the world who may not fit the ethnocentric criteria for chosenness.

Decolonization then, so far as it concerns Afroasiatic diasporic religions, is not the type considered in progressive postcolonial scholarship: a space of inclusion – sharing power and resources with intentions to embrace the contributions of various epistemologies. Instead, it is akin to what Fanon describes, a violent recovery of epistemological and national assets (the Bible and Bible Religion) from European colonial powers. Perhaps with the exception of the Holy Qubtic Church, Black Bible Religions do not concede to the notion of pluriversality or, as Walter Mignolo articulates, 'truth with parentheses' (Mignolo, 2021).

> Some Black bible-reading religions seek to de-colonize Christianity or mainstream Bible religion by rejecting a colonial version and rediscov-

ering the most accurate and authentic Bible religion. In this sense, they aim to detach (visualize removing someone's hand from an object with force) the grip of colonialism from God talk, hermeneutics, education, ritual, and day-to-day living – to reveal what is under the big white hand. (Louis in Louis and Goodliff, 2023)

In this sense, Colonial Christianity is replaced with Afroasiatic diasporic religion as more authentic, authoritative and appropriate for Black peoples.

Out of order: The final authority

Unlike the type of decolonization that I have discussed earlier, which seeks, in part, to redistribute power through contextualization, the emphasis among the de-churched is to return to the realization that the religious power lies with the origins of Black people and their sacred writings (which include the Bible), not in the European interpretation of plagiarized documents. The Afroasiatic diasporic religions seek to discover and provide a corrected translation of the biblical Scriptures through ritual, historical re-examination and cross-referencing with other texts such as the Apocrypha, using their lived experience as a hermeneutic. While the latter method has liberationist undertones, there is an amalgamation of interdependent approaches at play, where research and revelation are held in tension. Although diverse in doctrine and interpretation, among each of the representative religions is a preservation of the life, ministry, death and return of Christ. Much like mainstream Christianity, most of their teachings are fashioned and shaped around the life of Christ (Farrakhan, 2002): for the Nation of Islam, for example, this seems to be a strategy for engaging Christian listeners as Jesus, to them, was a great teacher but not Allah. In this sense, although their resulting interpretations do not meet the standards of Christian orthodoxy, there are two connecting points within the Protestant tradition that may help us to understand how Scripture is being used methodologically – *Sola Scriptura* and *Sensus Plenior*.

Sola Scriptura was a key element of the Protestant Reformation in the sixteenth century. It 'denotes the conviction that scripture is the one and only criterion for Christian faith and living, and beliefs and practices are true and truthfully Christian if and only if they correspond to the witness of the whole of scripture' (Maarteen Wisse in Burger et al., 2018, p. 20). However, this is not the stance of all Protestants – variations have developed over time, such as *Prima Scriptura*, the Methodist and Anglican approach, which says it is the primary authority but is complemented by experience, reason and tradition as secondary authorities. Martin Luther, John Calvin and others, in their liberatory actions against the centralized religious authority of the Roman Catholic Church, created an added layer of complexity to the hermeneutical process when bringing the power of interpretation to all people led by the Holy Spirit (in line with the Protestant notion of the priesthood of all believers). We see similar attitudes towards emancipation among the de-churched. The Holy Qubtic Church provides a version of the Bible that they claim to be the original ancient African biblical texts that predate Christianity, upon which the present European Christianity has built a foundation. KaHun Anju Sa ra, High Priest of a community in Barbados, says:

> You see, for too long, we as a people have been feeding off of the watered-down, bleached-out versions of what is being called the scriptures today. Whether it was the Alexandrian Greek orthodox scriptures, whether it was Constantinian Greco-Roman orthodox Scripture, whether it was the King James anglicized scriptures, we have been feeding off the watered-down bleached-out misinformed, misinterpreted version for so long that we as a people have emulated these scriptures by being out of place, being watered down, and even bleach ourselves from time to time – amun? (KaHun: Anju Sa Ra, 2016, YouTube)

The Original Books of the Bible are taught as a religious manual that meets the specific needs of African peoples:

> As a teaching Church, we teach the words of The Most High with simplicity and understanding, using the proper translations from the original languages. This is done in the hopes that, once one has gained a full comprehension of what the scriptures are actually saying, the knowledge can then be applied to our everyday lives in a practical and effective manner. (https://www.holyqubticchurch.com/)

Standing alone among the Afroasiatic diasporic religions referred to in this study, the HQC is the only religion that does not emphasize eschatological events as a primary focus; for them, uncovering the most authentic translation of Scripture is to have a guide for everyday living, as opposed to making sense of the Black experience and the return of the Messiah or God's judgement on Babylon.

Unlike the Roman Catholic authority, which centralized truth claims and biblical interpretation, the reformers could all participate in the interpretation process of the Holy Scriptures – the sole authority on salvation and spiritual life so long as it was in the form of literalist or plain Bible reading. This requirement led to various competing interpretations and denominational factions, and we are no closer to establishing universal truths for all believers, even under the premise that Scripture interprets itself (*sacra scriptura sui ipsius interpres*). On the other hand, this theological requirement also demonstrates a sense of democracy that, in theory, welcomes the contribution and participation of all believers. Brad S. Gregory, in *The Unintended Reformation: How a Religious Reformation Secularized Society* (2012), suggests a historical view which interprets commitment to *Sola Scriptura* as anarchistic.

> From the very outset of the Reformation, the shared commitment to *sola scriptura* entailed a hermeneutical heterogeneity that proved doctrinally contentious, socially divisive, and sometimes (in the German Peasants' War, the Anabaptist Kingdom of Munster, and the English Revolution) politically subversive. (Gregory, 2012, p. 92)

Sympathizers of *Sola Scriptura* argue that their religious perspective cannot be sufficiently interpreted using humanist philosophical methods and perspectives.

Historically, this has resulted in a deliberate disengagement with progressive theological discourses and hermeneutical processes, which reflects the conservative aversion to radical philosophical trajectories. Interestingly, Gregory's analysis is that adherence to *Sola Scriptura* is described as uncharacteristic of conservatism – radical. However, Keith A. Mathison, in *The Shape of Sola Scriptura*, argues that this corrective hermeneutical measure is part of a historical tradition that leads back to the early church fathers and a small selection of creeds that were a result of early church councils. He suggests that in the Church's formative years, '[t]radition was simply the body of doctrine committed to the church by Christ and His Apostles whether through written or oral revelation' (Mathison, 2001, p. 275). Hence, despite the internal conflicts, the Reformation and its subsequent position on Scripture can be seen as a *liberation* specifically from the Roman tradition and power – not the type of radicalism that seeks to create an entirely new system having dismantled the old.

As a hermeneutical premise in evangelicalism, *Sola Scriptura* focuses on where to place religious authority which acts as a precursor to establishing fixed doctrine and religious truths. The reports made by the Evangelical Alliance Commission on Unity and Truth among Evangelicals (ACUTE) make explicit that the evangelical theological approach seeks answers to issues from within Scripture:

> [T]he concept of 'evangelical theology' thus refers to method as much as conclusions, a method which is governed by the question: 'what do the scriptures say?' Such an emphasis helps evangelicals to live within a diversity of opinion on a range of theological issues which are not perceived as threatening the fundamentals of Christian faith, since they can justify widely differing views on baptism, for example, as equally motivated by a concern to be faithful to the teaching of Scripture. (Hillborn, 2001, p. 12)

Wisse in Burger, 2018, Chapter 2 argues that an objective approach to Scripture, or the objectivity of *Sola Scriptura*, which some argue is subject to divine revelation, is dishonest about the part that the interpreter plays in its interpretation and the humanity of the authors of the Scriptures. The contention that many scholars have with plain readings and a commitment to *Sola Scriptura* is that those who interpret and teach accordingly are relieved from the duty of qualifying their interpretation. The in-house factions themselves act as a process of testing and judging interpretations but, in theory, do not welcome outsiders' contributions. In this sense, then, fundamentalist, literalist interpreters who adhere to *Sola Scriptura* monopolize a power over interpretation that is hard to engage with and challenge.

Israel United in Christ (IUIC), a (Black) Hebrew Israelite Camp, believes that the Bible is exclusively for Israel, of which they are descendants. An IUIC elder teaching a brief history of Israel says, 'The Bible is only for us and written to us' (IUIC: A brief story of Israel, 2020, YouTube). He goes on to verify his assertion by quoting Psalm 147.19–20:

> He sheweth his word unto Jacob, his statutes and his judgments unto Israel. He hath not dealt so with any nation: and as for his judgments, they have not known them. Praise ye the LORD. (KJV)

It is common among many (Black) Hebrew Israelite groups to teach the exclusivity of the biblical texts; their adherence to the Mosaic Laws most notably marks their nation-building process. The Bible is the major asset in BHI communities; it is the sole reference in their teaching and public preaching. Of all the Afroasiatic religions in this study, the BHIs seem to take the Bible – the King James 1611 translation – most seriously and literally. Apocryphal books are also included in many (Black) Hebrew Israelite biblical canons, which refer to them as historical and prophetic in function. The IUIC website describes biblical teachings as a remedy for the sick:

Blacks and Hispanics must learn the truth that they are the Biblical 12 tribes of the Nation of Israel. Disobedience to God's laws has been the root of all our troubles. Blacks and Hispanics everywhere suffer the same racial, social, economic problems worldwide. Voting has not helped us, Christian churches have failed us. It's time for a change. In these last days, we must give the Bible's medicine to sick people, then and only then will things begin to change. (https://israelunite.org/ 2020)

Part of the awakening process and returning to this Nation of Israel is to commit oneself wholly to God's laws. There are various interpretations among the camps about what constitutes God's laws across the Old and New Testaments. These are particularly influenced by one's Christology – some BHI's do not believe Jesus to be God incarnate; however, the common aspiration is obedience. Obedience is what BHIs teach to be the key to emancipation from the judgement of God – slavery, subjugation and oppression over the last 400 years.

Despite the challenges of its internal workings and relational tensions with those who do not adhere to *Sola Scriptura*, what it does accomplish is a sense of religiosity, which some may consider medieval and others traditional in the apostolic sense. This preservation of religiosity, the revelation of the Word and Spirit, is what is more difficult to see in modern and postmodern theological methods. Douglas A. Oss, in 'Canon as context: The function of sensus plenior in evangelical hermeneutics', says:

> Evangelicals must reject the concept that the needs of the modern man determine the meaning of the text and thus also its application. At the same time it must be acknowledged that we are 'trapped' within our historical situation and there is no escape. So in one sense, sharing in the meaning of a text by way of application cannot avoid historical conditioning. Yet in the fusion of the biblical and modern 'horizons,' it is the modern horizon that must be subject to refinement, not the horizon of the text. Authority resides in the text not with the interpreter. (Oss, 1988, p. 119)

While the interpretation process undergirded by *Sola Scriptura* is imperfect because the interpreters are imperfect, it is the premise that is valuable to the religious reading – the text is the sole authority on matters of Christian faith despite the condition of the interpreter.

> *When I ask certain questions, the Church is like, 'Oh, you're not meant to ask those questions', and I think that's where the Church fails 'cause Jesus always answered questions, even whether people were tryna trap him or not, and I think that as a church we shouldn't be embarrassed to say we don't know. Because there's some things that the Church just doesn't know, the Bible just doesn't say: the Bible doesn't say how old Adam and Eve were, the Bible doesn't say how many female siblings they had and how did Cain get a wife, the Bible just doesn't say a thing, and I think we try and make excuses and do what have you and it causes frustration in people, Black people for the sake of this discussion, and they leave the faith.* (Participant A, 2017, Out of Kemet)

Participant A highlights an institutional dialectical inconsistency with Scripture; he rightly asserts that on various occasions in the New Testament Jesus answered the questions of his followers and opposers, and so to be subject to a tradition that is subject to the authority of Scripture should mean that embracing Jesus' methods of teaching should be present among his believers. As explained earlier in the chapter, the issue lies with the churches' selectivity. Because the topic of ethnicity and 'race' is topical in the political landscape, it can be rejected alongside the identity politics and liberal political philosophies that offend a core theological 'colourblindness'. Many apologetic programmes have excelled and invested in debating mainstream science and alternative religions. However, they have only recently come to attend, in hostility, to the in-house issue of 'race' and the alternative apologetic arguments provided by these Afroasiatic diasporic religions that have come out from under the evangelical influence.

Out of line: A single message

Another hermeneutical premise found within conservative evangelicalism is *Sensus Plenior*, which has been complementary to the development of systematic theology. Oss asserts that *Sensus Plenior* is necessary for 'proper hermeneutical methodology' beyond the limits of 'a rigid grammatical-historical exegesis' (Oss, 1988, p. 106):

> *Sensus Plenior*, here defined, refers to the recognition of the canon of Scripture as a single and unified literary work. Because it is one book, no part of the book can be properly understood apart from the whole. Therefore, reflection on the whole of Scripture becomes a vital and central aspect in the hermeneutical process. And one's understanding

of a passage will be deeper and clearer as the result of being seen in the light of the whole. This may include levels of meaning that were not part of the conscious intention of the human author, but which are included in the expressed meaning of the publicly accessible text and which are part of the canonical text. (Oss, 1988, p. 106)

This premise is also complementary to *Sola Scriptura* because fuller meanings of the text, including prophetic meanings,[1] can be uncovered by searching the Scriptures, not dependent on outside sources. *Sensus Plenior* functions to confirm an initial interpretation of a passage by seeing how it holds up alongside the rest of the biblical texts, which function as a divine and integrated message.

The foundational premise for *Sensus Plenior*, according to Oss, is as follows:

- God is the author of Scripture and he himself is the ultimate epistemological context for understanding the meaning of Scripture.
- Only the Bible in its canonical form is the normative and authoritative source of theological data.
- The nature of progressive revelation is such that the meaning of the Scriptures became deeper and clearer as the literary corpus of the canon increased.
- The canon has an organic unit that is demonstrated in its harmony of doctrine, perspective, and faith. (Oss, 1988, pp. 111–12)

From a de-churched perspective, there remain in the online debating spheres concerns about the normalized Protestant canon and the rejecting of deuterocanonical books (Tobit, Judith, Baruch, Ecclesiasticus, Wisdom, First and Second Maccabees) and also other apocryphal books such as the *Book of Enoch* found within the Ethiopian Orthodox Canon. Despite this, Black Bible Religions read the biblical Scriptures as a single text, regarding each book and letter (those they accept) as confirming the others and as a record of their origins, nation-building, judgement and redemption. The Rastafari believe that the Bible tells their story in that of the Israelites captured and enslaved because of their disobedience and idolatry. Their interpretation is that their historical experiences directly correlate to the biblical account of the Israelites and are thus one and the same story. For example, the Rastafari liken white skin to the affliction of leprosy, as seen in the biblical accounts of Moses and Miriam, where they are struck with leprosy, and their skins, on separate occasions, become white (William David Spencer in Murrell et al., 1998, p. 328). In the first instance, Rastafari would use this reinterpretation to support the idea that the biblical characters were Black (having dark skin); but, further to this, some would perpetuate the idea that white skin is a curse or a punishment. In this way, they also turn the curse of Ham, for example, on its head so that whiteness becomes the curse rather than blackness. Many 'Rastafarians believe they were the very Israelites depicted in the Bible' (Spencer in Murrell et al., 1998, Chapter 19).

Sensus Plenior is not primarily concerned about the presupposition and participation of the human author because it considers the Scriptures to be of divine authorship. In this case, one must assume that, under the sovereignty of God, the Scriptures confirm and affirm one another, and that, with the support of the necessary scholarship, one can uncover the more profound meaning beyond their face value. It requires a belief that God has orchestrated every aspect of the coming together of the canon, from inspiration to in-text interpretation and its historical canonization. Raymond E. Brown, in *The Sensus Plenior of Sacred Scripture*, defines it as such:

> The *Sensus Plenior* is that additional, deeper meaning, intended by God but not clearly intended by the human author, which is seen to exist in the words of a biblical text (or group of texts, or even a whole book) when they are studied in the light of further revelation or development in the understanding of revelation. (Brown, 2008, p. 92)

The premise of *Sensus Plenior* is important in conservative evangelicalism because it functions as a tool to identify Messianic prophecies throughout the Old Testament. Evangelicalism centres itself around the life, ministry, death and resurrection of Christ – particularly in the substitutionary atonement which, they would claim, Old Testament scriptures foretell. Statements such as, 'The new is in the old concealed; the old is in the new revealed,' by the fourth-century African theologian St Augustine of Hippo, are generally accepted by evangelical teachers such as R. C. Sproul to confirm that this line of theological inquiry was part of early Christian thinking and interpretation and thus a trustworthy line of hermeneutical inquiry (Sproul, 2005, www.ligonier.org). However, *Sensus Plenior* has also been a point of contention in the development of evangelical hermeneutics, which had been dominated by the grammatical-historical method (what the author meant in consideration of his historical context). While scholars who adhered to this method were keen to identify the single meaning of the text, *Sensus Plenior* creates the space for 'fuller' or 'deeper' meanings to the text. This undermines the role of the Scripture's historical context, and the author energizes the hermeneutical process with a mysterious spiritual dimension that can also be seen in the *Sola Scriptura* concept with its necessary engagement with the Holy Spirit. However, Oss argues that *Sensus Plenior* does not need to undermine the single meaning if one re-evaluates the narrow scientific approach.

> Therefore, while maintaining the view that meaning in texts does have parameters beyond which the exegete cannot go, it is also necessary to postulate that meaning in texts is multi-dimensional. The 'single meaning' in a text refers to its unity of meaning, with all of its dimensions being connected to the results of grammatical-historical exegesis. (Oss, 1988, p. 115)

Oss suggests that the grammatical-historical method can work well with the *Sensus Plenior* premise as the deeper meanings would bring depth to the initial exegetical interpretation and not contradict its meaning.

The Nation of Islam's approach to the Bible suggests that there are also hidden meanings in the text, which are remedied by divine revelation. The NOI attempts to sever its links with Christianity but maintains ties to the Bible or Hebrew Scriptures and acknowledges Jesus as a central religious figure, consistent with mainstream Islam (Curtis, 2009). Elijah Muhammad taught that the Bible (the collection of books as a whole), although not holy as the Qur'an is holy, contains truths and prophecies that speak to the 'so-called-negro' experience. He teaches that the Bible has been corrupted and misunderstood to 'blind the black man' (Muhammad, 1973, p. 94). Partial severance is a common trend among these Afroasiatic diasporic religions; much of their biblical teaching deals suspiciously with the hidden truths that have been made obscure by the reinterpretation and tampering of the European Christian Church. In the case of the NOI, the correct interpretation had been divinely received by the late prophet and leader Elijah Muhammad. He says: 'The Bible means good if you can rightly understand it. My interpretation of it is given to me from the Lord of the Worlds' (Muhammad, 1973, p. 88).

Muhammad acknowledged the symbolic integrity of the New Testament insofar as it speaks specifically about Black people and their present state:

> The New Testament and Holy Qur-an's teaching of a resurrection of the dead can't mean the people who have died physically and returned to the earth, but rather a mental resurrection of us, the black Nation, who are mentally dead to the knowledge of truth; the truth of self,

God and the arch-enemy of God and his people. (Elijah Muhammad, 1973, p. 967)

This interpretation is consistent with the notion of 'woke' that I have presented in the first chapter, a religious awakening that leads to action and redemption. In this way, the Bible acts as a mobilizing force, a catalyst towards rediscovering truth and strengthening the 'Black nation' to realize its divine purpose on earth.

Out of step: Contextualizing

Another methodology where we can see points of convergence is in the theological application of postcolonialism and how it concerns itself with the implications and legacies of colonialism among the 'other' – in the British context, the Black and Brown peoples who are descendants of the enslaved and colonized. Applying this approach to biblical hermeneutics means that it is most necessary to engage with the historical context in which conservative evangelicalism was birthed and interrogate the movement as a theological arm of the European colonial empire. Furthermore, postcolonial biblicism subverts the authority of this Protestant movement with alternative hermeneutical methods that illuminate dominant powers at work within the interpretation and the text itself. Conservative evangelicalism comes under interrogation not simply because it was birthed during the time of European global dominance but because, for one, European conservatism seeks to protect and preserve European tradition and institutions (which included the aristocracy and the Church); and, two, evangelicalism resists the influence of contemporary philosophical frameworks (often non-European) in their hermeneutical processes – liberatory or not. From a postcolonial point of view, what this has meant is that the experiences of the marginalized, oppressed and enslaved have been ignored at best and intentionally terrorized at worst due to these social, religious and political positions. As evangelicalism progressed and has come to the fore of Western Christianity, it is considered complicit in dominating the third world and its diasporas. Although one could argue that the principles of evangelicalism are complementary to the participation of all believers, including non-Europeans, its hermeneutical principles in practice have not been perceived as inclusive of alternative readings and perspectives. Any claim to read Scripture objectively (see *Objectivity in Biblical Interpretation* by Thomas Howe (2015)) and interpret universal meanings is slow to acknowledge the interpreter's preconceptions as contextually biased. Sanders and Woodley, in *Decolonizing Evangelicalism*, say:

> Western Christianity's preoccupation with its own extrinsically categorical worldview within a systemic binary leaves little for other possibilities. Postcolonial theologies, then, should recognize and repudiate the histories of oppression that disregarded the rights of the others and often failed to recognize the ubiquitous theologically influenced systems that uphold colonialism's theological grip. (Sanders and Woodley, 2020, Chapter 1)

Anthony Reddie suggests that ongoing participation with conservative-inspired church traditions has affected the ability of Black Christians to flourish holistically:

> The malaise that afflicts Black Christians in Britain can be described as 'Religio-cultural-theological-dissonance'. In using this term, I am pointing to a historic phenomenon where Black Christians have imbibed the blandishments of imperial mission Christianity to such an extent that the operative basis of their Christian faith proceeds as a form of negated Blackness or even anti-blackness. (Reddie, 2012, p. 64)

The de-churched phenomenon can help one see evangelicalism as a de-churching movement, not pulling away from belief in God, Christ or the Bible but from the domination of the institutional Church and mainstream scholarship. The preservation–liberation framing translates well for the evangelical context on several counts: first, the rediscovering of the authority of Scripture as foundational to Bible religion; second, a severance from the colonial Church (although many argue it is not a complete severance, I am speaking of its early intentions); third, internal diversity that is framed by central tenets and internal gatekeeping (within the ADR frame, diverse perspectives and internal debates are a form of gatekeeping); fourth, the preservation of ancient church creeds; and fifth, a commitment to activism.

The phenomenon can also perhaps shed light on an alternative interpretation of the Black Church's commitment to conservative religiosity. Seen through the preservation–liberation lens and the examples of the ADR, perhaps conservative evangelicalism is appealing to Black churches because it is both liberative and preservationist at its core. Although one cannot negate the colourblind theology that seems rife in conservative evangelicalism, the five points of convergence with the

ADR and de-churched phenomenon suggest the possibility of an Evangelical Theology of Black Liberation.

Conclusion

The Out of Kemet? session is particularly provocative because it considers claims that are aimed at the foundations of the Christian religion and its historical validity. Beyond its doctrinal claims, many in the Black Conscious Community are turning towards the revised history that suggests Europeans have stolen ancient African esoteric principles and given them white face. This type of attack against the mainstream, in effort and concept, can be paralleled with the efforts of dismantling and decolonization, and so I have drawn out from the de-churched and the teaching of Black Bible Religions a nuanced approach to decolonization. This approach does not seek to dismantle for the purpose of redistributing but to reclaim and replace what is considered a lie with what is true, right and perceived as original. It has all the favour of Fanon's imagery of a violent exchange between victim and perpetrator with a single victor – in this case, the victim.

The teachings of Black Bible Religions and the expectations of the de-churched show us that, in approach, they have a high view of Scripture; so I juxtaposed these notions with the conversative reading conventions *Sola Scriptura* and *Sensus Plenior*. Looking to the Scriptures as authoritative over not only religious practice but also the historical narrative of Black people, the de-churched are open to teachings that claim to reveal the hidden and deeper meanings of the Bible text, the untainted Scriptures revealed to chosen prophets but obscure to the mainstream whom the Scriptures exclude. In this chapter, we begin to see that Black Bible Religions are caught in a tension between the reading and knowing conventions often found among the evangelical conservative schools of thought and the necessary contextualizing mechanisms displayed in postcolonial theology.

Note

1 Here I'm talking specifically about foresight as opposed to the socially critical.

The Black Face of the Early Church (transcript samples)

I think one of the things we've got to understand is the power of religion. I think we see it as just a church ting, but it's almost something that's in the atmosphere, in our perception, in our culture, and its Christianity is deeply bound up with the notion of hierarchy, a racial hierarchy; it's almost just assumed as we don't often recognize it but it's deeply embedded in our past consciousness, and not just in Black subconsciousness but in White subconsciousness as well, that this – at the top of the racial ladder sits a White God. And actually, to deconstruct that, to get that out of your head, is liberating; it's absolutely liberating. It gives us permission to challenge the very way our social order has been constructed. It has been constructed with this underlying assumption. And every now and again, it rears its ugly head. How many people have seen the Black Panther movie? So I was having a conversation with someone, we're talking about it, and I was saying that one of the things it does – this projection of Wakanda, although it's this Afro-futurist view, this technologically advanced society, that actually is reaching back into history into this idea that actually there were these great historic African kingdoms. It's not something that just sci-fi, it's actually rooted in history. And the person I was talking to was like 'oh what African – name an African kingdom' like they didn't exist, and I was really shocked – a White friend of mine, who I knew quite well, but this dismissal of any notion that there was these great historical African histories that they've been written out of. So people's view of African and Blackness is, you know, receiving aid, you know ... (Participant/Pastor CAW, The Black Face of the Early Church, 2018)

I was eight. I got sent back home, so I went to live in the Caribbean. So seeing the difference between me and other friends growing up in Dominica at my age, being that for me I had all the Black stuff, the latter part of primary school, all my high school I learned all about the Caribbean, I learned Black history, I learned everything. I didn't learn about

Shakespeare and Queen Elizabeth, I never heard them things, so my perspective to a lot of people my age is a lot different. When I see younger Black people now, I find the struggle for identity is kinda similar to the Americans, in the sense that Americans obviously came from Africa at some time but as the generations go by they're losing the history, they're losing knowing where they come from. There's so many people that they've never been back to their country in Africa, never been to the Caribbean. Don't know anything about Jamaica, St. Lucia, wherever they're from, Nigeria. Don't know the language, don't know how to cook the food, they just lose all their culture, and their kids are gonna be worse off because they're not going to their countries on holiday, they're going to Spain and all these kind of places. (Participant D, The Black Face of the Early Church, 2018)

Participant/Pastor CAW: And I think one of the things that, umm, traditional Christianity has done is made us suspicious and mistrustful of our own heritage, so that is the 'other'. This is the established truth, and everything else is to be other, to be wary of, whether that's African spirituality, African traditions, or, ummm, so we're wary of it. So there's no need to have fear, it's worthy of the investigation, umm, you know, it's not something you're gonna suddenly find yourself stepping into a room full of demons and all sorts.
Participant HB: Yeah, a lot of it's Black culture, so I'm open, completely open with it – it's just a lot of the things that they practise. I asked my mum the other day about women wearing trousers; I was like 'Mum, if I wear trousers, am I going to hell?' She's like 'Yes', you know, things like that, and I'm just like, it's one of those tin-head moments, you're just like 'what?' So I don't know what cross of information and the practices what they're doing, because all through the culture, if you bring it back to Black culture and find out history, I'm all for it, I wanna know what they know, but when they started crossing that with it and making it part of something that's when I have to be, 'What is this all about?'
Participant HB: It's the crossing out of everyone else is what I don't fathom because I grew up multicultural; I've got a mixture of friends from all everywhere, and I like that, and I like knowing about people's different backgrounds. And I'm not gonna cast them out just because you don't follow a certain law or because God said you're not one of the chosen people, but we're still here living on this earth all together, and I'm still gonna love like God said, 'You need to love everyone,' so I'm going to love everyone, so that's when I don't understand why you, why they felt that no one else is … ' (Participant/Pastor CAW and HB, The Black Face of the Early Church, 2018)

4

The Black Face of the Early Church

Participant HB: It was more when you brought up the whole Israelite thing; I was brought up in church, we two [indicating her sister] grew up in church together, but from the age of 19, it was probably when my family started coming out of church, questioning the Bible, our thoughts were everywhere, and we took a step back instead of going into it more, and then discussing it an' finding out—
Eleasah: With your parents?
Participant HB: Well with my whole family, yeah, my brothers and sisters. That was it, every Sunday go to church, that was the routine like, so we all just took a step back kind of just wondering about ourselves like, 'Okay we don't go church anymore'. It was weird on a Sunday, to wake up and like – lie down. So yeah, now my mum, in like the last year she gone to this Israelite thing.
Eleasah: Hebrew Israelites?
Participant HB: Yeah, sorry, I'm not sure what you really call it because I dunno; there's some things with me because I've not … I dunno, it just hasn't – I dunno, something with me. I'm not kind of at peace with it or something like it. It's 'cause it's too … I don't even how to describe it because it's that kind of—
Participant/Pastor CAW: Mmm, it's different, isn't it?
Participant HB: Yeah, it's different.
(The Black Face of the Early Church, 2018)

This session looked at the contributions of African theologians, bishops and thinkers in early church history, which directly impacted the foundational theologies of mainstream Western churches today. In each session, I put up timelines and maps that helped to put our conversations into a historical and geographical perspective. For example, when talking about the 'Council of Nicea' conspiracy, which many de-churched and ADR claim is the time that Roman Christians devised the repackaged biblical text and declared Jesus as divine, I can demonstrate other historical events that may support or challenge these ideas, such as the evidence of biblical canons that predate AD 325 as well as what some of the leading theologians understood as the earliest Christological doctrines. Equipping the participants with this background knowledge I felt levelled the playing field for those in the room, all then able to interrogate some foundational information.

I pay particular attention to Tertullian and Origen as examples of African Church fathers who significantly influenced mainstream Christian theology today. I presented them, in contrast, to demonstrate the variety of theological ideas during the early history of the Church and the fundamental implications and application of their ideas, so that I could help the participants connect with their own theological ideas and those of early African Christians. Tertullian is known for coining the term 'Trinity' to reflect the triune nature of God, Father, Son and Holy Spirit, whereas Origen is known to have introduced gnostic ideas into his Christian doctrine; his approach to allegory and deeper meanings in the text, I felt, would resonate most with those de-churched who considered Christianity to be a descendant of an earlier African religious tradition – such as the claims of the Nation of Islam and the Holy Qubtic Church.

This session aimed to consider how one's identity is connected to one's religion or religious identity and, further to this, the power of knowing one's religious history. We see that ADR are keen to demonstrate the continuity of their religion with ancient religions that had been destroyed and forgotten through the enslavement experience. They are also keen to develop strategies for nation-building, showing self-determination on a communal level, pooling resources, striving for excellence and building a type of independence within wider Western society that restores dignity to the diasporic community. Ethiopianism is the root of this thinking; it worked on both spiritual and practical levels. In this chapter, we explore Ethiopianism and how it has manifested as nation-building for Black Bible Religions and causes intrigue among the de-churched, as well as how globalization shapes the growth of these new religious movements.

Consciousness raising

To support the Participatory Action Research, I employed a method from feminist consciousness-raising groups from the 1960s which focused on slowing the pace of the conversation and allowing participants the time to talk, think, process, and complete their contribution. This slower pace of re-processing and sharing interpreted experiences allowed people to tell their stories and share in considering what had happened during the session, something they might have learned, or an idea that had piqued their interest. In this way, I was also empowered to politely request that people who had spoken before or made a habit of interrupting others should give room to allow others to speak and complete their contribution. Interestingly, this became a significant part of the analysis because many of the participants felt that, during their church experiences, their voices were not valued, their questions were left unanswered, and their unconventional contributions were dismissed. Having discussed this issue in a more general way with the group helped create that sense of sharing, even when it came to allowing people to express an idea or experience fully.

Another significant aspect of consciousness-raising that has contributed to the research and programme is the format of the group sessions. Focusing on a particular theme each week rather than an utterly unstructured discussion allowed for the participants to think and speak deeply on the topics. 'The group format typically consisted of a round of personal experiences and reflections on the week's theme, followed by an integrative session in which the group sought to combine their accounts into a structural picture' (Firth and Robinson, 2016, pp. 346–7).

Consciousness-raising was a communal activity requiring the group to bring together their individual experiences and consider this qualitative data as critical signifiers. This type of formatting aids in analysing and developing a strategy that works for both the sessions and my data analysis.

By combining these approaches, I designed my five-session programme that focused on the religious teachings and challenges within the Afroasiatic diasporic religions. These programmes were designed to have safe, transparent, listening conversations and consider solutions for decolonizing the mainstream Church.

Ethiopianism

From a historical perspective, Afroasiatic diasporic religions have roots in Ethiopianism, a Black religious framework that brought together a literalist, institutional, genealogical, historical, liberative understanding of Scripture during the legal enslavement of African peoples in the Caribbeans and the Americas (Jalata, 2009; Price, 2003, 2014; Quirin, 2011; Shepperson, 1953; Shilliam, 2016). Although multifaceted in its function as a social and political movement, this Black religious framework is the root of a Black Christian theology and Afroasiatic Diasporic Religion. As early as the eighteenth century, Prince Hall, abolitionist and founder of Black freemasonry (Johnson, 2011), became known for his liberatory interpretation of Psalm 68.31, 'Princes shall come out of Egypt; Ethiopia shall soon stretch out her hands unto God' (KJV). His prophetic interpretation of this verse became foundational for many Ethiopianists who sought the emancipation of enslaved, segregated and oppressed Black peoples and believed God had appointed Black people as the key to the successful emancipation of Africa (Kay, 2011).

Rastafari is an example of one of the religious trajectories built upon Ethiopianism; many Ethiopianists became followers of Ethiopian Emperor Haile Selassie (born Ras Tafari Makonnen in 1892), believing him to be God incarnate and a descendant of King Solomon and the Queen of Sheba. It was believed to be the fulfilment of the scriptures that describe the Messiah as a descendant of King David, such as Jeremiah 23.5–6:

> Behold, the days come, saith the Lord, that I will raise unto David a righteous Branch, and a King shall reign and prosper, and shall execute judgment and justice in the earth. In his days Judah shall be saved, and Israel shall dwell safely: and this is his name whereby he shall be called, The Lord Our Righteousness. (KJV)[1]

An Ethiopianist approach to Scripture draws upon a genetic and ethnic link between King David of the Old Testament, Jesus Christ of Nazareth, and Haile Selassie, Emperor of Ethiopia. This situated Africans within the biblical narrative literally, liberating Christ from the triumphant hands of the colonizer and returning him to his people. Charles Price would argue that this was a natural development of Ethiopianism: 'Ethiopianists combined race, scripture, historical experience, religiosity, and social criticism in ways that made enduring and compelling ideas of a Black Messiah or Christ possible' (Price, 2014, p. 419). Ethiopianism developed a critique of the mainstream European Church and provided alternative interpretations which, I argue, went deeper than a creative emancipatory framework to demonstrate the importance of ethnic genealogy, biblical historicity and religious institution.

ADR's religious teachings challenge mainstream Christian interpretations; the alternative interpretations appear corrective rather than functioning purely to resist and critique Colonial Christianity.

> Cults or new religions are diverse and complex organizations whose significance cannot be gauged without reference to the sociocultural and religious situation of the second half of the twentieth century. (Saliba, 1995, p. 8)

While Ethiopianism extends beyond Saliba's time constraints, Ethiopianist Black religious movements undeniably grew in prominence due to subjugation and Christianization by European colonizers and missionaries. Ethiopianists believe that the Book of Revelation spoke of the destruction of the systems that oppressed them and worked towards a vision that saw Africans unified and returning to their place of origin. As a result, Ethiopia became a symbolic home of the disenfranchised, a central idiom whereby Black people could find affirmation and claim a legitimate ancient history and powerful ancestry (MacLeod, 2014).

Ethiopianism formed a more solid cluster of ideas in the nineteenth century among preachers and intellectuals such as Henry Highland Garnet, Martin Delaney, Edward Blyden and Alexander Crummell. In 1829, Robert Alexander Young published a pamphlet called *The Ethiopian Manifesto*, in which he called for a theocratic body politic, a social and political order that would promote and work towards the welfare of Ethiopians (Black people) in America. The manifesto reflected the Bible-mindedness many Black people in the West were believed to have upheld; Young spoke of the imminent freedom from slavery that would be achieved by the 'power of words and the divine will of God' (Hayes, 2000, p. 105). Those who subscribed to the ideology saw Ethiopia as either a place to return to or a place to invest in; their theology worked as resistance against oppressive White forces and turned their focus back to Africa. By grounding their roots in Ethiopia mythically, believers could develop and maintain a morally rooted sense of Black identity and Black redemption (Price, 2009, p. 32).

Ethiopianists developed a mythical connection to Ethiopia (both the country and the greater continent of Africa, believed to be referred to as Ethiopia in biblical Scriptures), not necessarily claiming direct genetic connection but rather a new theological hermeneutic that recognized the displaced African, an affirmation of their experience, history and ancestry – 'the creation of history and identity that contested white racism and bias' (Price, 2009, p. 39).

Blyden was one of the first Black scholars to document the various African figures in the Holy Bible and demonstrate African participation in the unfolding of the biblical revelation. In an 1882 discourse, *Phillip and the Eunuch*, he homed in on the account of the Ethiopian Eunuch in Acts 8, suggesting, first, that it was God's will that the Eunuch would be the one to bring the message of the gospel to his people in Ethiopia, and, second, that the prophetic writing of Isaiah at the centre of the account was tied to the future experience of Black people:

And there was something symbolic, also, of the future sad experience of his race – and at the same time full of consolation – in the passage which he read. It was holding up Christ as the 'man of sorrows and acquainted with grief,' as if in anticipation of the great and unsurpassed trials of the African. These were to be the words of comfort and uplifting to these people in their exile and captivity. They were to remember that if they were despised and scorned, a far greater than themselves had had a similar experience. (Blyden, 1993)

Although most commonly known as the father of Pan-Africanism, Blyden made a poignant contribution to the formation of Ethiop-centric ideologies; he formalized grassroots theology which, up until this point, had been largely driven by preachers and activists.

As a concept, Ethiopianism resists White religious hegemony and employs an ethnoreligious hermeneutic. It is a crucial player in this conceptual framework as it clearly describes the religious ideas present in the teachings of the Afroasiatic diasporic religions. Price confirms this:

Wherever Ethiopianism has taken root, three main factors animate it: White hegemony, especially over liberty, knowledge, and religion: a desire for varying degrees of autonomy in economic and political affairs; and a sense of injustice and moral wrong related to Blacks enduring White injustices, especially slavery and apartheid. (Price, 2003, p. 35)

Ethiopianism is widely recognized for the influence it has had on Black Religion and political activism. Price credits the development of Afroasiatic Diasporic Religions to Ethiopianism:

In Ethiopianism, we find precursors to beliefs and practices associated with Black nationalism proper. This does not mean that Ethiopianism caused the practices; rather, it points to a genre of Black efforts in disparate places and times to grapple with their complicated relationships with White-dominated societies. (Price, 2003, p. 37)

Price extends the influence beyond religious ideas – Black emancipatory movements are indebted to the Ethiopianist model and underpinning principles. In the decades that followed the legal emancipation of enslaved Africans, Black nationalism maintained prominence; however, as diasporic relationships with White-dominated societies continue to be complex and unstable in the twenty-first century, Black nationalism is not at the fore of public racial justice conversation. The protest is for reparations and to belong to White-dominated societies as equals; and conversations about being compensated through a repatriation process, or given land and regions exclusively for the use and governance of Black peoples within the white-dominated societies, are less centralized.

Ethiopians saw God through a new lens as the God of the Ethiopians, who saw their oppression and commissioned them as agents of the gospel – a missiological and historical mandate. Their Christology eventually evolved into the belief that Emperor Haile Selassie was the reincarnated Christ. There were also ideas of exclusively inherent qualities being put out by activists and thinkers of the time. George Fredrickson, in *Black Liberation: A Comparative History of Black Ideologies in the United States and South Africa*, presents religious romantic racialism as a key trait in Ethiopianism. He posits that the movement centres on the notion that Black people have exclusively inherent qualities; he looks back to the work of Emmanuel Swedenborg, a Swedish philosopher and mystic in the eighteenth century who believed that out of Africa would come a 'purer church', as Black people are more spiritual in nature than the latest phase of the true Church inhabited by Europeans. Further to this, Swedenborg suggested that Black people are most naturally inclined to Christianity because of their God-given temperaments and characteristics: believing, affectionate and altruistic. Fredrickson suggests that David Walker, who resided in Boston and published *An Appeal to the Coloured Citizens of the World* in 1829, was influenced by Swedenborg's ideas. The publication is most recognized for its militancy and its call to an uprising against White oppressors, but what is perhaps more significant for this study are the conceptions of Black moral supremacy and Messianic destiny.

> It is my solemn belief, that if ever the world becomes Christianized, (which must certainly take place before long) it will be through the means, under God of the Blacks, who are now held in wretchedness, and degradation, by the white Christians of the world ... (Walker, 1829–30)

Walker, like Swedenborg, also draws a comparison between the nature of Whites and that of coloured people. He postulates that even Christianity could not alter the 'essential nature' of White people, calling them an 'unjust, jealous, unmerciful, avaricious and bloodthirsty set of beings, always seeking after power and authority' (Walker, 1829); in this sense he justifies his ideas that it is the God of the Blacks that is the salvation of the world. It is these notions that help us to connect threads through history to contemporary liberation theologies that promote a Black theological Messiah – the genealogy of Black Liberation Theology.

Nation-building

Nationalism generates important questions for ethnic communities seeking to articulate their feelings and actions politically. The context of nationalism in this study is Black British de-churched peoples who seek a Black religious framework in which they can flourish culturally, religiously and politically. Nationalism has served the purposes of both left- and right-wing social politics. Those on the right wing of nationalism seek to preserve historical/traditional national traits and interests, while left-wing nationalism seeks to revolutionize the traditional meanings of 'nation' and the systems in place to uphold those historical traditions. In this light of nationalism, then, several vital questions arise: what is a nation? Is a nation to be defined by common philosophies, ethnicity, culture, religion or origin? Particularly concerning minority communities who may be a part of a state voluntarily or involuntarily, are cultures, religions and customs at stake if people become nationalist about the state they dwell in? Is their ability to successfully integrate and reap the benefits of their local nationality affected if they have nationalist affections for another nation or state?

Black nationalism in the eighteenth, nineteenth and twentieth centuries was marked distinctly by its attempts to define Black racial identity in consideration of their position as a minority or underdog group within European states and colonies. As descendants of enslaved Africans who were displaced and involuntarily relocated to Britain, the Americas and the Caribbean, many attempts have been made to develop and promote a non-assimilationist identity marked by culture, origins, experience and struggle. In its most practical form, this has led to the independence of African and Caribbean countries from the ruling of European colonial powers. However, before this began to occur, Black philosophers, thinkers and activists had begun to think ontologically about Black identity and nationhood. Part of the development of these ideas was the task of defining Black identity; for example, in *The Souls of Black Folk*, originally published in 1903, W. E. B. Du Bois asserted the concept of 'double consciousness', the conflict of two souls, that begins with his personal experience of being African and being American, 'looking at oneself through the eyes of others, or measuring one's soul by the tape of a world that looks on in amused contempt and pity' (Du Bois, 1994, p. 8).

This description speaks to the individual experience of the African diaspora in the West, making sense of a new reality, a liminal reality away from one's ancestral home and yet not accepted by one's new hosts. Double consciousness has become a tool for exploring the Black reality in the West and the Black community's distorted connection to ancestral histories and cultures. Paul Gilroy furthers this discourse by using the postcolonial concept of 'hybridity', a new perspective on identity which dismantles a purity/autonomous narrative because all are involved in a diverse society (Gilroy, 1993). In this way, double consciousness becomes wider than America and the African American reality and the essentialization of Blackness with Afrocentric perspectives. Moreover, it serves as a tool that aided Black Theology in moving beyond a patriarchal aversion to neo-colonial capitalism and general systemic violence. Together with feminist/womanist theologies, as mentioned previously, complex concepts of identity are being formed by the unique experiences of being who you are, where you are, and considering where you have come from and your place in society. The concept of hybridity in postcolonialism acknowledges and works with varying input points and complements the method of self-differentiation, where colour and gender are not enough to create a complete Black identity.

Du Bois's framework allowed Black thinkers to develop ontological blackness, which was a new and separate identity from their ancestors' purely cultural and ethnic identities in Africa. The tension that double consciousness highlights from a political standpoint in later movements centred on measuring success and the type of action towards a Black nationalist reality. On the one hand, some Black people, particularly in America, Britain and the Caribbean, wanted equality, to be considered an 'American' or 'British' – which may also be termed assimilation. On the other hand, Black organizations were lobbying for, protesting for, and actioning various levels of autonomy, which may also be termed 'self-determination'. Marcus Garvey is the prime example of a Black nationalist who sought to empower Black people by developing a Black economy rooted in and serving both Africa and the diaspora. Garvey, among others, carved a route for the descendants of enslaved Africans to engage with or return to the continent, illuminating the potential for continuing the journey voluntarily as a diaspora by reconstructing African nationhood or nationality.

Civilizationism looks at the realizing of higher forms of social, intellectual and behavioural norms within a community. What makes this a complex discourse is the varying r-o-u-t-e-s and r-o-o-t-s through which this can be realized, as well as the ethical implications of civilizing a community. First, in response to colonial/imperial oppression, Black African communities have sought to re-establish the journey towards being civilized that was interrupted by colonialism and slavery, taking civilized and civilization as the journey towards and markers of a sophisticated society, as opposed to barbarianism.

Civilization derived from the universal theory of human social and cultural progress that emerged in the eighteenth- and nineteenth-century Europe and was often used as a rationale for imperialism and colonialism. (Fredrickson, 1996, p. 69)

However, William R. Scott and William G. Shade in *Upon These Shores: Themes in the African American Experience 1600 to the Present* (2000) put forward the case of African Civilizationists who sought to produce a sterling civilization in Africa as a vindication of the abilities of the African race:

Nonetheless, Christianity, Marxism, and bourgeois democracy all assumed the existence of universal truths, which had been discovered, not devised by Europeans, and therefore could not be rightfully appropriated by them. The truths of human progress, currently arrogated to themselves by white supremacists, were just as properly the cultural property of Africans, who should busy themselves with reclaiming their legitimate heritage. (Scott and Shade, 2000, p. 69)

What these two texts are showing us is that the issues surrounding civilization are not the ways in which it is measured according to geographic location but the cultural norms that are defined as civilized. For example, Europeans and Africans both have legacies of art historically, but if either one assumes the monopoly on defining the level of sophistication based on its own cultural perspective, then it claims the monopoly on defining what is civilized. African Civilizationism appears to work towards re-establishing its own kind of civilization through arts, education, sciences and documentation (for example), moving away from Eurocentric norms.

W. E. B. Du Bois, however, has a slightly different perspective, arguing that by developing the 'Talented Tenth' educating Black elites, the Black community could be mobilized to take their place among the civilized in America. Derrick P. Alridge, in a comparative study (2007), identified Du Bois's commitment to education and, more importantly, the education and leadership of Black women. Du Bois saw a broad education curriculum, vocation and liberal arts as a form of liberation that would secure the Black community's ascent to being accepted as civilized and contributing to the progression of the Black race in American society while upholding ideological African values and Black historical racial pride:

The great deficiency of the Negro, however, is his small knowledge of the art of organized social life – that last expression of human culture. His development in group life was abruptly broken off by the Black Codes, and suddenly wrenched anew by the Emancipation Proclamation. He finds himself, therefore, peculiarly weak in that nice adoption of individual life to the life of the group which is the essence of civilization. (Du Bois, 1898)

Leonard Harris in 'Honour, Eunuchs and the Post Colonial Subject' (Eze, 1997) uses the life of Jacobus Eliza Joannes Capitein (1717–47) as an example of a postcolonial subject: a former slave who was permitted to be educated and ordained by the Dutch then later sent as a missionary to Ghanaian natives. Harris suggests that Capitein's Christianity or religiosity was the main factor in his blindness to the suffering of his people. Capitein's hope, detailed through his 'postcolonial' writings and speeches, was in the civilizing of the entire world through the Christian colonial forces that had saved him from his fallen state. 'Capitein argued that slavery was compatible to Christian doctrine' (Harris in Eze, 1997, p. 252) – through this civilizing of the entire world would come the end of slavery. Harris's observations of Capitein conclude that Christianity became his complete identity, and he no longer saw himself as a Native African; he had been civilized. This paper argues that this postcolonial thinker, Capitein, is a prototype of a neo-colonial trajectory for the Black community of Christianity today. No longer does the body of the Church need to be predominantly White in skin tone; instead it is filled with bodies in submission to Euro-Christian hermeneutics that maintains the status quo of White superiority. This aspect of Civilizationism, whereby Western modernity/Euro-centricity is the baseline for a civilized society, is the type, this paper argues, that encourages the adoption of a prosperity gospel and mimicry of mainstream Christian hierarchical structures among church leaders. Upon seeing the successes of his captors, Capitein is converted to a capitalist model of expansion and hierarchy, which he sees as the outstretched redeeming arm of God. The colonial powers ordained Blacks and delegated the responsibility of teaching, in moderation and through a colonial lens, the gospel of Jesus and the testimony of the prophets. In direct parallel, what we see in many Black churches in Britain is a mimicry of these campaigns, specifically within the theological framework of a prosperity gospel. By adopting a theology whereby wealth reflects God's favour, the prosperity gospel ignores the oppressive social/political forces that strategically keep communities in poverty. Rather than protesting for social change and resisting colonial ideologies, they affirm individualism.

David Maxwell in 'Delivered from the spirit of poverty?' quotes Paul Gifford's response to a prosperity gospel within churches in Africa:

> By advocating the gospel of prosperity it [born-again Christianity] dissuades adherents from evaluating the present economic order, merely persuading them to try to be among those who benefit from it. With its emphasis on personal healing, it diverts attention from social ills that are crying out for remedy. Its stress on human wickedness and the fallen nature of 'the world' is no incentive to social, economic and constitutional reform. By emphasizing personal morality so exclusively, it all but eliminates any interest in systemic or institutionalized injustice. By making everything so simple, it distracts attention from the very real contradictions in the lives of so many in Southern Africa. (Gifford, 1991, pp. 65–6)

Despite this contribution, Maxwell concludes that the prosperity gospel is a positive soother in the realms of hardship: 'While liberation theology promises to pull people down into violent struggles ... Pentecostal practice at least offers them some realizable advance in their livelihoods' (Maxwell, 1998, p. 370). Having conducted research with a community in Zimbabwe that has been transformed through the adoption of a Pentecostal belief system, Maxwell found that, alongside the new Pentecostal theology, a prosperity gospel aided the development of the people within the church. The family structures became more stable, debt decreased, money management improved, and habits such as smoking, drinking alcohol, prostitution and gambling were being traded in for more community-conscious activities.

Maxwell's opinion of Liberation theology is superficial, as, it seems, are his insights for the impoverished community. While Black Liberation Theology ideals regarding Black people and economic advancement are in their early stages, its protest is for social reform, which incurs longer-lasting economic and social benefits for communities such as those in Maxwell's research. The blindness caused by Christianity that Harris suggests caused Capitein to be hardened to the demise of his people in Ghana can also be seen through the practice of a prosperity gospel that offers temporary emotional highs and little yield – rarely enough to transform the economic advance of future generations.

During the research process, I began to consider the issue of 'wealth' and 'power' as posited by Black liberationist theologians. I struggled to create a firm link between their Marxist position and what I perceived in the Black community to be, as Kehinde Andrews (2018) considered it, 'soft nationalism', and an economy within an economy that was essentially capitalist. Black Liberation Theology is often critiqued by the Christian 'right' for taking a Marxist position that challenges the structures of power in the form of classes in society and lends itself to a socialist stance. The main argument is that Black Theology situates Black identity in victimhood and draws upon Karl Marx's use of oppressed/oppressor to analyse social realities for Black people: White people are inherently deemed as 'rich' oppressors and Black people as the poor and oppressed.

Within this framework, Black theologians have developed a criticism of White supremacy and neo-colonialism across the Black Atlantic. Cone engages this conversation with a critique of capitalist powers, these powerful institutions that continue to hold Black communities in poverty; and on Marxist thought, he says:

> The Christian faith does not possess in its nature the means for analysing the structure of capitalism. Marxism as a tool of social analysis can disclose the gap between appearance and reality, and thereby help Christians to see things as they really are. (Cone, 1984)

Cone suggested that one can use Marxism as a tool, regardless of its atheist roots, to aid the theological quest of demonstrating the injustices perpetrated by the White ruling powers over the poor Black oppressed. In *For My People* (1984), Cone calls for Christians of the third world to redefine Marxism to serve their purpose – to shed light on the evils of those in power. In *The Future of Liberation Theology: An Argument and Manifesto* (2017), Ivan Petrella criticizes the way Liberation theologies have poorly conceptualized capitalism. Petrella contends that by reasserting and rearticulating the core themes of their theology, they have maintained a critique of capitalism that is fast becoming redundant. While it has been and can be argued that capitalism has been used to support colonization and slavery, Petrella calls for a revision of this objection according to the realities of today, saying that liberation theologians must consider the opportunities that capitalism affords all peoples to develop new historical projects. Here, the new task is to re-theorize capitalism and rework it into socialism so that Liberation theologies can finally contribute practically to the development, empowerment and enrichment of poor peoples. Although Petrella speaks primarily about Liberation theology in impoverished countries (in Latin America), the sentiment can also apply to Black Liberation Theology, which is developed in impoverished communities within an economically developed country.

Petrella's contribution brings this conversation back to the relevance of Black Theology in this current dialogue about the social development of the Black community. While activists may argue that, statistically, Black people are the underdogs in Western society, it could also be argued that, more than ever, we are seeing a fast-growing Black professional and middle class developing, along with Black millionaires and internationally renowned celebrities, not to mention prominent politicians – and that the nature of capitalism supports all this. While one observes a significant rise in individual success and prosperity within the Black Atlantic community, Black Theology is concerned with collective success and liberation. Cornel West challenges Black theologians to consider the nature and notion of the liberation they seek for Black peoples and to go beyond 'getting theirs'; he says, 'If this is the social vision of Black theologians, they should drop the meretricious and flamboyant term "liberation" and adopt the more accurate and sober word "inclusion" (West, 1979, p. 879). In *Black Theology and Marxist Thought* (1979), West draws our attention to the systems and processes developed by Marxist thinkers to ensure participatory democracy. These models claim to ensure liberation from a capitalist system that provides prosperity for the few, instead intending to redistribute wealth equally. West asserts that this is in line with the spirit of Black Liberation Theology: it is not enough to want to succeed in the existing systems; the aim must be to introduce a new radical system that redistributes power.

Considering Cone and West's dialogue with Marxism this way, fiscal wealth seems to have become a distasteful concept in Black Liberation Theology. It is often affiliated with the wealth of neo-colonial powers, the government, large corporations and old families that have benefited from the enslavement of Africans. This attitude towards personal wealth and capitalist methods for betterment is contrary to the attitudes of many within the Black Conscious Community, the de-churched and the ADRs. Their desire is to utilize capitalism to become wealthy by competing, creating successful businesses, and to develop a thriving Black economy within the larger Western economy – without the need for 'big government' intervention. Black Theology's concept of liberation is still embedded in the action of resisting, uncovering and surviving and, in my opinion, struggles to translate into day-to-day action for flourishing and economic empowerment. Although West claims that Black Theology does not elaborate on the ideal society, it is certainly opposed to American mainstream ideals considered 'conservative'.

This is but one example of the 'right' and 'left' tensions referred to earlier. I believe I have captured others in this work, primarily theological and methodological approaches to Scripture conceptualized for contemporary meanings of conservative and liberal or progressive. Afroasiatic religions have much to contribute to this discussion theologically, especially using the preservation–liberation framework. Such religions are neither radical nor submissive to existing British systems. However, because of their high view of Scripture, their ideals find connection points in both pools – I believe this has inspired their communities to build businesses, contribute to community development and seek self-sufficiency.

I contend that progressive or liberal theological premises underestimate the power of plain reading and authoritative truth assumptions within Black ethnoreligious movements towards the solution-finding process, anti-racism and community empowerment. Unless they propose a humanist overhaul of Black Christianity, which I suspect is the desired end goal for many, Black theologians should continue to regard in a positive light the ethnoreligious connection to Bible-based religions that birthed much of its resistance efforts during legal subjugation. Losing connection with the cultures, traditions, interpretations and religious verve that underpinned these resistances to cosmopolitanism and wholly new British identities threatens the ethnoreligious institutions that have strengthened oppressed peoples to survive and build in hostile environments.

The (Black) Hebrew Israelites reject an ontological view of blackness and instead seek to mobilize a nation of people united by their ethnicity and religious heritage. 'Building a nation, not a religion' is a key sentiment demonstrating an intentional separation from the West's Christendom and Judaism. Ontological blackness defines the African diaspora according to their experiences of oppression and strategies for survival and overcoming (more on this in the next chapter). However, the BHI perspective refuses to be defined by those experiences and regards them as a judgement outlined by the Hebrew God, according to their prophetic/historical reading of Deuteronomy 28.

> And it shall come to pass, that as the LORD rejoiced over you to do you good, and to multiply you; so the LORD will rejoice over you to destroy you, and to bring you to nought; and ye shall be plucked from off the land whither thou goest to possess it.
>
> And the LORD shall scatter thee among all people, from the one end of the earth even unto the other; and there thou shalt serve other gods, which neither thou nor thy fathers have known, even wood and stone.
>
> And among these nations shalt thou find no ease, neither shall the sole of thy foot have rest: but the LORD shall give thee there a trembling heart, and failing of eyes, and sorrow of mind:
>
> And thy life shall hang in doubt before thee; and thou shalt fear day and night, and shalt have none assurance of thy life. (Deut. 28.63–66 KJV)

The slavery experience for the (Black) Hebrew Israelites is a result of idolatry and disobedience, and neither assimilation nor localized self-determination is considered a method for emancipation. The BHI refuse the governmental authority of the countries where they dwell, instead considering true repentance and a mental/spiritual awakening (realizing one's true identity as an Israelite) the only necessary task. Gilroy says, 'The politics of "race" in Britain is fired by conceptions of national belonging and homogeneity which not only blur the distinction between "race" and nation but rely on that very ambiguity for their effect' (Gilroy, 2013, p. 45). Gilroy counters a nationalistic strategy of resistance by developing a transoceanic perspective through which we can view iconic Black thinkers such as Du Bois, Black intellectuals who were deeply embedded in European society, cultures and environments and, as a result, were heavily influenced by European philosophy. A key argument in this text is that the Black diaspora is an archetype of cosmopolitanism, a body of peoples that cannot be reduced to a single nation, culture and history; while connected by the experience of enslavement and subjugation, there is a wealth of new cultures, histories and movements that are a result of resistance, unwavering strength and self-determination.

Gilroy's call to a new cosmopolitanism in *Against Race: Imagining Political Culture Beyond the Colour Line* (2000) dissolves ethnic and culture-driven nationhood, which is argued to be a separatist enterprise, and explores the possibilities of post-racial realities in space, place and political communities. He hypothesizes that cosmopolitanism allows all peoples to thrive as equals and be free from modernist conceptualization of culture and geo/historical origins. Gilroy's work dreams of future societies and envisages cosmopolitan cultures rather than ethnically routed/rooted ones to move our socialization beyond 'race' talk and view one another as citizens of the earth rather than of nation-states. He supports this argument by surveying historical moments in which racial sciences, cultures and ethnicity have been sources of selective superiority and oppression, demonstrating how European cultures have been nationalized and politicized, acting as measuring rods of civilization and worth. This criticism is not only aimed at White European institutions but at the Afrocentric (and ADR) communities who retaliate with corrective campaigns claiming Africa to be the originating cradle of many scientific discoveries, and to have been robbed of their prestige.

> It makes the conspiracies that covered up the theft into a principal issue. This counternarrative of progress is accompanied by a degree of temporal disturbance. It says in effect: 'we were ahead of you on

the ascending escalator of civilization until you displaced us by illegitimate means'. These depressing cycles contribute to the climate in which authoritarian and antiliberal passions can take command of the political imaginations. (Gilroy, 2000, p. 340)

Afroasiatic Diasporic Religions, at the core, do not intend to civilize or improve civilizations outside of their own; as these religions locate themselves explicitly as a 'lost tribe', they are focused on awakening the lost rather than improving the social and political conditions of the host nation. Reverend A. J. Varmah, head of the Holy Qubtic Church, insists that Black people reclaim the Bible religion as African religious heritage:

> So we must reclaim our religious heritage by African standards, by African eyes, African ears, African tongue, African ideals and structure. The reason the religion is so important to reclaim – to remove the Africa out of Judaism – reclaim it back, all of the African components found in Judaism reclaim it back, all of the African components found in Judaism, we've gotta take it back. All of the African components that's been sprinkled and bleached within Christianity, we have to take it back. (Reclaiming our Religious Heritage, Got Kush TV, 2020, YouTube)

According to the Holy Qubtic Church, the Bible is the religious text of Ancient Africans – the Ta Ma Reans. They teach that foreign nations have taken the text and reappropriated it for their own ethnic groups. The call to reclaim and recover the truths that have been distorted and reappropriated in order for Black people to flourish comprises the religious teachings that bring freedom. Again, this perspective is linked closely to nationhood and genealogy, the religion not being for all people but for an exclusive community – designed for and by a particular ethnic group. 'White Man's Religion' is a fitting term for this type of conversation because, according to Black Bible Religions, distinctions of religions and whom they belong to are foundational to liberation. Mainstream Christianity claims that Christ died for all, according to the Bible, and is therefore in theory an inclusive religious framework; however, the experience of Black people through enslavement, segregation and ongoing discrimination within Christian institutions, according to the ADR, says that Christianity is indeed a 'White Man's Religion'.

Black Bible Religions thrive on group mobilization but do not require mainstream elevation; the more the group are marginalized, the more affirmed they become. Rastafari, the Nation of Islam and Hebrew Israelites, in particular, have grounded their movements in 'us' and 'them', setting themselves apart from what they perceive to be the dominant society (often termed Babylon) as a prophetic voice. Drawing from Old Testament Hebraic narratives, the participants in these movements believe themselves to be the chosen children of God; their identity, thus, is divinely inspired or ordained. These groups embody an essentialism that goes beyond genetic traits; the divine essence sets them apart from other people groups. In these movements, scientific inquiry and history become tools for uncovering hidden or lost truths about the true identity of Black people and are used to directly resist the identities that the Black community have taken on during their enslavements and subjugation. New Religious Movements such as these present an epistemological conundrum; their identities are presented as fixed (as Hebrews, for example), yet the source of this knowledge comes from contextualized readings of their holy texts. They seem to fall in between Coherentism, where knowledge is social and limited to experience (Nelson, 1990, p. 40) and the correspondence theory of truth, where truth corresponds to or with a fact (David, 2022). These movements developed during experiences of ethnic oppression, inspired by the hidden knowledge revealed to religious leaders who have sought to uncover the truth/facts concerning identity through study. In this sense, their beliefs confirm Gilroy's criticism: they believe themselves to be rediscovering cultures and religious traditions that predate modernity and would go so far as to argue that the West was civilized by learned African peoples.

Western scholarship, including some Black scholarship, is limited to its philosophical 'dispensations' and fails to take ADR sufficiently seriously so long as it is understood only within European philosophical thought. Particularly for Gilroy, this is perhaps due to the lack of attention to Black Religion.

> No less than their predecessor Martin Delany, today's Black intellectuals have persistently succumbed to the lure of those romantic conceptions of 'race,' 'people,' and 'nation' which place themselves, rather than the people they supposedly represent, in charge of the strategies for nation building, state formation, and racial uplift. This point underscores the fact that the status of nationalists and the precise weight we should attach to the conspicuous differences of language, culture, and identity which divide the Black of the diaspora from one another, let alone from Africa, are unresolved within the political culture that promises to bring the disparate peoples of the Black Atlantic together one day. (Gilroy, 1993, p. 34)

Nationalism can be described as the attitudes, feelings, and actions of those who care passionately about the nation they belong to and protect that nationality's integrity. Ernest Gellner describes it as a 'political principle, which holds that the political and the national unit should be congruent' (Gellner, 1983). Nevertheless, it also considers the nationalist notions of minority communities within larger nation-states. This consideration reflects the movement of groups (voluntary and involuntary) who have ties to their previous dwelling or a historical place of origin. These minority groups may not seek to have complete political control of the state in which they live but strive for recognition, equality, and certain levels of autonomy within the wider state. In this general sense, the nation means the body of people, and the state is the governmental and geographical parameters of the region.

Gilroy's futuristic gaze compels him to desire Black scholarship to enter the broader arena of academia as members of this cosmopolitan reality, not to focus on what has been lost or stolen but to use the tools, experiences and lessons learned on the historical journey from Africa to the Black Atlantic and the substance of these Pan-Africanist claims to contribute to scientific enterprise, the evolution of ethics and cosmopolitan politics. He says, 'It is my hope that not Europe and North Atlantic but the postcolonial world in general, and South Africa in particular, will in due course generate an alternative sense of what our networked world might be and become, a new cosmopolitanism centred on the global south' (Gilroy, 2006. p. 289).

Conversations about ethnocentrism often overlap with nationalism, bearing negative links to racism, prejudice and hostility which cause it to be generally regarded as an undesirable phenomenon (Bizumic, 2015). Ethnocentricity describes how people view, perceive and judge the world according to the values, morals, practices and standards of their ethnic community.

I looked up something, for example, um, African – I think it was Bible school or something like that – and I found that in Kenya and I found that it was still led by someone of European descent, and Uganda – still by European descent, and it's like why do we need that ... there's that element. It's an interesting one for me because, for me, it's more a 'on this earth' thing, does that make sense, and interacting [with]people, other Christians who are not Black. I think my concern is that as a body – as a Christian body – there seems to be a disconnect within that, understanding that as a Black person. I can worship God in a certain way which may not be the same as what you do, but it equally, it's not – there's an element of it done in an African way – it might be

> *voodoo evolved, do you know what I mean? Whereas the White way is the righteous way, and for the Bible, for me, the Bible didn't come from your culture anyway. The Hebrew culture wasn't the same as modern-day Western culture. So kind of coming across that and also helping for me, the reason why I'm here is – I don't personally, there's some little gaps in my knowledge, that doesn't influence my salvation if that makes sense personally, but there are some friends who it does. And helping find where some of their challenges are and filling those gaps, discussing it with my fellow brothers and sisters, I can better understand where they're coming from.* (Participant KA, The Black Face of the Early Church, 2018)

In much of the earlier literature focused on the ethnocentric nature of 'tribes', 'clans' and 'native peoples', these orientalist ventures failed to see that all people and nations, including (to great success) European peoples, are ethnocentric and can only view the practices, beliefs and morals of others in contrast to their own. The study of ethnocentrism itself is cloaked in universalist ideals and ethnic superiority that is disturbed by asserting ethnocentric traits in others.

> Ethnocentrism is conceived as an ideological system pertaining to groups and group relation. A distinction is made between *ingroups* (those groups with which the individual identifies himself) and *outgroups* (with which he does not have a sense of belonging and regarded as antithetical to the ingroups). Outgroups are the objects of negative opinions and hostile attitudes; ingroups are the objects of positive opinions and uncritically supportive attitudes; and it is considered that the outgroups should be socially subordinate to ingroups. (Adorno et al., 1950, p. 104)

In an interview on Speakers' Corner, Leo Muhammad was asked if he believed in an 'ethnostate', and, if so, whether it was feasible.

> Yes we do, in the sense that we believe in the humanity of all people, we believe that human beings should be able to live together regardless of creed, or class or colour; however, the problem is this, black people have been crushed to the ground and destroyed as a human reality where white people, yellow people, brown people have their own landmasses and their own nation-states that they can take ownership of, mostly black people found in the Western hemisphere, we have been disenfranchised from having our own. So, in this reality, we have to create an ethnostate, where in that reality, we finally have something that we can call our own. But the idea is not to do that to the

detriment of somebody else. We believe that white people should be entitled to have their own, Chinese people should be entitled to have their own, brown should be entitled to have their own, and we should be entitled to have our own. (Muhammad, 2018, 0.30secs)

Afroasiatic religions are typically ethnocentric; we have seen in the data how they refer to identities anchored in geography, genealogy, ancient cultures and traditions, languages and religions. Although academic literature acknowledges African origins, roots and connections, unlike Garvey's aspirations of literal and cultural repatriation, diaspora talk is focused on who Black people have become and struggle to be in European nation-states. Contrary to this ongoing notion, though seemingly less popular in academic circles, the Afrocentric and Pan-Africanist trajectories which peaked during the civil rights era have persisted among the ADR and the de-churched. These schools of thought centre their attention on the ethnic particularities of African peoples (religion, culture, politics and philosophy) and use these particularities to inform, empower and guide the diaspora to resist White supremacy and preserve the historical/geographical connection between the diaspora and their continent of origin.

The ADR's relationship to older religions is significant; they seek to reject the colonial and Eurocentric Christian religion and assert a corrective – an ethnocentric religion. Unlike the hermeneutical processes of postcolonial and Black liberationist methodologies, Afroasiatic religions in Black Britain do not seek to relativize or contextualize biblical interpretations and dismantle the ethnocentric approach. Instead, the claims are to *correct* false and erroneous interpretations and *preserve* the ethnoreligious narrative that returns Africans, Asians, Hebrews and their descendants – Black people in the West – to the centre of the biblical narrative.

According to the ADR, as they understand it to be outlined in Scripture, personal identity is not dependent on the experience or acceptance of the dominant culture, host country, or native peoples outlined in the Black ontological project. The Israel United in Christ BHI Camp in London challenges the Christian idea that God's people are anyone who believes; instead, through their interpretation, God's people, the true Israelites, are the only people God refers to as his own. This is an excerpt from some street preaching that took place in London:

Reader: Psalm 147.19 *He sheweth his word unto Jacob*
Preacher: *He sheweth his word unto Jacob, Jacob is the progenitor of the Nation of Israel, come on*

Reader: His statutes and his judgments unto Israel.
Preacher: His statutes and his judgements unto whom?
Reader: Unto Israel
Preacher: Unto Israel, the so-called Blacks and Hispanics come on
Reader: He hath not dealt so with any nation
Preacher: Uh-oh – who has not what?
Reader: He hath not dealt so with any nation
Preacher: The Heavenly Father is only dealing with the Israelites, so you can understand
Reader: And as for his judgements, they have not known them.
Preacher: And as for his judgements, they have not known them – meaning his judgements are for the children of Israel for breaking his commandments. That's why we went into slavery; that's what we're here to teach you. Come on. (The Israelites: cutting the Christian lies, IUIC London (2018) [YouTube 01.27–02.00])

A large part of the identifying process is to ground Black people's humanity in ethnic origins, geographic locations, clans, family lineage and religious heritage. This is most notable in the strong separatist nationalism that works within the host country until redemption is realized or the community repatriates. It is not to say that people who are a part of these religions do not participate in society, but that their teachings suggest that their religious framework/narrative should have more authority over their choices and modes of operation and ambition for Black people than the ideals, morals and values of the country in which they live. This approach has a significant appeal to the de-churched: the sense of ownership and participation in an ethnoreligious community that teaches 'chosenness' and disregards any sense of unworthiness one may experience on account of being Black or 'other'.

Globalization

Considering new directions for the study of New Religious Movements, Liselotte Frisk draws attention to globalization. Following the suggestion that New Religious Movements have a responsive mechanism, Frisk argues that globalization creates fertile ground for the rise in religious fundamentalism:

The process of relativization gives rise to the dual and simultaneous process of search for, on the one hand, particularistic identities, and on the other hand, universalistic identities, a process which could also be expressed religiously. Globalization is thus producing universalism and cosmopolitanism, but also, as a reaction, the assertion of particularistic identities, as opposition to the conception of the world as a series of culturally equal, relativized, entities or ways of life. An example of this resistance or particularism is religious fundamentalism, reacting to the cultural complexity of a globalized world as disturbed and dangerous, taking refuge in renewed and purified traditions. (Frisk in Zeller, 2014, p. 274)

Frisk refers to New Religious Movements that seek to form religious identities that are not necessarily ethnic-specific but are marked by spiritual and religiously ideological markers. In this sense, globalization in the twenty-first century means that people worldwide can join New Religious Movements if they have access to technology, specifically the internet, and share this new religious identity. This type of connection means that there is also greater scope for people to make the religion adaptable to their natural social and cultural environment instead of geographically specific cults where there is perhaps more of an assimilation process. Here, it can be seen that both universalistic and particularistic identities develop simultaneously. For example, the Afroasiatic religions I have selected for this study are typically ethnocentric, focusing on reclaiming an ancient ethnoreligious identity; in this way, it is not so easy to uncover the type of universalism that is associated with globalization. There is little to no sense of accommodation and tolerance of other religions. While some may argue that the principles of Rastafari have been embodied by people all around the world – the commercialized 'one love' Rastafarianism – at the core and certainly at the root of Rastafari is a genealogically informed religious perspective that challenges the legitimacy of universalism.

In Afroasiatic diasporic religions, mechanisms of globalization undeniably play a fundamental role, most notably using social media and the internet to transmit teaching to the various camps throughout the Black Atlantic (Frisk in Zeller, 2014, p. 274). In this way, they can generate and nurture an ethnoreligious identity throughout the diaspora. According to their claims, they could be considered transnational by nature due to the intervention of enslavement:

Many new religions could be seen as examples of such transnational cultures. Members are residents of different countries, but have a feeling of commonness, and of sharing of a history and a destiny with other members worldwide. (Frisk in Zeller, 2014, p. 275)

The Black Atlantic is perhaps the best phrase to describe the boundaries of its transnational nature. As we shall see in the penultimate chapter, the term Black Atlantic intends to capture the scope of Black diasporan reality and geography and the existing/evolving/hybridized religious, cultural, social and political particularities. While these religions are generally exclusive to Black/African/Asian ethnic groups, they still qualify as transnational.

Catrina Kinnvall, in her 2004 article 'Globalization and Religious Nationalism: Self, Identity, and the Search for Ontological Security', contends that globalization creates the best environment in which nationalist religious identity flourishes. She says the destabilizing effect of globalization's lack of certainty 'challenges simple definitions of who we are and where we come from' (Kinnvall, 2004, p. 742).

Globalization and other facets within postmodernity move away from fixed concepts and labels that have helped create a sense of certainty in building identity – historical, religious and geographic connections that carry unique traditions and cultures. Kinnvall argues that this insecurity, created by the ever-growing dominant global culture that undermines socially constructed religious, cultural and geographic boundaries, drives communities to what is familiar and grounding – religious nationalism being a prime example. Religion and nationalism function to provide security in response to globalization and insecurity by calling into question and challenging how society contends with reality. Kinnvall reminds the reader of how scholarship talks about religions and their beliefs as a social construction, leaving behind medieval cosmology. Religion and nationalism often work well together in fundamentalist religious expressions because they serve as longstanding institutions, vehicles that carry a people's theological, historical and genealogical identity.

> The construction and reconstruction of historical symbols, myths, and chosen traumas supply alternative beliefs to everyday insecurity. The more inclusionary such beliefs are, the more exclusionary they tend to be for individuals or groups not included in the definitions of these beliefs. The construction of self and other is therefore almost always a way to define superior and inferior beings. Superior, are those on the inside (of the religion or nation) who represent purity, order, truth, beauty, good, and right (order), while those on the outside are affected by pollution, falsity, ugliness, bad and wrong (chaos) ... The inside (the home) can bring order from the chaotic outside. (Kinnvall, 2004, p. 763)

Kinnvall poses thought-provoking questions for this study about Afroasiatic diasporic religions as constructionist and reconstructionist religions. The religious teachings depict their beliefs as spiritual revelations and as prophetic (as opposed to an inherited tradition). Being 'woke' in this sense bears the responsibility of defining the details and scope of the religion being delegated by God, who reveals the truth through the Bible and his prophets. However, it cannot be denied that these religions were birthed in a time of insecurity, struggle and oppression, and that the core messages are responsive to enslavement, subjugation and oppression.

In trying to locate these Afroasiatic religions within the broader religious scholarship, given their relatively recent emergence and apparent response to people's historical and current social conditions in (and around) those religious communities, describing them as New Religious Movements seems most fitting. On the one hand, their religious genealogy is rooted in the Christian–Ethiopianist traditions, yet they claim to have a more ancient and pure form of spirituality and religion that centres on the concepts, prophecies and histories detailed in the Hebrew Scriptures and Christian Bible. On the other hand, the constructionist lens itself generates huge questions that would lead this thesis down the path of 'legitimizing' and 'authenticating', which I do not intend to entertain. I intend to privilege the voice of the religious teachers and adherents themselves; many, I assert, do not consider their beliefs to be anything less than a transcendent epistemology.

Kinnvall identifies the importance, for many religious people, of distinguishing between identity and beliefs rather than embracing fluidity or intentional pluralism. What Kinnvall alludes to in this text is the value that many religious people place on essentialist identities:

> The more essentialist such interpretations can become in establishing links with past events, such as the historical significance of a place or a building, the more successful they will be in terms of inclusiveness and exclusiveness – in creating boundaries between self and other. Many such places (churches, temples, mosques, gurdwaras, synagogues) constitute controversial and contested sites and are often the sites of competing narratives and historical 'facts.' They are parts of the chosen trauma (or chosen glory) that define self and others in historical terms. (Kinnvall, 2004. p. 760)

Being able to make distinctions between Afroasiatic diasporic religions and Colonial Christianity, for example, is fundamental to their ethno-religious identity and purpose in the diaspora; the boundaries and exclusive nature of the belief systems are what reveal the criticisms of other competing religious traditions.

Conclusion

The prevailing themes of this chapter are encapsulated in the term Ethiopianism, a religious, social and political phenomenon birthed among the Black Bible-reading oppressed. It was a mobilizing force that evolved into the political and religious movements we have seen challenge racism in the West from the era of legal enslavement to the present day. It is a movement that is fuelled by the conviction that God sees and detests the injustices against Black people; drawing upon the themes and narratives of Scripture, Black Bible Religions seek to re-establish nationhood among Black people whose identity is more than the 'other'. Inspired by the enterprise of Garvey, the mythologies of Shabazz and Tama Re, ADR can offer the de-churched a religious experience that aspires to gather the lost and restore the diaspora to the nations of their ancestors, ruled only by the God they worship. This process begins by utilizing the resources of the dominant nations (such as the internet, social media, the education system and business opportunities) to build wealth and evangelize those not yet considered woke. This is a direct challenge to mainstream teaching about the kingdom of God, the 'now and not yet' that leaves many believers awaiting freedom and emancipation in the afterlife.

Note

1 The King James Version 1611 Bible is the preferred translation among many adherents of Black Bible Religion and so I use this version when referring to their teachings.

Black Jesus, Black Theology (transcription sample)

How do you justify taking my tithe money and you do not present a programme that feeds the people, not just feeds the people but pays a few bills here and there? Do you understand what I'm saying to ya? You got red tape – I know people that need shoes for their children, and when they go through the admin side of things, there's so much red tape they're made to feel so embarrassed about it, they don't ask. It's alright for you to take my tithe money but what about the person who needs £20 for their Oyster [card] – do you understand? My dilemma is do I give you my tithe money or do I give my sister or my brother that £20? And I say I'd give you that £20. Do you understand what I'm saying to ya? So those sort of things in the journey is becoming increasingly distressing for me, and the change, yeah, I do challenge leaders, all the time, I'm in their face ... that bishops, elders ... and I'm constantly told 'oh you can't say that' and I say 'well you show me where I can't say it if it's in the word'. Yeah, it's a real ting, so I think there should be more of this. (Participant PA, Black Jesus, Black Theology, 2018)

Participant DH: Can I just say, I know I've just come in on your fourth thing—
Eleasah: Nah, it's okay, you're welcome!
Participant DH: I'm -----'s best friend, so I've been on this journey with her. And my experience is a bit, she invited me to church on numerous occasions, and as I say to her, she knows, I believe in God. I believe 100 per cent but the church environment, it scares me, and whether from the experience, going back to this lady, you know I grew up in the West Indies, and for me, I grew up in a Catholic environment, so it was everything was White Jesus, and that's what was instilled in me as well as, like she was, I was in a middle-class family, and it was Black, White, Brown you know ... And in the church, I never felt complete there, and as soon as I came back to England with my mum she was like 'oh you got to go back to church', and I was like nope! Not going to church. 'Oh,

but you grew up in a Catholic environment.' Nope! Hated it, hated it – walking into that ting with all those tings stuck up on the wall, hated it. Numerous occasions, I've been invited to Black churches – hate them. Can't think of anything worse, but my faith is still there. I still believe in God. I'm with my friend 24/7; she's preaching to me whatever, you know I know it's in there, but that environment absolutely scares me because, I dunno, I kind of look from the outside in, what I see I don't actually like. I don't like the whole, kind of, because you got two, two, um, two differences, because you got some churches where you've got the Holy Spirit and whatever which I find terrifying, and then you've got the other thing where you've got this man or woman stands there, and they're dripping in gold or whatever else and, you know, I don't get it because to me that's not Christianity, and to me, that's not what I wanna stand there – I wanna sit in a session like this and talk amongst like-minded people, and walk out of here and think 'oh I feel whole now'. It's not about, you know what I mean, going, clapping and singing – for me that's not Christianity, that's my personal opinion. So for me, things like this, and as well as that I'm learning about my culture and my blackness, so I'm feeling whole on numerous levels. I'm walking out of here feeling a bit more Black conscious and a bit more Christian, and I'm – do you know what I mean, so to me this and when I think we talk about our youngsters, if I was to sort of turn and say to my 22-year-old son now, 'Oh come let's go to church', he'd be like, 'What!?' as opposed to me saying, 'Come and have sit-down in this session' – do you know what I mean? I think this would be more inviting for him, it wouldn't be so much like, you know. I think sessions like this will work, and it will take time like everything else because the minute you put Black in front of anything, they think, 'Oh here we go, they come with their army', so we don't necessarily have to put a label on it; but for me, obviously, on the fourth week [everyone laughs], you know, sorry, but I think things like this can work and when people are kind of talking and expressing I think that works better than the whole kind of 'oh join us' and giving tithes, you know, I don't get all that. So for me, this is a nicer environment. (Black Jesus, Black Theology, 2018).

5

Black Jesus, Black Theology (Liberation)

Participant PA: I think the biggest issue for me is, um, there's no question about my blackness and relating to Christ; there's no questions about that. I don't; I'm not schizophrenic in my faith. However, my issue is having been in church for nearly 20 years or so ... and, um, everything I've learned on my journey up until now for me as in the way it's been taught in church, is based on a lie. It's based on deception. And I say that because it doesn't match up with what's in the word. I don't – not my faith, it's not about my faith, it's not about how I see myself and how I would pray and how I would encourage and all of those things – it's not about that issue. My issue is when I sit in church, and I listen to the sermons, and I watch what's going on in church life, there's two Jesus.
Participant M: Yeah yeah yeah, it's not matching up.
Participant PA: It's not matching up the word and the church, there's a void in between, so that's been my issue. The whole Black consciousness thing and the journey of that, I've been – not secretly, but I've not been as vocal about it; this journey's been going on for me since 2006. The questioning, the research, the how does this White Jesus relate to me, and he doesn't because it's an image of something or someone's perception of who that person should be. But if God has come for everyone, there should be Black Jesus, Chinese Jesus, and European Jesus. There should be an African Jesus. Do you know what I mean?
(Black Jesus, Black Theology, 2018)

The fourth session was designed to introduce the fundamental concepts of Black Liberation Theology. Here, I explore how Black theologians have attempted to reconcile their Christian identity with the Black lived experience and the relationship between Black realities and God's sovereignty. I use Jesus as the main focus of the session, allowing me to explore the Afroasiatic diasporic religions' perspectives on the Messiah of the New Testament.

It felt important to introduce Black Liberation Theology into the conversation because I realized that it had the potential to form bridges between the mainstream Church and Black Bible Religions for dialogical purposes. Although I would argue that ADR has more in common with conservative Christianity than it does with progressive Black liberationist scholarship, the growth of ADR and BLT have similar roots and refer to the same key historical Black figures. This, I hoped, would lead the group to think about solutions moving forward. It is my observation that Black Liberation Theology has struggled to manifest itself practically in Black-British Christian spaces, so I presented some questions for the participants to consider, as the Participatory Action Research method has the potential to generate new ideas and breakthroughs:

- What is your initial response to this overview?
- How does this interact with other ideas about a Black Jesus?
- Is Black Jesus necessary for revelation?
- Does a theological Black Jesus work?
- How could Black Theology be put into practice?

Afroasiatic religious adherents seek a religion that is integral to its Afroasiatic roots. White Jesus for Afroasiatic diasporic religions is not simply a matter of contextual representation but a direct dismissal, cover-up and colonizing of the true biblical religions. ADR's concerns with uncovering historical *truth* are embedded deeply in their religious imagination.

Postcolonial and Black liberationist theologians such as Carter (2008) and Jennings (2010) would agree with Afroasiatic diasporic religions that the European Church's terror and violence towards Black people are rooted in Christianity being Europeanized. Thus, in the era where science and theology were formally racialized, these knowledge bases have come to despise, undermine and reject the Black body. Black Liberation Theology asserts the need for the Black Christ, a Messiah who sides with the poor and the subjugated. Drawing upon the life and ministry of Christ as described in the Bible, BLT recognizes that Christ was born into a colony, committed his ministry to meet the needs of those on the margins of society, and was then unjustly imprisoned and executed. Black Liberation Theology posits that God sides with those who suffer in much the same way throughout history – specifically Black people under the subjugation of White supremacy.

> To know God is to know God's work of liberation [o]n behalf of the oppressed. God's revelation means liberation, an emancipation from death-dealing political, economic, and social structures of society. This is the essence of biblical revelation. (Cone, 1970, p. 48)

James Cone, often referred to as the father of Black Theology, equates justice for the oppressed with the revelation of God, typically the scope of a Black liberationist approach. Reddie, building on the work of Cone, asserts that Black Theology's focus is on developing resources that reflect, respond to and document Black experiences:

> Essentially, Black Theology is not concerned with protecting assumed truths or with providing a spiritualized understanding of history and human experience. Rather, its central concern is the need to provide the necessary resources for fruitful and flourishing living for all people, but particularly for Black people of African descent. (Reddie 2012, p. 27)

What this highlights is that Black Theology does not have an emphasis on the conversion element of Christianity, conventionally understood as the intentional effort to convince people to submit to Jesus Christ as Lord and Saviour, but instead aims to use the biblical texts to develop a methodology for social and political justice both in the Church and in wider society. The blackness of Christ, then, is a central theme that espouses this Black political theology, but it is not a blackness that is linked to ethnicity. Instead, it is a reflection of Christ's choices, deeds and affiliations, as reported in the Scriptures. Christ was born among, worked among, and sided with the poor, and this is translated in contemporary society as siding with the oppressed and, more specifically, contextually, with Black people.

Grounded theory and postfoundationalism

I employed grounded theory as part of the methodology, which means that while I began with a hypothesis, I developed my final theory from the data I collected in my field research as both participant and researcher. As mentioned before, as an insider, I must manage my intuitions so as not to warp the data with my presuppositions. Strauss and Corbin state that 'theory evolves during the actual research, and it does this through continuous interplay between analysis and data collection' (Corbin and Strauss, 1994, p. 273). This is evident in the various methodical approaches I developed throughout the research process to best understand this phenomenon.

Stalker et al. (2005) suggest that grounded theory integrates well with Participatory Action Research. Their research deals with highly sensitive and personal topics, but the consideration of power and relationships aptly applies to my research. Of their integrated methodology, they say:

> The integration of both approaches, started with a traditional grounded theory, which led into PAR, was guided by (a) the need to produce knowledge that is relevant to and acceptable by the professional community and (b) a consideration of the power differential between survivors and professionals. (Stalker et al., 2005, p. 1131)

Grounded theory develops my knowledge-generating fieldwork (PAR) into a transferable theory applied to other contexts. Hammersley suggests: 'Grounded theorizing seeks both to represent concrete situations in their complexity *and* to produce abstract theory' (Hammersley, 1992, p. 21).

Grounded theory methodology requires a coding process that supports the integrity of my data analysis – induction, deduction and verification (Hammersley, 1992). I began by considering broad themes in the transcribed audio data, such as 'racism', 'White supremacy', 'Black power', 'origins', 'mis-education', 'transparency', 'knowledge', and 'true religion', and comparing them with my conceptual framework, intuitions and religious teaching from the Afroasiatic religions. This was a cyclical process, with each cycle refining my interpretation into something that was not only original but shed new light on the phenomena of Afroasiatic Diasporic Religion and Black-British identity formation.

Generating my theory from the data allowed my interpretation to be sensitive to the political and social events shaping my thoughts and those of the de-churched, such as the Black Lives Matter movement, the presidency of Trump, Brexit, and the Windrush scandal. Corbin and Strauss support this approach:

> One of the methodology's central features is that practitioners can respond to and change with the times – in other words, as conditions that affect behaviors change, they can be handled analytically, whether the conditions are in the forms of ideas, ideologies, technologies, or new uses of space ... when we carefully and specifically build conditions into our theories we eschew claims to idealistic versions of knowledge, leaving the way open for further development of our theories. (Corbin and Strauss, 1994, p. 276)

Building conditions into this research process has been consistent. A key example is the notion of citizenship, which had initially been considered more broadly as a communal social model to describe the social features of Black Religion. However, as events around Brexit and the Windrush scandal developed, I was drawn to consider more precisely what Afroasiatic diasporic religions contribute to the concept of being Black and

British. This trajectory became a significant feature of my findings – this tension of acceptance and citizenship in Britain, yet this appeal to Afroasiatic origins.

Martyn Hammersley in *What's Wrong with Ethnography?* (1992) questions this idea of theory emerging from the data, asking, 'On what basis can an ethnographer decide which theory is emerging?' (p. 71) Having come to a now satisfying answer, he suggests that 'we are often left with an appeal to intuition'. The case for this research is that I have designed a conceptual framework that best conceptualizes the diversity of concepts that describe what is emerging most prominently in the data. As mentioned in the previous chapter, conservatism (conceptualized) focuses on the preference for institution, tradition and religious authority, which, although very broad, works well to theoretically describe participants who demonstrate a preference for a type of institution, a sense of tradition or religious authority.

A postfoundationalist rationale considers context, interpreted experience and traditions that inform religious values to be credible sources of knowledge. It moves beyond a foundational approach that relies on a self-validated knowledge source, the Bible, to produce absolute truths. Foundationalism is problematic because the transmission of those 'truths' is clothed in human language (which evolves). A postcolonial theory posits that Eurocentric powers have monopolized interpretations of these truths. Foucault suggests that what one knows reflects who has the power (Foucault, 1991). The de-churched and Afroasiatic diasporic religions are inspired to recover knowledge and tell their divine history – *returning, correcting, and discovering*. So there is an engaging, contested space that postfoundationalism can accommodate, the decolonial process of dismantling Eurocentric epistemologies, often associated with foundationalism, and the foundationalist perspective of Scripture evidenced in the data pool (the group discussions) and among the ADR.

Postfoundationalism, as it pertains to theology, is a useful theoretical tool that aids the analysis; although not the key processing tool, it helps me to manage the tensions described in earlier chapters about the academic view of a constructivist religious phenomenon and the raw beliefs of the religious adherents themselves. Both Participatory Action Research and postfoundational practical theology prioritize the local contextual experience over the grand narratives and louder voices on specific issues. In this sense, they are the ideal tool for spaces where personal identity and communal politics are inextricably linked.

Afroasiatic diasporic religions such as Rastafari, the Nation of Islam, Hebrew Israelites and the Holy Qubtic Church movement all hold individual/communal and religious/socio-political identities in their appropriate tension. The programme was designed to facilitate those tensions by welcoming individuals into a space where their interpreted experiences and stories become the tools for more comprehensive social action. In challenging one's idea of Black identity, religious identity and Black religious identity, I hoped to uncover the basic building blocks for ADR identity formation in the British context.

Participatory Action Research challenges participants' epistemologies, making it a complementary method to postfoundationalist practical theology. It provides the opportunity to re-evaluate how one knows and understands one's world and the social issue that focuses on the research experience. In addition, the participants can create new realities and contexts by consciously exploring alternative knowledge methods, specifically knowledge grounded in their experiences.

As alluded to in the introduction, the Black Bible Religions I have selected for this study can be understood conceptually in a preservation–liberation framework. This means that I have demonstrated religious interests in preserving a sense of authoritative truth forms, ethnocentric traditions and other social/religious institutions as a basis for identity formation. At the same time, I have also demonstrated from the socio-political perspective that these religions were birthed in response to dominant Western Christianity in the context of suffering and oppression.

> Postfoundational theology … fully acknowledges the role of context, the epistemically crucial role of interpreted experience, and the role of tradition in shaping religious values. Theological reflection in postfoundationalism also points creatively beyond the confines of the local community or culture toward a plausible form of cross-contextual and interdisciplinary conversation. (Park, 2010, p. 2)

The postfoundationalist rationale also resists the groundlessness that non-foundationalist rationale champions. A non-foundationalist approach asserts that knowledge and meaning have no fixed value and are entirely relative to the individual experience (Park, 2010). This approach does not fit well with ADR because they are rooted in holy texts that serve as a source of truth and knowledge. Postfoundationalism acknowledges the limitations of these extremes and sits in between the two, working with both the fixed and the fluid. This way, one can understand the discourses that influence one's theology. This process is complemented by interdisciplinary dialogue; by engaging with decolonization or conservatism, one's theological reflection becomes enriched and allows people of different beliefs to find common ground.

Ultimately, a postfoundationalist reflection ensures a re-evaluation of epistemology, and this is central to the reflective process:

> As we have seen above, the creative fusion of hermeneutics and epistemology in postfoundational critical theological reflection occurs through the processes of interpreted experience, use of rationality and transversal reason and interdisciplinary conversation. All of these elements of postfoundationalism are critical to a practical theological process. (Park, 2010, p. 3)

Healy captures the need for a conceptual framework:

> The transition to postfoundationalist is marked by a loss of faith in these erstwhile certainties, with significant consequences for how we construe the epistemological project. Thus, sustained challenges to traditionalist foundationalist presuppositions have resulted in a loss of faith not only in indubitable foundations, but also in atemporal truths, superordinate legislative standpoints and infallible algorithmic procedures for adjudicating knowledge claims. (Healy, 2007, p. 135)

This research requires respect for foundationalist thinking because it will be represented in the data; the research is not about legitimating specific beliefs or authenticating identity formation processes but seeks to understand the motivating factors behind the phenomenon, and postfoundationalism is a supportive theoretical tool for the preservation–liberation conceptual framework and the grounded theory process.

In the last session of the programme, I gave an overview of how New Religious Movements, such as the Nation of Islam or Rastafari, teach and promote a Black Christ. One of the participants became interested in religion's self-validated sense of knowing, and he began his contribution with (paraphrase), *'Who makes this stuff up? How can Elijah Muhammad know that the earth and the moon were once joined together trillions of years before Adam?'* (Participant PH, 2018); other Christian members challenged the participant on what he believes in (how he would describe his belief system). He responds by saying (paraphrased), *'I believe in myself, I believe sometimes I am right, sometimes I am wrong ... and I believe in energy – science backs it! Energy has been around as far back as we know; everything is held or bound together by energy ... '* (Participant PH, 2018). I used this opportunity to build a bridge between the rationale of believing in science and faith by bringing up the notion of miracles, explicitly a miracle performed by Elijah in 2 Kings 6. In this account, Elijah throws a piece of wood out into the water to retrieve an axe head that had sunk to the bottom. This story could be viewed in one of two ways: an act of God (a miracle) or a matter of science and energy (theories of), but as observers of biblical accounts and scientific theories, what we have to work with at ground level is the language to convey the eventualities – human transmission. If one believes in ultimate truths, miracles by faith and scientific theories could be divided by language and power. However, on the level of experience, context and tradition, the dissimilarities lessen; not only is the adherence to the understanding a matter of 'faith', but principles guide the practice of miracles and science. Thus, this concept of energy becomes less of a divide between the scientific and the foundationalist Christian and rather a matter of language, metaphor and transversality.

Liberation?

Following an introduction to Black Liberation Theology in the East London group, the programme participants initiated a focused conversation about Christianity, the Church and finance or resources. In particular, the participants seemed to feel angry about the Church's inability to meet the needs of the poor in the congregation despite teaching about Jesus' ministry, which heavily engaged with the poor. This group was concerned not so much with Christ's appearance (like some of the other groups), but that the Jesus of the Bible was the 'Jesus' they would encounter through the Church's ministry to the local community. These concerns led the participants to value the safe, relaxed, inclusive, open discussion made available through the BCCF programme. Their hope was to replicate the setup with the view of engaging the younger generation in Christianity that spoke directly to their social and cultural needs.

Michael T. Miller in his 2020 article 'The African Hebrew Israelites of Jerusalem and Ben Ammi's theology of marginalisation and reorientation' touches on a contention that I will explore further in the next chapter: the notion of marginalization and identity as the 'other', 'poor', 'oppressed'.

> The marginalized Black Americans, the oppressed lower strata of American society, were the focal point of Ben Ammi's thoughts and the major actors in his narrative. The African American Israelites were always the centre of the narrative – this had been concealed and distorted by the satanic agenda of the Euro-gentiles, but since the Israelites began their movement back to righteousness, the world has

adjusted around them. This eschatological reordering, brought about by the revealing of divine truth, has demonstrated where the centre and margins actually lay all along: the AHI were the centrepiece. (Miller, 2020, p. 14)

Miller highlights a common characteristic among these four movements: they see themselves as central to the biblical narrative, which translates as central to contemporary society. Despite being considered marginalized and oppressed, their eschatological viewpoints on future glory and redemption reveal their true identity as people chosen by God. Miller makes an interesting observation on new Black religious movements' relationship with Liberation theology:

> The poor are the locus of Gutiérrez's theology but only to the extent that they are seen from the outside, and they are liberated from their poverty in order to incorporate them into the mainstream of privilege; to get what the others already have. In fact, one could argue that liberation theology fetishises poverty in order to release the poor from it; once liberated, they are of no further interest. In these respects, it is radically different from Ben Ammi's theology which is faithful to the biblical narrative of a single chosen people around whom the world should and will orient themselves. (Miller, 2020, p. 15)

Black Liberation Theologies seek to centralize the Black lived experience as a theological resource through which all people can see God's preference for the poor and oppressed and understand salvation through the self-determination of Black people themselves. This is unlike the centralizing of the New Black Religious Movements (or ADRs), which centralize Black people in a way that does not become redundant if Black people are no longer oppressed or marginalized and whose legacy is not limited to resistance and self-determination. Miller argues, quoting James Cone, the father of Black Liberation Theology, that 'blackness signifies oppression and liberation in any society' (Cone, 1997) and that Black Liberation Theology is not exclusive but situational; hence 'there is no special role for African Americans' in the ways that can be outlined by Ben Ammi in particular and these other New Religious Movements in general (Miller, 2020).

Miller contends that Ben Ammi's theology did not require the intervention of social reforms because his 'theodicy of deserved punishment' also outlines and foretells the African American's return to righteousness (Miller, 2020). This interpretation can again be extended to the other movements whose eschatology is framed by literalist-prophetic Scripture readings, not by intellectuals and activists who eschewed social reform. Interestingly, these movements are a rich resource for those seeking and shaping social reform, and the preservation–liberation framework makes sense of how the legacy and presence of Afroasiatic diasporic religions are holding an apocalyptic, dispensationalist hermeneutic in tension with the notion of community or social reform.

A Black Messiah

Although there is no ADR consensus on his divinity, each of the Afroasiatic diasporic religions is reverent of the person of Christ/the Messiah. Among the Hebrew Israelite camps, there are conflicting ideas on the divinity of Christ. For some, he was a major prophet, a Black man from the land of Israel; in this school, they reject the triune nature of God (Father, Son and Holy Spirit). Some consider Christ (Yahawashi) to be God incarnate, but what is generally accepted, however, is his Black ethnic appearance. Many camps refer to The Book of Revelation 1.13–16 as evidence:

> And in the midst of the seven candlesticks one like unto the Son of man, clothed with a garment down to the foot, and girt about the paps with a golden girdle.
> His head and his hairs were white like wool, as white as snow; and his eyes were as a flame of fire;
> And his feet like unto fine brass, as if they burned in a furnace; and his voice as the sound of many waters.
> And he had in his right hand seven stars: and out of his mouth went a sharp twoedged sword: and his countenance was as the sun shineth in his strength. (KJV)

Here, many BHI preachers consider this a description of a black-skinned man with afro-textured hair, and they use this as central to their arguments against White images of Christ. In much of their literature, online content and learning resources, Yahawashi (Jesus) is portrayed as a powerful, muscular, dark-skinned warrior-priest, ultimately rejecting the traditional European's effeminized, meek and gentle rendition of Jesus.

According to Barratt (1997), Barnett (2006), Murrell (in Murrell, Spencer and McFarlane, 1998) and others, Rastafari was specifically birthed from the recognition of Haile Selassie as Messiah, although the death of the Ethiopian emperor brought this fundamental belief into question and has caused division within the community. In 1930, Tafari Makonnen Woldemikael was crowned emperor of Ethiopia, taking up the formal title of Haile Selassie I, meaning 'power of the Trinity'.

Through mainstream media and the eyewitness accounts of travelling Black free men and women, Ethiopianist preachers in Jamaica were able to develop a new theology, the divinity of Haile Selassie I. Ethiopianists who followed the teaching of Marcus Garvey, believed to be a prophet, were awaiting the Black King and Messiah. Although it has become historically difficult to prove the moment Garvey had proclaimed that a Black Messiah would come out of Ethiopia, it is largely accepted that local preachers, Garveyites and others were awaiting salvation to come to them from across the Atlantic. The new religious movement came to be known most famously as Rastafari, which refers to another name of Haile Selassie, 'Ras' meaning head and 'Tafari' being his birth name. The Rastafari, the followers of Haile Selassie, believe him to be God incarnate and a descendant of King Solomon and the Queen of Sheba. This idea is linked to biblical Scripture, where Christians and Rastafari believe the text to prophesy the coming of the Messiah from the line of King David, Solomon being David's son. The Rastafari Christ has genealogical and eschatological trajectories that, despite the disappointment of Selassie's death, continue to capture many followers' religious imagination. Howell says:

> His Majesty Ras Tafari is the head over all man for he is the Supreme God. His body is the fullness of him that filleth all in all. Now my dear people, let this be our goal, forwards to the King of Kings must be the cry of our social hope ... Forward to the King of Kings. (Howell, 1933, p. 5)

In the same way that Rastafari have been able to reimagine themselves outside of the dictatorship of colonial powers, they have reimagined God as Black, and many maintain this link through the belief in the divinity of Selassie, the Black/African Messiah. Rooting their claims in the biblical Scriptures, Rastafari have developed agency for Black people, a non-subservient role in which God has chosen them to realize salvation through adherence to Haile Selassie, coming against twentieth-century Babylon and seeking repatriation back to Ethiopia (Africa) (Sugirtharajah, 2006 edn).

Redemption is equally contested among Afroasiatic diasporic religions. Rastafari, the Nation of Islam and the Black Hebrew Israelites take a more dispensationalist approach to redemption as inextricably tied to the biblical eschatological texts, anticipating a gathering of God's chosen people. Many (Black) Hebrew Israelite groups teach that the Bible prophesies a time of European dominance before the return of the Messiah and gathering of Israel to the promised land; standard scriptural references used to support these perspectives are:

> And they shall fall by the edge of the sword, and shall be led away captive into all nations: and Jerusalem shall be trodden down of the Gentiles, until the times of the Gentiles be fulfilled (Luke 21.24 KJV).

And:

> For all nations have drunk of the wine of the wrath of her fornication, and the kings of the earth have committed fornication with her, and the merchants of the earth are waxed rich through the abundance of her delicacies.
> And I heard another voice from heaven, saying, Come out of her, my people, that ye be not partakers of her sins, and that ye receive not of her plagues. (Revelation 18.3–4 KJV)

Many in the Hebrew Israelite community believe that the 400-year enslavement prophesied in Genesis is to be re-read in terms of the enslavement of Black people, estimating the return of Christ to be 2019. Popular Hebrew Israelite YouTube personality Donte Fortson contests in his book *The Black Hebrew Awakening: The Final 400 Years as Slaves in America* (2018) that 400 years of bondage in Egypt is incomplete, according to the years and dates provided in the Old Testament, and that Hebrews lived peacefully in the land for some of that time.

The Hebrew Israelite leader Ben Ammi taught that the anti-God/anti-Christ individual in the Book of Daniel 7.23 is spiritually and prophetically the European nations.

> I beheld, and the same horn made war with the saints, and prevailed against them;
> Until the Ancient of days came, and judgment was given to the saints of the Most High; and the time came that the saints possessed the kingdom.
> Thus he said, The fourth beast shall be the fourth kingdom upon earth, which shall be diverse from all kingdoms, and shall devour the whole earth, and shall tread it down, and break it in pieces. (Daniel 7.22–3, KJV)

These dispensationalist methods of interpretation are not unlike those that can be found within conservative evangelicalism.

The Nation of Islam's eschatology is primarily focused on the 'mother plane' or 'mothership' in the War of Armageddon, a small mechanical planet armed with bomber planes to destroy Allah's enemies, specifically unbelievers and the White 'race'. This idea is drawn from Ezekiel's vision of a wheel within a wheel:

> Now as I beheld the living creatures, behold one wheel upon the earth by the living creatures, with his four faces.
>
> The appearance of the wheels and their work was like unto the colour of a beryl: and they four had one likeness: and their appearance and their work was as it were a wheel in the middle of a wheel.
>
> When they went, they went upon their four sides: and they turned not when they went.
>
> As for their rings, they were so high that they were dreadful; and their rings were full of eyes round about them four.
>
> And when the living creatures went, the wheels went by them: and when the living creatures were lifted up from the earth, the wheels were lifted up.
>
> Whithersoever the spirit was to go, they went, thither was their spirit to go; and the wheels were lifted up over against them: for the spirit of the living creature was in the wheels.
>
> When those went, these went; and when those stood, these stood; and when those were lifted up from the earth, the wheels were lifted up over against them: for the spirit of the living creature was in the wheels. (Ezekiel 1:15–21, KJV)

Elijah Muhammad and Malcolm X presented their correction of the Bible texts within the context of America's social tensions, wars and politics about racial injustice. While the Nation of Islam would claim the method of truth to be revelatory, Wayne Taylor in 'Pre Millennium Tension: Malcolm X and the Eschatology of Nation of Islam' brings this revelation into the broader field of Black eschatology and compares the NOI theology with that of the Black Ethiopianist Christian churches. He posits that Elijah Muhammad builds upon the connection between the experience of the Hebrews in Egypt and the enslavement of Africans in America by trying to satisfy the failure to reach the promised land past physical emancipation (Taylor, 2005). The War of Armageddon and the Promised Land narrative become subject to the end of the world rather than to slavery. The Nation of Islam extends the story beyond slavery and into a cataclysmic physical judgment of America. Taylor suggests that the imagery of the mothership represents Elijah Muhammad's mechanical universe in that the revelation/interpretation surfaced during the era of the 'space race' between America and Russia (Taylor, 2005, p. 57). He says that 'they racialized their eschatology by conflating the white race with biblical devils' (Taylor, 2005, p. 62), supported by the racialization of God, who is Black. Despite Taylor's constructive interpretation, the plain reading of the teaching speaks of a severe and personal judgement against America.

Before the revival of these formalized ideas from Elijah Muhammad, Wallace Muhammad, his son, reinterpreted the NOI's eschatology, which was later rejected for its original vision. Wallace Muhammed's eschatological claims were similar to that of St Augustine's Millennialism; this interpretation considers the Book of Revelation as an allegory in which the millennium begins with the birth of Christ and is fulfilled through the Church. In this same sense, the Muslim community became the representation of the Black Millennium (Lee, 1996), upon which Wallace Muhammad expounded on the meaning of community instead of the destruction of White people.

In a similar vein to the interpretation of Elijah Muhammad, Rastafari interprets the biblical terminology of Babylon to mean that White supremacy would be consumed and overthrown upon the final return of the Messiah, the redemption, and the rest of the chosen people. The colonial, imperial European empire led by the government and supported by the pope has become the signifier of Babylon, the wicked and oppressive power mentioned in various places throughout the Bible. Kebede et al., in their 2000 article 'Social movement endurance: Collective identity and the Rastafari', suggest that cognitive liberation and movement/culture boundaries are critical methodologies found within the development of Rastafari. In this work, the scholars describe cognitive liberation as having two elements: first, 'system attributions' whereby Rastafari blame the governing systems for their oppression, poverty and lack of opportunity, and, second, 'political efficacy' whereby they have created a means of doing politics that works outside the parameters of mainstream political activities such as voting. Renaming the West as Babylon is evidence of this thinking: 'Babylon constitutes a symbolic delegitimation of those Western historical values and institutions that have exercised control over the masses of the African diaspora' (Edmonds in Kebede et al., 2000, p. 24) Kebede et al. further suggest that movement and cultural boundaries within Rastafari are signified by wearing dreadlocks and symbolic colours in their clothing (red, green, gold and black). In one way, these choices create an aesthetic identity, and in another way, they signify their politics, dreadlocks being statements against colonial aesthetic conventions and, for some Rastafari, a homage to a scriptural guidance system that is above the law and conventions of the 'White man'.

Some scholars may deem Rastafari escapist and apathetic, but Kebede et al. argue that Rastafari's action-politics is directed at their purpose as free Black men who oppose Babylon and will repatriate Ethiopia. This same notion can be appropriately applied across the Afroasiatic diasporic religions.

The Holy Qubtic Church, in contrast to the (Black) Hebrew Israelites, teach an esoteric Christ. According to Reverend Dr A. J. Varmah, the Head of the Holy Qubtic Church, Jesus was schooled in Africa while taking refuge in Egypt. There, he learned African history and spirituality and bore the Ka-restian consciousness.

> The Living Messiah says that he will come amongst the people, not as an individual but as a what? A consciousness, not a spirit. A personality, a consciousness, I stand at the door of your heart, and I knock. That's what the Scripture says, right. And what does it say, the heart, the heart is the seat of what? Your emotions, and your emotions is a direct reflection of your personality. How you respond to something ... so this word Christ, somebody was bringing it in, and they knew when they were bringing it, there was already a Ka-rest ... (Ancient Africans in the Bible, 2010, YouTube)

The teaching dictates that becoming like Christ is to follow the example of Jesus and grow toward the Ka-rest consciousness from Tama-Re (ancient Africa), and it is in this process that salvation is found. The Holy Qubtic Church website says:

> Thus, as your level of awareness grows, you will become more in tune with The Karast (Christ) Consciousness, working to bring salvation to all members of humanity, in varying degrees of genetic potency. So we welcome those of you, who are seeking true faith, to enter the gateway, which leads to atonement and salvation within The Holy Qubtic Church. (https://www.holyqubticchurch.com/, accessed 15.12.2020)

The theology of atonement takes on a new meaning with this alternative approach; it relies less on the ministry, personhood and death of Christ as on the idea that these activities imply an outward expression of the Ka-rest consciousness to be found in those who pursue it. Although a revered religious figure, Jesus in Afroasiatic Diasporic Religion is not necessarily as central as in mainstream Christianity. This, in part, is due to alternative salvific perspectives: attaining salvation through the law or an elevated consciousness.

Seeing Black and being Black

A tradition of Black Bible scholars is dedicated to uncovering the Black presence in the Bible, clarifying that Hebrews were not White and Jesus (Yeshua) was a person of colour (McCray, 1990, Burton 2007, Wright 1995, Adamo, 2001). However, this is not the crux of the Black Liberation theological method – it does not sufficiently respond to the claims of the ADRs that Christianity is a 'White man's religion' and that Christ himself is a European deity or fabrication of White supremacist colluders. Ultimately, Black Liberation Theology aims to take an ontological approach to the blackness of Christ, which Anthony Pinn argues recreates the very issue that Black Theology claims to combat:

> Viewing these issues from the context of overtly religious thought, it is reasonable to say that Black religious studies participate in their ideological game by demonstrating the uniqueness of Black religion in opposition to White religious expression. Ontological blackness denotes a provincial or 'clan-ness' understanding of Black collective life, one that is synonymous with Black genius and its orthodox activities and attitudes. (Pinn, 2004, p. 44)

Arguably, ontological blackness provides a safe space for Black religio-cultural assets to be documented, evaluated and analysed, having been understood as products of experience, context and continuity. These processes are essential as they allow Black religious scholars to handle these assets with care, connection and conviction rather than hostility. However, an ontological approach is not sufficient for the de-churched who demand evidence-based answers to validate the foundational claims of the faith. Black Liberation Theologies commit themselves to theologizing and politicizing blackness as death, struggle, life and hope. For example, for Cone, Black Theology was a direct combatant against America's White Jesus. Cone describes the mascot of whiteness (White Jesus) as a stumbling block for Black people:

> If Jesus Christ is white and not black, he is an oppressor, and we must kill him. The appearance of Black Theology means that the black community is now ready to do something about white Jesus, so that he cannot get in the way of our revolution. (Cone, 1970, p. 111)

Marcus Garvey's approach to making distinctions is through an Ethiopianist lens, so, unlike the other ADRs who suggest more concrete genealogical/historical connections, Garvey does not necessarily make a firm connection between Hebrews and Black people.

> If the White man has the idea of a White God, let him worship his God as he desires. If the yellow man's God is of his race, let him worship his God as he sees fit. We, as Negroes, have found a new ideal. Whilst our God has no color, yet it is human to see everything through one's own spectacles, and since the White people have seen their God through White spectacles, we have only now started out (late though it be) to see our God through our own spectacles. The God of Isaac and the God of Jacob let Him exist for the race that believes in the God of Isaac and the God of Jacob. We Negroes believe in the God of Ethiopia, the everlasting God – God the Father, God the Son and God the Holy Ghost, the One God of all ages. That is the God in whom we believe, but we shall worship Him through the spectacles of Ethiopia. (Garvey in Jacques-Garvey, 2009, p. 29)

Here, Garvey is concerned about the appropriate lens through which Black people see and understand the God of the Bible. An obvious precursor to formal Black Liberation Theology, in some sense, there is relativity in this approach that is not shared among the other ADR religions, yet they share the determination to define religion that is unique to those who are descendants of enslaved African peoples.

Carter, a third-wave Black theologian, considers the Jewishness of Christ that steers away from what Pinn alludes to as a simplistic Black vs White competition; he mirrors some of Cone's ideas in *Race: A Theological Account* (2008), where he explores the origins of a 'race' or racialized imagination. Carter's work suggests that modern theology was the root of racialized imagination, which contributed to or is responsible for the assertion of White supremacy and Black inferiority. Carter suggests that, while there is much to celebrate about Cone's contribution to Black Liberation Theology, he has repackaged and re-centred the essence of whiteness by creating a 'blackness'. By relying on the 'strength' and 'courage' framework given by Paul Tillich, Carter says, 'Cone does not challenge the way in which I-ness as a structure of identity-in-self-possession – that is, as construed in zero-sum terms – repeats the problem, albeit dialogically' (Carter, 2008, p. 191). The issue of Black Jesus in Black Theology is an epistemological one; how one knows, and names, Christ and oneself has remained subject to Eurocentric methods of naming and claiming in theological education in the West and beyond. Carter roots the theological exploration of Jesus Christ in a tangible and genetic ethnicity and, as a result, steers the conversation towards the quest for a historical Jesus. He also critiques the whiteness of Colonial Christianity and the blackness of Black Liberation Theology which has, it can be argued, become a stumbling block in the landing of Black Liberation Theology in the Black church body. Carter contends that reconnecting Jesus with his historical people is a valid form of decolonization needed within the discourse.

> But in modernity, as looked at from the underside, this ditch is the ditch of coloniality, which itself is the ditching of racial imagination built upon the severance of Jesus from the covenantal people of Israel and thus Christianity from its roots in the reality of YHWH's historical transcendence toward the world through YHWH's covenant with his people. (Carter, 2008, p. 192)

In this way, Carter has demonstrated that Black Theology has the potential to build bridges between Hebraic-Afroasiatic religions and cultures, grounding the theory in a resourcefully rich tension of past and present identities. This is different from glorifying the gentile conversion, which Carter suggests is central to our Western theological imagination. By drawing the de-churched away from dominant Christian imaginings and criticisms (particularly with slavery) momentarily, the potential to sever Christianity from Christendom's White supremacist campaigns offered alternative ways of understanding Christianity as a religious tradition rooted in ethnic identity and geography.

The womanist theologian Dianne Steward says:

> Even in instances where theologians may not be interested in examining slave religion, preferring instead to limit the scope of their research to studies of Christian religiosity among the enslaved, African diaspora studies research and competency in the African religious heritage will facilitate more carefully nuanced interpretations of Christianity in the lives of enslaved Africans. (Stewart, 2004a, p. 80)

A Black liberationist approach speaks to the contextual nature of Afroasiatic religions, which share historical, social and religious experiences. BLT systematically and theologically seeks to liberate Black people and Christianity from White hegemonic religion by reimagining the person of Christ as a Black Messiah through experience, but ADR demands that Christ be identified as Black through the Scriptures. Progressive approaches to the decolonization process question the Bible's credibility

BLACK JESUS, BLACK THEOLOGY (LIBERATION)

and the integrity of human (male) authorship. Renita Weems, a postcolonial and womanist theologian, calls into question the dedication of Christian believers to texts that can be considered violent towards them:

> The interests of real flesh-and-blood black women are privileged over theory and over the interests of ancient texts, even 'sacred' ancient texts ... the Bible cannot go unchallenged in so far as the role it has played in legitimating the dehumanization of people of African ancestry in particular. It cannot be understood as some universal, transcendent, timeless force to which word readers – in the name of being pious and faithful followers – must meekly submit. It must be understood as a politically and socially drenched text invested in ordering relations between people, legitimating some viewpoints and delegitimizing other viewpoints. (Weems, 2016, Chapter 1)

Weems illuminates an interesting contention of understanding centred on the role of the Bible and the enslavement of 'African ancestry' in particular. An in-depth study of slavery in the biblical context reveals that the systems of slavery are not parallel to that of the enslavement of Africans in the European transatlantic slave trade. While slavery is an undesirable position, Weems' assertion does not consider the social function of slavery in Hebrew society as a means of getting people out of poverty – which, it can be argued, is redemptive and not dehumanizing. There are undeniably controversial issues of gender inequality for female slaves (particularly women who are sold by their fathers and cannot opt to be freed after seven years but are instead enslaved for life), and the undeniable exploitation of enslaved people by individual persons, which deserves critical engagement; however, it is an unsatisfactory conclusion that the Bible is responsible for the enslavement of Africans in the sixteenth century. Weems here highlights the chasm between the faith-based religions (assumed to be erroneous) and the politicized theology that I argue the ADR aims to fill. Weems goes on to demonstrate the challenges of Protestant/Reformed perspectives on approaches to Scripture for the Black woman:

> To see African American Protestant women's devotions to the stories of the Bible as a continuing example of a naïve attachment to the principle of *sola scriptura* or as a slavish belief in these texts as the divinely revealed word of God, the sole authority in all matters religious, is to traffic in partial truths and to be overly determined about a far more complex and subtle aspect of gender, reading and culture. (Weems, 2016, Chapter 1)

Weems suggests that submission to its religious authority is an incomplete and unjust approach and asserts theological violence towards marginalized peoples that is manifested in socio-political systems of dominance. Clarence J. Martin, in 'Womanist Interpretations of the New Testament: The Quest for Holistic and Inclusive Translation and Interpretation' (1990), draws our attention to the more technical aspects of interpretation and translation. Here, Martin confronts 'texts of terror' (a phrase coined by Phyllis Trible, 1984), such as the use of slavery in the New Testament. This womanist theological hermeneutic does not set about redeeming these 'terror texts' but instead highlights them as problematic and, in many cases, seeks to relieve them of religious authority. The hermeneutic requires that the readers humanize the authors of the texts and 'amplify the voices of *all* persons who are marginalized in the text' (Martin, 1990. p, 53) so we can consider how they may have been complicit in the oppression revealed in their religious writings. Holding past and present religious thought in tension, Martin says:

> A womanist critical biblical hermeneutics, then, must not only critique the tendencies of the biblical writers and traditional processes themselves, but must also analyse contemporary scholarly and popular interpretations and appropriations of those traditions, and the underlying theoretical models. But that is not the end of the story. A womanist biblical hermeneutic must clarify whether the *doulos* texts, potential 'texts of terror' for Black people, can in any way portend now possibilities for our understanding of what actually constitutes the radicality of the good news of the Gospel. (Martin, 1990, p. 60)

By highlighting the context in which the authors of the biblical texts lived, focusing on 'texts of terror', a womanist hermeneutic asserts its capability to recognize and resist present-day manifestations of intersectional violence and oppression. The womanist framework is so entrenched in *experience* that it applies its varied hermeneutical principles to the day-to-day experiences of Black women in the Church and the wider society. This allows womanist theologians to use their religious and theological critique for socio-political purposes; the Bible becomes (after much dismantling) a critical anthropological resource towards understanding the strategies of people in power and the suffering, strength and resistance of the oppressed. This approach to Scripture (or culmination of various approaches in conversation) seeks to relieve Christianity from its authoritative religious text and emphasize theologically rooting its moral perspectives in knowledge generated through the experiences of the oppressed.

With a particular focus on the approach to Scripture, the Afroasiatic diasporic religious voice, and arguably the voice of the de-churched, while suspicious of specific translations, do not reduce the authority of the sacred text to a mere cultural resource. Instead, what we have seen in this study is a reverential attitude and dependency on the Bible to uncover the true religion of God's chosen people. A constructivist view would argue that ADR bring their experience to their Bible reading, but the ADR argue that the Bible makes sense of their experiences because it is prophetic (foreseeing) and a product of their ancestors' experience of the Most High (God).

Conclusion

It is clear that Black Bible Religions and Black liberationist thought have much in common – common epistemological ancestors, common fuels and common enemies – but it is the methods and, at times, outcomes that are at odds with one another. What this chapter demonstrates is the ways in which Black Liberation Theologies and Black Bible Religions are symbiotic and not synonymous. Of course, Black Bible Religions produce theologies of Black people, but their teachings and aspirations require intellectual input that is interested in establishing fixed truths and fact-finding, yet allows for the mysterious revelation of their leaders to shape the final interpretation. Black Liberation Theologies' obligation to the poor rather than the chosen, to the oppressed rather than the soon-to-be-victors, and to context rather than eschatology, means that it has little to offer the de-churched whose questions are of origins, nationhood and personal/national redemption.

State Your Case (transcript sample)

I find that insulting when I hear that [Black people are only Christian because it was forced upon them] coz it tells me two things; it tells me one thing that people believe that Black people were that weak to let someone make you feel something, and at the same time, make you keep going on believing. We find it hard to now get someone to believe something, let alone when someone is forcing you to do something, while they're beating you, killing your family – all this stuff. And it's manipulation. It's manipulation of the Scriptures that they use to justify what they were doing but to manipulate something you had to know something in the first place. So I know that if we go back before slavery, in Africa, back back back, I don't know if anyone has been to the Pan-African centre here in London, and, uh, if you go you will learn, there is so much that you will find out about Black people that it's amazing. Even one of the richest to this day, the kings, one of the richest people ever to live is a Black man. And, um, I say all this to say, there's so much greatness there, and to feel that someone's kind of made you believe something I find insulting, we're not the only enlightened species, all of the sudden we're enlightened because it's 2016 and all of the sudden we realize actually 'no it was all a lie'. (Participant DS, State Your Case, 2016)

You know when you think about Jesus, you see a White man on a cross with a beard and long hair and that's gonna affect the way, the way that you view Jesus, it's gonna affect the way that you view Christianity. You know, I remember witnessing at some point some guys say to me, 'Nah that's a White man's religion … I don't do that', and it's – again, it's really the person who holds the bigger stick is the one who sets the rules. Yeah, there were loads of Black Christians way before White Christians, but when you think about it like, for example, I'm rambling, but if you think about it, you got Hollywood, you got Nollywood. Hollywood, yeah, they got the explosions, they got the marketing, they got so much millions, and they can't tell you about all the movies that's taking place. And then you've got Nollywood, nobody really knows about it unless you watch it, and I think that the people that have the most money control the image. They control the way that you look at things. That's why I think certain people can suggest that Christianity is a White man's religion because the people that hold the biggest stick are the ones that are often gonna have the biggest say about it. (Participant RU, State Your Case, 2016)

Participant MI: I wanted to say something, um, something you said [indicating participant NA]: you said, um, we didn't have this racial designation and especially in our history a lot at that time, the people. So let me just bring up some names: the Moors, the Hamidians, the Carthaginians, the Tamagaru, the Copts – those are the ancient Egyptians – the Hebrews, the Babylonians, the Sumerians, the Phoenicians, the Ethiopians, the Cushites – these were all Black people. So naturally, there's that notion of sameness, so the thing that stands out distinctive among the groups is their culture, their language or their dressing, something to that effect. So what happens is, when you read the Bible, you don't see a lot of physical descriptions of these people except maybe what somebody was wearing or what they were holding, something to that effect, that would have been the distinctive marker of the religion or culture – not what they looked like, because everyone at that time, prior to the Cyprian, Greek, Turkish, Roman, Asiatic, basically all those people in the Middle East or Northeast Africa and the rest of the continent were all Black, so that notion of sameness. So there was never need of me saying 'Oh a Sumerian is Black, or this person is Black'. So the point is that there was no need of that description in the Bible, you know what I'm saying? But if you read history books, you will find that. But because obviously with the Bible, the issue is, because those descriptions aren't there and they're not solid – tactile, you know, written down – it leaves space for other people to put their own images, do you see what I'm saying? It leaves room, like for example: I debate a lot of Arabs and Europeans when they try to debate me about the Moors, 'cause when it comes to the Moors, there are pictures, primary sources of the Moors, where they lived, how they looked at that time, during the Islamic Era and before, so my point is there was written accounts of what they looked like – their skin, their nose, their hair.
Participant NA: Shakespeare
Participant MI: Not just Shakespeare, the French, the Italians, the Greeks did it, the Romans did it – so many people actually described them, even the Arabs did, so my point is there's no real case to argue with that one. But with the Bible, because there were so many people that looked the same because they were Black, there was no actual physical description of a lot of these people – of what the Hebrews looked

like, of what the Egyptians looked like, of what this group or that group looked like – so that has left a wide berth for these people to appropriate it and whitewash it. And so again, because we're looking at this object of race which is a European concept, it is really a European concept, but it wasn't that Black people were oblivious to race; we were very proud of our blackness, it's just that we didn't – it wasn't the be-all and end-all of our existence, so that's what I wanted to say about that. (State Your Case, 2016)

6

Geography, Genealogy and [g]ods

The question here has to be worded, so we can make these kinds of critical analyses and come to intelligent conclusions. My point is if I were to go Ghana and tell a typical Ghanaian that that's Jesus on the right, yeah [image of Black Jesus], he would look at me as if I were insane. That's a fact, yeah, and that's what we have to deal with, so the whole, we're getting two things mixed up as well. The White Jesus was used for a purpose; yeah, it was deliberately used to manipulate, like you said earlier [pointing to Participant DS]. (Participant NA, State Your Case, 2016)

Although the sessions I designed were built as a response to criticism of the validation of the Scriptures themselves, it was often the case that participants would use biblical Scriptures as a form of evidence and support for their argument. During the earlier development of the programme, I facilitated a one-off event called 'State Your Case', which invited anybody interested in Black consciousness and Christian faith to take the stage and deliver an argument that would then be open for dialogue. There were two reasons for this approach. First, regarding my research, I wanted to make sure that the hypothesis I was developing was being built on the relevant topics. Second, in line with the ethos of Participatory Action Research, I wanted to demonstrate its capacity to allow others to take the lead in the sessions and determine the topics and themes to be explored. Despite the positive levels of interest I received when advertising the sessions, only one person signed up to 'State His Case', a Black Christian male in his late thirties, who took an apologetic, evangelical approach to dismantle some of the arguments the conscious community/ADRs had made against Christianity.

This chapter will feature more transcriptional input than the other chapters; this session was one of the last in the Central London location, and the data pool was rich after weeks of discussion and developing relationships. It was very important throughout this investigative process that I had a strategy for facilitating group discussions, particularly on a sensitive topic that dealt with suffering, discrimination, identity and religion. My hope for the sessions was that people would feel that they could share safely, without the need for censorship and allowing the group to assume their unique shape. So, I begin this chapter by outlining my methodical guide for facilitating group discussions. I then move on to conceptualize 'conservatism' and 'evangelicalism' in a way that allows one to consider them as authentic Black reading and epistemological conventions, distinct from White conservatism in its ideals and outcomes but with obvious points of convergence: the need to *dissent, recover and re-establish*. The final sections are committed to discussing the religious (and political) teachings that influence the need of the de-churched to be rooted by geography and genealogy and what it means to be made in the image of God.

Group discussion

In *Pedagogy of the Oppressed* (1970), Paulo Freire introduces a critical pedagogy to the academic platform. A revolutionary work from Brazil (considered part of the 'third world'), this challenged how education existed, perceived love, and liberated the oppressed. Freire's dialogue as a form of transformation education is a vital tool for defining a pedagogical method for the BCCF programme, as it destabilizes all preconceived notions of 'teaching well'. Freire describes dialogue as a human phenomenon in which *true words* are the goal (action + reflection). The true word informs a work that informs a praxis that transforms the world (Freire, 1970, p. 68). Words that are not true, either lacking action or reflection, are merely verbalisms and are considered non-transformative.

Further thoughts on this were presented in a 1987 article, 'What is the dialogical method of teaching?', by Freire and Ira Shor, where Freire posits, 'Dialogue is the moment where humans meet to reflect on their reality as they make and remake it' (Shor and Freire, 1987b, p. 13). Dialogue, in this context, is more than just a conversation; it is a meaningful and transformative experience in the process of getting to the conversation, which is undergirded by the thought, language, aspirations and conditions of the student (Shor and Freire, 1987b, p. 11).

Freire's theory on dialogue speaks directly to small-group dynamics. In a series of instructions, he establishes a code of conduct to achieve dialogue in the transformative sense. There is no room for domination, one over the other, within dialogue; it is a safe space in which the word is the right of everyone (Freire, 1970, p. 69). Establishing these rights in dialogue gives everyone the right to be considered a human with agency; there is no room for a division of class or 'race'. Freire was mainly concerned with the evil of capitalism and was committed to educating the illiterate communities, contributing to the development of their countries throughout his career.

Dialogue demands critical thinking, which demands understanding of one's reality and the part one plays in that reality. This type of learning establishes equality among the group. In contrast, the banking method in which the teacher fills the receptacles (students) with static narrative (facts) denies the students the opportunity to truly engage with the narrative and experience the life behind the facts and how it relates to their reality. The banking method does not require critical thinking and minimizes students' opportunity to understand their reality and create new realities; it does not require the type of student participation that ensures holistic growth. In rejecting the banking method of transference and domination, the dialogical method affirms everyone's right to speak, in that it does not work without the contribution of sincere others to find true words that have action, that have been reflected upon, and that create new realities and ways that people can name the world and not be subject to being named (Freire, 1970, p. 69). The liberation within Freire's dialogue is present in the fact that people have the freedom to speak for themselves, to name their reality and to have that naming valued; 'those who have been denied the primordial right to speak their word must reclaim this right and prevent the continuation of this dehumanizing aggression' (Freire, 1970, p. 69).

One of the crucial moments within the dialogical teaching method is the space for the teacher to learn and relearn what they already know. It is not just liberation for the student that is the goal, but for the teacher: every time a topic is taught to build upon the reality of what they know, the experience is 'shaped by the subject matter and training of the teacher, who is simultaneously a classroom teacher, a politician and artist' (Shor and Freire, 1987a, p. 11). In this way, learning is not achieved through the accumulation of knowledge and facts but by making sense of the information according to one's lived experience and transforming those realities.

Freire's work is set within a framework of humanism, the pursuit of betterment as a human, experiencing and fulfilling human potential. He concludes that true dialogue cannot occur without these five virtues:

- Love – 'If I do not love the world – if I do not love life – if I do not love people – I cannot enter dialogue.'
- Humility – 'Dialogue, as the encounter of those addressed to the common task of learning and acting, is broken if the parties (or one of them) lack humility.'

- Faith – 'Faith in people is an *a priori* requirement for dialogue; "the dialogue man" believes in others even before he meets them face to face.'
- Hope – 'Hope is rooted in men's incompletion, from which they move out in constant search – a search which can be carried out only in communion with others.'
- Critical thinking – 'Thinking which perceives reality as process, as transformation rather than as a static entity.' (Freire, 1970, p. 71)

Freire's dialectical teaching method speaks directly to the nature of group dynamics within a small-group setting, which I feel is necessary for this programme. Dialogue provides a vehicle in which the like-minded and those who share similar experiences and interests can make sense of their reality and transform it into something better or more appropriate. In my study, dialogue can help those connected by a commitment to and hope for justice for Black people to name and rename their realities. This type of transformative communication requires a vision and an established goal for learning and action, which creates a sense of value for the group and its members. Applying the dialogical teaching method to the programme can create a sacred space for those within the learning space; however, its humanist bent does not resonate with the religious emphasis I envisage for this study.

During the group discussion, I began by sharing my own story of someone on a personal journey of understanding my faith in relation to my identity, and some of the broader issues of miseducation and whitewashing of Scriptures that I believe have shaped my understanding of God. It is crucial to clarify that, in the session space, we all become teachers and students and that, although there is initial educational input, it is still limited to operating as a tool to provoke ideas and questions and is open to criticism and further exploration by the participants.

Each group discussion should be considered a planned discussion (O'Reilly, 2008) or focus group, in that I methodically organized the gathering of the participants, and each section had a topical focus. The initial seminar section of the event, as mentioned before, was designed to provoke and stimulate ideas, questions, rebuttals and responses for the group discussion, which was the main focus. In the programme's pilot, I had anticipated an attendance of eight and was overwhelmed with a response of over 100 people. However, as I moved into the ethnographic data collection, where the sessions were topic-led, each session averaged 20 people per session. This seemed to work well because, while more dominant characters would often lead with their contributions, having such diverse responses among those considered more dominant seemed to give those considered 'quiet or reticent' (O'Reilly, 2008) more confidence to contribute.

In *Nobodies to Somebodies: A Practical Theology for Education and Liberation* (2003), Anthony Reddie details and discusses the process of developing a church- and child-friendly education programme that used Black Theology, Womanist Theology and transformative education as its frameworks. Reddie sought to develop materials that reflected the everyday life of the Black-British reality by devising activities, games and role-plays that featured African/Caribbean foods, music and colloquialisms. While acknowledging that Afrocentricity is problematic in its essentialism and romanticism of 'blackness' and Africa, he concludes that at the centre of Afrocentricity is the crucial resource of Black culture; it 'offers a critically important tool and framework for the task of developing an appropriate model or example for the Christian education of Black youth in Britain' (Reddie, 2003, p. 36). Reddie asserts that by infusing Christian education with Black culture, young people can be affirmed in their hybrid reality. He concludes that Black music is an essential tool to make this positive affirmation work as it is a key expression of Black-British culture and tells a more truthful story of the Black experience in Britain. By creating a space where both Black cultures and Christian education are at play, Reddie aims to create a safe space of affirmation and positive identification:

> These young people required specific, intentional education processes for their emotional and psychological wellbeing ... they needed additional education and theological interventions that would assure them it was acceptable to be 'Black' and more starkly 'non-white'. (Reddie, 2003, p. 145)

What is apparent is Reddie's intention to develop a programme that encourages emotional and psychological well-being through the affirmation of Blackness and the relationship between God and Black people as made in his image. Inspired by James Cone's systematization of Black Theology and through the support of a Black Theology group during his research, Reddie used Black Theology as one of the major frameworks for the programme.

The programme works as a praxis for liberation as it emerges from the margins (Reddie, 2003, p. 7) and seeks to establish justice for the oppressed, the overlooked Black youth within mainline British churches. Part of the liberative process was to give the young people an opportunity 'to see aspects of their cultural and familial world reflected as the norm', countering the British institutional stigma of 'other' (Reddie,

2003, p. 145). Reddie draws upon Shor and Freire's reflections on the learning process and transformative education. Reddie argues that this notion of defining truth through a mutual explorative relationship between the student and teacher is able to improve the student's ability to develop agency and understand history, particularly Black history, of which the delivery and interpretation are often policed. Reddie uses dialogue to draw upon the benefits of transformative education within his programme; he found that the young people became literal and figurative actors within the teaching and learning process.

Moving beyond Freire, Reddie details how he uses the ideas of Grant Shockley to devise group activities that encourage the young people to define their world 'instead of being named by it' (Reddie, 2003, p. 87). For Christian education to be effective, it must wrestle with God's response to the present Black reality. Black Theology's answer to this humanist theory is that 'God sided with the oppressed in his manifestation as an oppressed Jew' (Cone, 1969). For Freire's theory to be truly transformative in religious spaces, it must meet with a framework that affirms the Black experience and develops action for liberation shaped by a religious perspective; the preservation–liberation framework meets this requirement.

Black Bible conservatism

In the previous chapters, I've discussed notions of conservatism present in Black Religion, primarily intended to be a criticism of Black Christian reading conventions and, more broadly, nationalist and patriotic stances. Conservatism, in many ways, has become synonymous with racism and colonialism. While considering its historical implications, there are grounds for conceptualizing conservatism that speak to anti-radicalization, a preference for institution and religious authority. Although many consider the Black Bible Religions to be radical, their reading conventions and bent towards institution and preservation of tradition say otherwise.

Conservatism as intellectual discourse or ideology is largely contested; a simple singular definition has yet to be produced because it is most simply understood for what it is not rather than for what it is. Its very nature rejects abstract theories and ideologies, so it cannot be sufficiently discussed accordingly. This being said, Samuel P. Huntington, in *Conservatism as an Ideology* (1957), persisted in using an ideological framework to demonstrate the nature of conservatism in a way that makes it helpful to discuss alongside the ideologies it opposes. While acknowledging its historicity, Huntington suggests that conservatism stands alone as situational and autonomous in its mechanisms.

Often termed 'reactionary', historical conservatism was formally birthed as a response to the French Revolution in the eighteenth century, which succeeded in overthrowing France's aristocratic rule and attempted to implement a liberal democratic system. It demonstrated the deep-seated frustration of the everyday person, both rich and poor, who did not have access to political power and influence due to the institution of feudalism. The writings of Edmund Burke, *Reflections on the Revolution in France* (1790), were a key catalyst for further defining conservative attitudes that, as with all intellectual thought, have varied perspectives and ambitions. While there is no space or need to herald Burke as the authority on conservatism, the context from which his opinions have developed is significant for understanding it's mechanisms. Daniel O'Neill, in *Edmund Burke and the Conservative Logic of Empire* (2016), summarizes Burke's ideas in a few sentences, that while in itself the interpretation of Burke's ideas is not supremely authoritative, they do provide critical points for this defining process and a strong trajectory that can be traced to conservative views of the twenty-first century.

> Burke adhered to a view of history as a civilizing process that stressed the fundamental importance of the landed aristocracy and organized religion for human progress and development. Conversely, he rejected as philosophically absurd and politically disastrous basic liberal notions such as natural human equality and declaration of universal individual rights, he consistently lampooned any notion of political and social equality between sexes or between the higher and lower orders. (O'Neill, 2016, p. 169)

O'Neill first highlights Burke's view of society as an evolutionary process toward good, which is undergirded by the dependence on institutions such as the Church and aristocracy to aid this 'civilizing process'. Second, he illuminates its aversion to abstract ideologies that aim to solve entirely the inevitable inequalities among citizens in the country. Conservatism is known for its 'slow reform' approach to society and politics in that, as mentioned before, it takes a historical view that society becomes better and more civilized over time and not through revolution but through evolution. So while, for Burke, society must make changes and requires improvement, these improvements can and should be made through the mechanisms of tradition, institution and religion. Society, in this view, has been described as a social contract which liberal politics sought to dismantle by applying abstract theories to complex human lives. Burke, on the other hand, posited:

> Society is indeed a contract … [But as] the ends of such a partnership cannot be obtained in many generations, it becomes a partnership not only between those who are living, but between those who are living and those who are dead and those who are to be born. Changing the state as often as there are floating fancies … no one generation could link with the other. Men would be a little better than flies of summer. (Burke, 1776)

Burke is alluding to the need for tradition and continuity, saying that tradition grounds humanity and provides a mechanism through which society can learn from mistakes and maintain what has proved to be successful. Huntington picks up on this idea; he says, 'the essence of conservatism is the rationalization of existing institutions in terms of history, God, nature and man' (Huntington, 1957, p. 457). He means that, aside from Burke's response to the French Revolution, conservatism in its own right functions as a resisting force to the dismantling of existing institutions in any society. According to Huntington and others, conservatism is not about protecting aristocracy or the Church in particular but about preserving and valuing any long-serving institutions as vehicles of wisdom and experience. This situational perspective concludes, then, that while conservatism is usually only active when the need arises – when there is an ideological resistance against the existing institution – what can also be seen through Burke's response to the French Revolution are some principles that complement yet go beyond a simple love for institution. The following is a summary of conservative principles concerning societal progress:

- Man is basically a religious animal, and religion is the foundation of civil society. A divine sanction infuses the legitimate, existing social order.
- Society is the natural, organic product of slow historical growth. Existing institutions embody the wisdom of previous generations. Right is a function of time: 'prescription', in the words of Burke, 'is the most solid of all titles …'.
- Man is a creature of instinct and emotion as well as reason. Prudence, prejudice, experience and habit are better guides than reason, logic, abstractions and metaphysics. Truth exists not in universal propositions but in concrete experiences.
- The community is superior to the individual. The rights of men derive

from their duties. Evil is rooted in human nature, not in any particular social institution.
- Except in an ultimate moral sense, men are unequal. Social organization is complex and always includes a variety of classes, orders and groups. Differentiation, hierarchy and leadership are the inevitable characteristics of any civil society.
- A presumption exists 'in favour of any settled scheme of government against any untried project ... ' Man's hopes are high, but his vision is short. Efforts to remedy existing evils usually result in even greater ones. (Burke paraphrased in Huntington, 1957, p. 456)

Working within these premises, conservatism can then be said to be a response and resistance to any ideology that seeks to usurp these premises. So it is not the case, then, that conservatism is the opposite of liberalism – there are examples, particularly with fiscal conservatism, of overlap; rather, it is against anarchy, radicalization and revolution – in brief, against the complete disregard for the existing institutions of the society. Nor is it the case that conservatism is always pro-monarchy or aristocracy; applied to North American society, conservatism is pro-constitutionalism as they have never had a monarchy. However, it is the case for British conservatism, whose foundational institutions are the monarchy and the Church.

In *Conservatism: Dream and Reality* (2017), Nisbet considers the constant struggle between tradition and new ideas and innovative philosophies towards a perfect society. Conservatism does not seek perfection but is committed to tradition:

> Given our normal predilection for the more exciting Enlightenment mentality of the Voltaires, Diderots and d'Holbachs, it is easy to miss, in the histories, this counter-force to the high rationalism and individualism of the Enlightenment. But it is there all the same, a product at one and the same time of the *Church* and its still considerable numbers of philosophers and theologians committed to orthodoxy instead of ideas of natural religion and natural ethics which had sprung out of the natural law movement of the seventeenth century. The more that *philosophes* declared the enlightenment of their doctrines of natural rights, the more the philosophers and historians in the universities – all religiously oriented, of course – appealed to the traditions which had sustained Europe for more than 1000 years. (Nisbet, 2017, p. 20)

Afroasiatic religions could also be considered as gatekeepers of the religious orthodoxy, deferring to an ancient and traditional ethnoreligious institution; the preference for identity formation being generated through a genealogical, traditional or mythological historical gaze is typically conservative.

> Basic to conservative politics is its view of the role of history, 'History' reduced to its essentials is no more than experience, and it is from conservative trust in experience over abstract and deductive thought in matters of human relationships that its trust in history is founded. (Nisbet, 2017, p. 38)

Kieron O'Hara, in his 2016 article 'Conservatism, Epistemology and Value', explains how conservatism supports a variety of social models:

> In a relatively egalitarian society without a hierarchical structure, a conservative position would defend *against* hierarchy and inequality. Even in a hierarchical and unequal society, a conservative's line might be that social stability will be promoted by ensuring that power or resources were shared a little more widely. (O'Hara, 2016, p. 425).

The point here is that conservatism defends historical institutions, an act of preservation – and is situational, so it allows for differences of opinions, systems and governmental structures by geography:

> An ideologue who focuses on a particular end detects its absence in existing society (which is so complex that no end will be entrenched enough to satisfy its adherents). This then becomes a key aim of the ideologue's policy, because of his one-dimensional yardsticks of what constitutes a successful society. On the other hand, the conservative eschews the idea of society having ends at all, and so – though he may well be critical of existing society – he can also appreciate its positive aspects without contradiction. (O'Hara, 2016, p. 431)

Conservatism, considered conceptually, is the balancing feature of this conceptual framework that best supports the ADR preference for tradition, religious authority and institution. The progressive intellectual contribution to the current extreme polarization of the British political landscape has been identity, representation, recognition and rights. With organizations such as the Black Lives Matter movement at the helm of Black progressivism in social spheres, people of colour are challenging the existing democratic political system which, they argue, is founded upon White Supremacy, patriarchy and exploitative capitalism (including the enslavement of African and Indigenous peoples). As its leading contender in many ways, conservatism has become synonymous with racism, White Supremacy, imperialism, colonialism and intolerance. Defining the principles of conservatism conceptually is essential to this study because I suspect that it describes the political/social attitudes of many, if not most, Black British Christians and those who can be described as de-churched. Not that they are racists and complicit in their oppression, but that Black history, ancient African and Caribbean cultures (proverbs and morals), family traditions, religion and continuity are essential features that govern and protect Black life.

We see conservative leanings in the social and religious attitudes of the Afroasiatic Diasporic Religion. Influenced by the teachings of Elijah Muhammad, who described the original man as rulers of the universe, the NOI community is committed to personal reform from slavish behaviours.

> In short, being a real Muslim meant exhibiting those behaviours so often associated in the United States and black America with middle-class respectability and being 'civilized'. For Members of the Nations of Islam, these protestant-like habits did not signify a capitulation to the norms and ideas of American Protestantism but instead became evidence of a properly Islamized and mentally resurrected black person. (Curtis, 2014, Chapter 6)

In the nation-building identity formation process, it seems that rooting oneself in an established historical timeline, an ethnic group, and a religious tradition with mechanisms for preserving these cultures and roots defines the point of convergence between Black Religion and conservatism. Judith Weisenfeld in *A New World – A-Coming: Black Religion and Racial Identity during the Great Migration* (2017) documents African Americans who re-identified themselves formally during their migration to the northern states of America. Referring to the 'Moorish Americans' or 'Ethiopian Hebrews', Weisenfeld demonstrates a 'religio-racial identity'. This transformation or reclamation shows us that religion was essential for many Black people in maintaining a sense of self beyond being Christianized. In this way, religion, particularly Afro-Hebraic religion, functions as an institution, a carrier of traditions, ideas, and truths:

> Even as they promoted different configurations of an intertwined religious and racial sense of individual self and shared history, the group held in common a conviction that only through embrace of a true and divinely ordained identity could people of African descent achieve their collective salvation. (Weisenfeld, 2017, Introduction)

Weisenfeld also considers the notion of ethnoreligious recovery:

> Rather than position the groups under consideration in this volume in relation to a presumed normative centre by labelling them 'cults' or 'sects' or isolate them from broader cultural and religious influences as new religions, I examine them as windows into religious challenges to conventional racial categories and explore what participation in the movements meant for members. (Weisenfeld, 2017, Introduction)

Weisenfeld looks at the narrative taught by Black religious leaders that lays the foundation of articulating knowledge of self and racial-religious identity formation, demonstrating the Ethiopian Hebrew religions' 'path to self-knowledge and understanding of peoplehood that articulated a literal connection to a sacred geography' (Weisenfeld, 2017). The ADR adhere to the cosmological teachings that would locate Black religious individuals, the Negro, the White man and the rest of the world, be it divine, supreme, raceless or determined by their dis/connection to past experiences – a cosmology that outlines the role of the leadership, prophets, men, gods and messiahs.

Black religions distinguished and maintained the 'new religio-racial selves', with performative actions such as dress, food choices, change of names and rituals within their new theological frameworks – returning or being 'restored to their true, original nature.' (Weisenfeld, 2017, Part II). The significant final section details how these groups defined and built their communities, families, location for living and relationships outside of their communities.

The structure of the study outlines personal and communal transformation that begins with the experience of being Black in twentieth-century America, which is influenced by Bible-based religious teaching. Interestingly, many African American migrants in the twentieth century sought to officially record this transformation on paper by the changing of name and ethnicity while physically journeying to new territories.

> I use the term 'religio-racial identity' to capture the commitment of members of these groups to understanding individual and collective identity as constituted in the conjunction of religion and race, and I refer to groups organized around this form of understanding of self and people as religio-racial movements. (Weisenfeld, 2017, Introduction)

The data shows that 'White Man's Religion?' prompts the need to make distinctions between European Christianity and the religion of the Bible. To make these distinctions, both the de-churched and ADR communities seek to 'recover' and 'reclaim' ancient Afroasiatic religion grounded in ethnicity and 'nationhood'. In this sense, Colonial Christianity is a stolen religion – the national and spiritual property of communities in the Afroasiatic region. The key solutions presented by the ADR lie in knowing the truth, obedience to God as described in the Scriptures, and participation in correcting and challenging the false religion – much like what we see with evangelicalism.

Evangelicalism

The emergence of Black Urban Apologists, ministers, teachers, pastors and influencers from evangelical Christian spaces that tackle the claims of the de-churched constitutes a movement towards defending core Protestant Christian claims while equally challenging racism and silence within their denominations. The Black Urban Evangelical space is best equipped to re-engage the de-churched, but this can be better understood by considering the historical emergence of evangelicalism; there are undoubtedly parallels between this religious movement and the Afroasiatic diasporic religions.

Evangelicalism emerged in Britain and New England in the eighteenth century and, like conservatism, was part of Protestant resistance against the liberal theological developments in Church and society. It also resisted the domination of Roman Catholicism and its emphasis on the tradition of the Church as authoritative on matters of faith and practice. Hindmarsh says:

> The rising evangelical movement was distinguished first and foremost by its appeal to men and women to be true and earnest Christians rather than nominal believers. 'Evangelical' was not thus a label used to distinguish something as 'not Catholic' and 'not liberal'. (Hindmarsh, 2018, p. 9)

Evangelicalism served as a criticism of the institutional Church and a revival of Christianity's divine or supernatural aspects that had become unpopular in the wake of the Enlightenment era and its empirical method for generating knowledge. The spirit of evangelicalism maintained that divine revelation did not discriminate and instead suggested all types of people were eligible for a personal spiritual experience and could engage with the divine revelation.

David W. Bebbington in *Evangelicalism in Modern Britain: A Modern History from the 1730s to the 1980s* (2003) suggests that it was a movement that ushered Protestantism out of the grips of the Enlightenment, and that is seen most notably in the works of Edward Irving, who was sympathetic to spiritual manifestations looking beyond scholastic methods for knowing the 'truths of revelations' (Bebbington, 2003, Chapter 3). Here, Bebbington suggests that evangelicalism is 'far more than a static creed', particularly by focusing on influential leaders within the movement; one can see that the internal differences and divisions produce a living dynamic that is responsive to the changing societies. Nevertheless, evangelicalism is generally known by the following principles:

- Conversionism – a call to personal repentance and moral transformation.
- Activism – a commitment to doing that which springs from the moral radicalism rooted in a sense of personal responsibility.
- Biblicism – the Bible as the supreme authority of faith and practice.
- Crucicentrism – a stress on substitutionary atonement; the sacrifice of Jesus Christ on the cross which enables the believer to access redemption. (Bebbington, 2003, p. 1713)

So, while there may be ideological and scientific influences, they must work towards and be subject to these tenets. Furthermore, any ideology that is subversive to the authority of Scripture is a hostile influence. Carl Raschke, in *The Next Reformation: Why Evangelicals Must Embrace Postmodernity* (2004), says:

> For reformers, Scripture is authoritative because it mediates God's magnificent reality to each one of us as a person on our own terms. Calvin described this process as the work of the Holy Spirit. Scriptural authority ensures that each one of us hears God as God, not through the filter of our own wants and expectations. (Raschke, 2004, p. 117)

What Raschke illuminates here is that while evangelicalism is insistent on believers being subject to the authority of Scripture, the interpretive process must allow for the intervention of the Holy Spirit for a divine revelation. Evangelicalism seeks to understand the Bible as the Word of God, a divine message and historical account, rather than a resource subject to one's needs, philosophical expectations, political affiliation and lived experience. Evangelicalism also emphasizes a personal conversion and redemption experience; combined with activism, it is hoped that society would experience the influence of evangelical biblical morality and the power of the gospel of Jesus. We see this emphasis in a report made by the Evangelical Alliance Commission on Unity and Truth (ACUTE), which released the following statement:

> An evangelical Christian is a Christian who lives under the authority of Scripture in all matters of belief and practice and who experiences a personal relationship with Christ founded in repentance and faith. Such a person will accept the fundamental doctrines affirmed by the ancient creeds and regard the history of the evangelical tradition as their history. (ACUTE, 2001, p. 14)

What can also be derived from this statement is the call to personal assimilation to evangelical history and tradition; an evangelical must participate in the ongoing commitment to the foundational tenets that have been preserved throughout the movement's history. Evangelicalism is a trans-denominational movement found within various Protestant traditions (Stanley, 2013, p. 11). This has meant that, throughout its evolution, interpretation of Scripture and perspectives on final authority have led to differences of judgement, most notably between Calvinism and Arminianism, but it has also made room for more liberal approaches to the tenets. Evangelicalism as a theological framework allows for differences within the boundaries of the tenets. Allister McGrath, in *Evangelicalism and the Fire of Christianity*, says:

> Thus, it has been asserted that Evangelicalism is as much about devotional ethos as it is a theological system ... Christian Orthodoxy, as set out in the ecumenical creeds, with a particular emphasis upon the need for the personal assimilation and appropriation of faith. (McGrath, 1993, pp. 52–3 in ACUTE, 2001)

The devotional ethos of the evangelical movement is in its commitment and submission to scriptural authority and the divine revelation of the Holy Spirit as working together towards a personal transformation. Although the ADR does not share central theological tenets, they have parallel emergence stories. Both religious movements come from under a dominant European Church seeking the true origins of the faith. In the case of the evangelicals, they were concerned about maintaining continuity with the early Christian Church, rediscovering the spirituality of Christianity as described in Scripture and severing ties with a dogmatic European religious tradition that seemed at odds with the gospel of Jesus. The evangelicals sought liberation, justice for the poor, inclusion of the other and religious space submitted to the authority of Scripture and not the pope.

Conservative evangelicalism, then, is the combination of an evangelical theological perspective and the social and political attitudes of conservatism. A particular twentieth-century development of conservative evangelicalism is seen in the fundamentalist movement, which embraced a distinction and distanced itself from the influence of liberalism in the evangelical movement. Despite its varied influences, evangelicalism is distinguished by its submission to the biblical Scriptures, as is canonized, as the sole authority of religious faith and practice. Thus, many evangelical people have sought to apply these religious distinctives to public policy.

Christian fundamentalism is commonly referred to as a religious development that took place from the late nineteenth into the early twentieth century, although it has been argued that fundamentalism, in its essence, can be seen throughout all known religious history (Baurmann, 2009, p. 46). Characterized by its dependency on certainty, religious fundamentalism, and in particular, Protestant fundamentalist Christianity, asserts absolute truth as a reality in response to theological liberalism, cultural modernism, and now postmodernism. Fundamentalism requires believers to read the biblical texts as historically accurate and the inerrant 'God-breathed' word of God. The five fundamental beliefs that undergird a fundamentalist epistemology were systematized in a collection of 90 essays written between 1910 and 1915 called *The Fundamentals: A Testimony to the Truth*, in which the Bible Institute of Los Angeles committed itself to exploring five key foundational beliefs: (1) biblical inspiration and infallibility of Scripture; (2) the virgin birth of Jesus; (3) Christ's death as atonement for sin; (4) bodily resurrection of Jesus; (5) historical reality of Jesus' miracles (Torrey, 2015). In this literature, conservative Christian thinkers engaged in an analysis of its tenets in the face of modern theological developments; an example of the approach demonstrates how they aimed to preserve the religious nature of biblical scholarship. Canon Dyson Hague says:

> In the first place, the critics who were the leaders, the men who have given name and force to the whole movement ['Higher criticism'], have been men who have based their theories largely upon their own subjective conclusions. They have based their conclusion largely upon the very dubious basis of the author's style and supposed literary qualification. Everybody knows that style is a very unsafe basis for the determination of a literary product. The greater the writer the more versatile his power of expression; and anybody can understand that the Bible is the last book in the world to be studied as a mere classic by mere human scholarship without any regard to the spirit of sympathy and reverence on the part of the student. The Bible, as has been said, has no revelation to make to unbiblical minds. It does not even follow that because a man is a philological expert, he is able to understand the

integrity or credibility of a passage of Holy Scripture any more than the beauty and spirit of it.

The qualification for the perception of Biblical truth is neither philosophic nor philological knowledge, but spiritual insight. The primary qualification of the musician is that he be musical; of the artist, that he has the spirit of art. So, the merely technical and mechanical and scientific mind is disqualified for the recognition of the spiritual and infinite. Any thoughtful man must honestly admit that the Bible is to be treated as unique in literature, and therefore, that the ordinary rules of critical interpretation must fail to interpret it aright. (Hague in Torrey, 2015, p. 3)

This substantial quote encapsulates a fundamentalist attitude towards scholarship, liberalism and Christianity. According to Hague, biblical scholarship can only be done successfully on the premise that the scholar is led by the Holy Spirit and is a competent intellectual. Thus, for a fundamentalist, the interpretive process is exclusive. Through a fundamentalist lens, many conservative Protestant Christians shaped a way of understanding and living in the world. So beyond the five key tenets, other themes come strongly to the fore as a means to combat the liberalizing of theology, such as personal morality (vs a social gospel), sexual and reproductive normativity (vs the affirmation and/or inclusion of LGBTQI+ and pro-choice narratives), and male-led churches/homes (vs female inclusion in church leadership roles, feminism and fluid family construction). Because of its unwillingness to bend to new ways of constructing knowledge (in the wake of the popularization of social sciences), fundamentalism is often associated with anti-intellectualism. Knowledge and understanding of one's reality come from divine revelation, Holy Scriptures and rationality (Baurmann, 2008, p. 46). In his analysis of fundamentalism and intellectualism, George Marsden says:

Yet perhaps even more important for the development of fundamentalism was the revivalists' tendencies to promote and reinforce a particular type of intellectual emphasis that is a tendency to think in terms of simple dichotomies. The universe was divided between the realm of God and the realm of Satan; the supernatural was sharply separated from the natural; righteousness could have nothing to do with sin. (Marsden, 2006, p. 48)

While people may contend that fundamentalists are anti-intellectual, a better description is that they are selectively intellectual in accordance with their spiritual and theological requirements for true Christian scholarship. For example, in the nineteenth and twentieth centuries, America saw a rise in conservative Christian theological seminaries to demonstrate their religious–intellectual engagement and their value in developing leaders and teachers who are 'biblically sound'. Conservative evangelicalism and fundamentalism reject intellectually creative ways of approaching Scripture because they are concerned with the spiritual salvific nature of the Holy Texts and view them as a work and tool of God to guide people towards redemption, right living and righteous judgement. In line with Burke's ideas of reality, conservative evangelicalism sees Christianity (religion) as the authority on moral order and not radical, revolutionary intellectualism.

Despite its emergence as resistance to dominance, with a promise for democracy and equality, the evangelical body has been critiqued for its resistance to any consideration of the contextual factors that have been a part of its own historical theological formation.

Black presence, Black bloodlines

Participant DS rejects the notion that Black people had been subjugated to the point that they lacked the strength and clarity to become genuine Christians willingly. Although he acknowledges the torture that enslaved Africans endured as part of their colonial Christianizing, he still believes that genuine conversion to Christianity is rooted in connections that the enslaved Africans may have had with the biblical religions before enslavement. Participant DS also brings to the fore an interesting point about what it has taken for Black people to become intellectually capable of discerning and resisting the power of Colonial Christianity. As evidenced earlier, Ethiopianism demonstrates only a part of enslaved people's resistance and intellectual capacity. However, he speaks more to this idea of 'woke' in the twenty-first century, suggesting that this generation possesses the qualities to chart a trajectory of dismantling Christianity as a religion of racism.

I parallel this conversation with those in the Black Conscious Community and their online rebuttals of the modernist/postmodernist or conservative/progressive dichotomy. Other participants who had several points on which they disagreed with Participant DS (including his approach and demonstration of historical evidence) also rooted their argument in the narrative of the biblical text. This is an example of a deep connection with the biblical text – that despite suspicion of the Christian religion, there is still a rooting phenomenon between the participants and the Bible, which is religious, ethnic and mythical. Although many of the participants demonstrate an interest in Afrocentric ideals, many of which give keen attention to Egypt or traditional West African belief systems, the Bible is still a significant backdrop to the story and unfolding history of Black people.

> *Participant NA.: You can make intelligent guesses as to what Jesus would have looked like, let's be honest, if you're gonna look at the book, umm, I mean, in the biblical story when he was born, you know Mary and Joseph took a trip to Egypt to hide from the King, whatever his name was; now how you gonna hide a White baby? In an environment where people are darker than dark, you know what I'm tryna say? It's not gonna work, so – if you read, if you read the Bible, you can make intelligent guesses as to what his skin tone would have been, you know what I'm saying. And to be honest, the construct of race is not important to the average African. You might not value it; you might think it's nonsense, but other people put a lot of significance to it. And that's another thing as well: we always look at these issues from an African mindset where we know 'Chancellor Williams said' the reason why we got into all this mess, this slavery is because of that mindset of embracing everything by being inclusive, always loving.*
> *Participant M: And not embracing ourselves – do you say, Chancellor Williams?*
> *Participant NA: Chancellor Williams yeah yeah yeah – you understand? So it's not –*
> *Participant M: Read his book, read his book.*
> *Participant NA: The African psyche does not see race; it's alien to us, you understand? But to other people, it's important so that's the biggest distinction I would make anyway.* (State Your Case, 2016)

Participant NA outlines a process of thinking that requires several significant assumptions; the first is that the Egyptians were dark-skinned African peoples. This is important among the de-churched, and it is one of the key arguments that fuel the religious movement's momentum – reclaiming what was stolen. Black academics, celebrities and activists have long resisted the whitewashing and European claim over Egypt that has been evident in the retelling of history through educational materials, movies and literature. As a result, Egypt has left a significant impression on the world because of its perceived magnificence as a well-developed social, religious and intellectual leader in the ancient world. Unlike those who may identify with the Kemetic Science movement, Participant NA does not align his genetic/mythic origins with the ancient Egyptians but acknowledges the Hebrews' common ancestry, likeness and geography with the Egyptians. Following this assumption, Participant N suggests one can positively identify that Jesus, his mother and his father were dark-skinned people who would have been able to blend with the local Egyptians among whom God sent them to hide from King Herod. This assumption illuminates the ethnic aspect of the biblical account, where perhaps emphasis may have been put on persecution in the early years of Jesus' life, obedience to God or a supernatural visitation from an angel. Participant N asserts that the mission's success lies with their ethnicity – the ability to blend in. The final assumption that is significant here is that you can make intelligent guesses if you read the Bible. This is significant because although Participant N was a very vocal, dominant voice in the group, he accepted that the information was there for anyone who reads the text. Participant N reads the accounts of Jesus historically (and literally) and, in doing so, has established the physical appearance and ethnicity of its central character, the nation to which he belongs and the surrounding nations, and uses this hermeneutic to rebut opposing European/colonial claims and re-readings of the text.

> *Participant DS: And it's Jewish culture; if you look at Jewish culture, the whole long hair wouldn't have been long hair because they don't do long hair – it's short hair. Like if you understand, looked into it now, like looked into some of the stuff then of what Jewish culture was like, there's a lot of imagery that you can know that it straight away kinda tears it down. They wouldn't have had long hair, even what the Bible says about long hair, it's not – it's for a woman to have, not a guy to have – so you gotta bring it back to the Bible.*
> *Participant NA: Look, sorry to interrupt, but the Jews of today are not the Jews of the Bible.*
> *Participant M: Tell them!*
> *Participant NA: You understand? But again, we get it confused because walking down Golders Green or Stamford Hill that's a representation of the Jewish people in —*
> *Participant DS: I don't think people think that though.*
> *Participant NA: No, they do, they do.*
> *Participant M: Oh, they do.*
> *Participant NA: That's a fact.*
> (State Your Case 2016)

This controversial topic (considered antisemitic), 'the identity of the real Jews', reveals the extent to which some de-churched Black people believe there is an agenda to remove Black people from the biblical narrative – to have them replaced by another group altogether. As we saw earlier

(p. 131), Participant MI follows this line of thinking by broadening the scope of the claim; he suggests that the Bible is absent of 'racial designation' because of the 'sameness' between *peoples* in the entire Afroasiatic region.

Black Bible Religions present their own sets of fundamentals that serve as the backbone of the tradition: first, that mainstream Christianity is distinct from true Bible religion and is a colonial re-working of ancient Afroasiatic truths; second, that Black epistemologies and sacred truths originate among the ancient cultures and traditions of Afroasiatic peoples; and, third, that Afroasiatic geography and genealogy serve to reveal who God's chosen people are.

The Holy Qubtic Church of the Black Messiah (HQC) seeks to direct 'Nubian-melaninites' (Black people) towards African religious traditions to remedy a diasporic identity crisis. Religious symbols and ideas that are often considered Egyptian, according to the Holy Qubtic Church, are the foundation of African religious knowledge. Much like the Nation of Islam, the Holy Qubtic Church traces its origins beyond conventional readings of the Genesis account and provides an alternative interpretation. Referring to The Original Books of the Bible – the ancient African biblical account – they teach:

> The Ba-Re-Shiyth gives the African account of the garden of A-Ten (Eden) that was recreated, replenished and reconstructed by the High Priest, Seer and Prophet Baba Ankh An Aton. In ancient times, it was referred to as A-Mir-Na, and was the place where the spiritual sciences would be taught to those students who had proven themselves worthy.
>
> Within these pages, you will also learn about the African Genesis story, which was really a refilling or replenishing event, that in time became confused as being the beginning of all creation. However, we as Ancient Africans knew that this was only the re-surrection, re-population and re-erection of a sacred city. (https://www.holyqubtic church.com/our-scriptures)

The Garden of Eden or A-Ten, then, is situated as part of ancient Egyptian and African history, not as an antediluvian creation myth, as is most readily accepted in mainstream Christianity and by many Rastafari and Black Hebrew Israelites. The Holy Qubtic Church looks to 'Tama-Re' (Ancient Africa) as their origin. Kahun Montu Tar (Dr Horace Wright), High Priest of the Holy Qubtic Church in London, says:

> Each race, nation, nationality has their own religion, and within their own religion, it helps and works for them. It helps to bind them; it

> helps to put, umm, a sense of morality in them, a code – a conduct that says we will respect and work by and for each other. It works for those who adhere to it. (Gotkush TV, 2019)

This claim draws the 'origins' conversation away from Canaan or Israel – as we see with the (Black) Hebrew Israelites – to Kemet (Egypt), but still keeps it in the Afroasiatic region. One of the interesting geographic points from the Holy Qubtic Church teachings is how they understand themselves in the broader divine reality. Unlike the other religions in which their adherents are central to God or Allah's plan for humanity and are the chosen people of the one true God, the Holy Qubtic Church teaches that each ethnic group will have a god or gods and a sacred text with teachings that are unique to them and can remedy their ills. Therefore, according to HQT, it is imperative that Black people in the diaspora reconnect with the religious teachings of their ancestors in order to function optimally in any society. There is less of an emphasis on repatriation and more on local gatherings in whatever part of the world the adherent resides.

These Afroasiatic diasporic religious communities have a deep tie between geographical, ethnic and religious origins. Together, they find an original home in the Afroasiatic region and the Biblical narrative that produces a sense of purpose, direction, and continuity that resists and negates the intrusion of Colonial Christianity. The Rastafari tradition builds upon Ethiopianism, which I discussed further in Chapter 4, and develops a more focused connection to the biblical Israelites. In this case, 'Ethiopian' and 'Israelite' are the same (Barratt, 1997, p. 111). There are two prevailing schools of thought; the first is that the Rastafari are 'reincarnated Israelites', which denotes a spiritual/mythical connection, a 'sonship', and 'personal divinity' that occurs through a spiritual birth (Barratt, 1997, p.111). The other school of thought takes a more literal turn and claims a direct genetic link via the tribe of the Falasha, followers of Menelik I, the supposed son of King Solomon and the Queen of Sheba (Wimbush, 2012), using Genesis 25.23 for scriptural reference:

> And the LORD said unto her, Two nations are in thy womb, and two manner of people shall be separated from thy bowels; and the one people shall be stronger than the other people; and the elder shall serve the younger. (KJV)

Some Rastafari believe that from Isaac, God created two peoples, Caucasians being the descendants of red-skinned and hairy Esau and Black people the descendants of Jacob. Rastafari seems to have literal and mythical origins in tension, both of which they believe affirm them as the true Israelites.

Prophet William Saunders has been recorded as one of the first in the Hebrew Israelite tradition to receive the revelation of African Americans' true origins while clearing his field in 1892. In his comparison of the Rastafari movement with (Black) Hebrew Israelites, Michael Barnett (2006) suggests that origins are determined by a combination of spiritual characteristics and geography within the various camps of the Hebrew Israelite movements. Hebrew Israelites claim that they are the people of Canaan, the Hebrews of the Bible from the 'Middle East' who were Black-skinned and not people of Africa. Instead, Africa is considered the wilderness the Hebrews found themselves in because of their disobedience and idolatry. This belief is based on their interpretation of Scripture rather than through widely accepted scholarly works. 'They find all the proof they need in the Bible. Invoking "Divine Geography," or a way of charting the world that is "pleasing to God"' (Markowitz, 1996, p. 193).

Since their enslavement in Africa, some of the Hebrew Israelite camps teach that the tribes can be identified by location: The Tribe of Judah – Negros; The Tribe of Benjamin – West Indians; The Tribe of Levi – Haitians; The Tribe of Simeon – Dominicans; The Tribe of Zebulon – Guatemala to Panama; The Tribe of Ephraim – Puerto Ricans; The Tribe of Manasseh – Cubans; The Tribe of Gad – North American Indians; The Tribe of Reuben – Seminole Indians; The Tribe of Naphtali – Argentina to Chile; The Tribe of Asher – Columbia to Uruguay; The Tribe of Issachar – Mexicans (https://israelunite.org/learn-the-truth/the-12-tribes-of-israel, accessed 09/06/2025).

Although these teachings are prevalent on social media platforms, it is not an essential belief; and many (Black) Hebrew Israelites reject this teaching altogether. The Hebrew Israelite religion differs from Pan-Africanism and Afrocentric religions because it has severed its African ties (Jackson Jr, 2005). Often found within the BHI teachings are varying degrees of the rejection of Africans and Arabs who sold the Israelites into slavery. Ultimately, the BHI teach that their relocation is a divine judgement resulting from the disobedience of which Africans and Arabs (and later Europeans) were tools to carry out God's punishment; the Gathering of Christ perspective found on their website is an example:

> Disclaimer: Before we take the time to reveal this understanding, we would first like to mention that we do not blame anyone for the atrocities that happened to our people. We understand that these things happened to us based on our disobedience (Deut. 32:15–21,

Deut. 28:15, Amos 3:1–2). (https://gatheringofchrist.org/twelve-tribes/, accessed 02/01/2022)

They support this notion through Old Testament Scripture, specifically the King James Version, much like the Rastafari:

> The LORD shall cause thee to be smitten before thine enemies: thou shalt go out one way against them, and flee seven ways before them: and shalt be removed into all the kingdoms of the earth. (Deuteronomy 28.25, KJV)

It is crucial for (Black) Hebrew Israelites to validate their Hebrew origins geographically as it is foundational to their identity formation as a nation. What we see with these Afroasiatic diasporic religions is more than a neo-religious construction; to them, it is the rediscovery of who they are to make sense of their communal divine purpose now that they have become woke from the slumber and trauma of oppression. Ben Ammi is an example of a Hebrew Israelite leader who repatriated to Israel with a Black Hebrew Community; I will speak more about this in the next chapter.

Imago Dei

> *Participant M: Yes, in Genesis, it's in the Old Testament and in the New Testament because Jesus repeats it. But my point I'm making is when we say we are gods, it is not for us – it's not to shock out and equate us with the Most High ... It is to say we are god in the person of the flesh; that's what it means.*
> *Participant NA: Yes, a reflection.*
> *Participant M: OK, let me give you an example, Genesis chapter 2, God says be fruitful, multiply, replenish, subdue, take dominion. That's what God does, the Most High, and God gave that mandate to us in flesh and blood to do the same thing on this domain that we call earth. To follow suit as he does in heaven, that's the mandate – okay God kills at will, so do humans, God creates, so do we – whether it's another human being, whether it's a business, whether it's a nation or an empire, we create. Do we replenish? So when something, when we run out of cakes we can go to the shop and buy some more, so what it's saying is to serve in the capacity of the Most High the way God does, the only difference is we have to work for it, the only difference is, and the by the way when he says gods they spell it with a small 'g', so you*

have to remember, that's the point, when someone says ye are gods it's not necessarily that it's false, but it's a matter of context it's not a matter of 'I can think of a thing' because God spoke everything into existence – we don't, we can speak an ideas and say 'I'm gonna start a clothing line' I've spoken that into existence but it hasn't manifested, I have to make it manifest. I have to learn how to sew, I have to learn how to market, I've got to get my website, hook up the pay pal, get my products, get people to come buy my stuff, you know, that's how I start a clothing line, do you understand. I've spoken into existence like God would, but the only difference is God manifests when he speaks, I would actually have to work. So when the Bible says 'ye are gods', especially for Black people who've been told they're not even human the last 500 years, that's not only truthful that's something we need to know, feel and hear and to have, so we know if 'ye are gods' children of the Most High, we can beat white supremacy, we can beat institutionalized racism, we can beat police brutality, we can resurrect Black Wall Street like we had in Tulsa Oklahoma and rosewood. OK and, this notion of, is there a Black superiority, I would say no, it doesn't exist now, and it didn't exist then. [Researcher: OK... making attempts to round him up!] Again, Black people just happen to be more topical, it's not like we had any notion of being better than another human being; if anything, if you read the Greeks, the Greeks themselves would say 'you see these Black people are better than us', so if anyone had a superiority complex of us it was the other people of the world. We need to read J. D. Rogers, Dr Joseph Ben Yachunnan, Dr John Henry-Clarke, Chancellor Williams, you need to read Dr Ivan Van Sertima, you need to read Priscilla Duncan Houston. (State Your Case, 2016)

Here, the participants challenge one another's interpretation of Scripture, which is unique among all the participant groups. These participants took up the challenge of apologetics with intentionality rather than discussing their experiences. Here, I witnessed a more rigorous teaching/learning experience. In this excerpt, we see how the participants are contending *Imago Dei*, being made in the image of God, and to what extent Black people or God's people can be considered 'gods'. The de-churched position in this group leans more towards what we see among the Afroasiatic diasporic religions, and scholars who teach self-determination – that to be like God, or to be a god, is the blueprint and impetus for realizing emancipation, for success, for victory over the oppressors.

> *Ummm, I do wanna make a different point about gods, but I do hope that helped. It's just a thing about Black people as gods – I think ultimately we are all gods. I really think that, not even in the sense of, as you say [indicating Participant M] 'making things manifest' – even right here and now we all have our own ideas about everything you know. Anyone can look in the Bible and say, 'Cool, I think it says this, I think this means this or this means that'; one of the things I learned when I left church is that we all have our own religions. You know, I went to a certain church, and I assumed that we all agreed on the same things, but we didn't, you know. Some people believed, 'Ahh this person is definitely gonna go to hell because he did this', and some would say, 'No he's not gonna go to hell, only god knows', but I really feel like we all have our own understandings of what we believe to be right and wrong. And so in my intimation, we're all gods, that's my understanding.* (Participant RU, State Your Case, 2016)

Participant RU takes a more pluralist approach to this concept, 'ye are gods', that the goal is to arrive not at the definitive meaning of the text but at the meaning that most resonates with the individual. Participant RU is unique in this perspective among the participants who have demonstrated concerns for a single truth. Pluralism does appear among the ADR, among the NOI and Rastafari in particular, in that they acknowledge the overlap or continuity of beliefs and histories of other religions. Yet this pluralism seems to serve the purpose of knowing the ultimate truth, of which other religions have a glimpse. Participant DS, the Christian, comes back to defend the Christian perspective. He suggests that the need to be 'gods' is a response to being oppressed and dehumanized.

> *I guess this is the problem; we've got so many manuscripts for the Bible alone, more than actually your historian books, more than can back up anything else, but we'd rather read from people that said something to us and we take that on board. I just wanna throw that out there as well, we say, 'Ahh, I read a book by this person or that person' and it just like but you won't kind of take the Bible for the word? And I guess as you said [indicating Participant RU] about the gods thing, like, the problem is the Bible: it says 'that's not – we're not gods', and for me, seeing what the Bible says and seeing what the devil's done is made us believe in any kind of way, shape or form that we are gods or we can be like God. That was the scripture that I was (reading) when Eve was being tempted, and he said, 'ye can be like God both knowing good and evil'; that was the scripture and the reason why I say that's a*

dangerous place to be. And even as I say that people shake their heads because people feel like no, in ourselves we wanna be superior, we wanna feel like we can do all these different things, but we kinda forget and then stop looking at God and the Bible as an authority and the one with the truth. So yeah, that's my response to couple things that you all were saying. (Participant DS, State Your Case, 2016)

These religions can be considered Afroasiatic because they each claim religious and genealogical origins in the Afroasiatic region. According to Elijah Muhammad in *Message to the Black Man in America* (1973), the NOI teach that Black people are the aboriginal (often synonymous with original) supreme beings of the planet. Their (terrestrial) geographic origin is from the once merged continent of Africa and Asia,[1] from within which the African Americans derive from the esteemed tribe of Shabazz. Having established the Nile Valley and the Holy City of Mecca, as it is now known, as sites of significance, the NOI maintain an Afro–Asian–Arab genealogy rather than the East, Central and West African route of its competing movement Rastafari. Nuri Tinaz in his 2006 article 'Black Islam in diaspora: The case of Nation of Islam (N.O.I.) in Britain', says:

> For African Americans and Afro-Caribbeans to become Muslim or a member of the NOI is to reclaim their lost religion and identity and to return to their ancestral faith which has been unknown to them over the years as a consequence of slavery, forced conversion and colonization respectively. (Tinaz, 2006, p. 153)

This teaching about the origin of Black people leads to the belief that Islam is the natural religion of Black people; it ties their spiritual and geographical journey to Islamic sites of origin. Further, the NOI teach that many enslaved Africans transported to the West were already practising Muslims. The NOI, in turn, teach that they provide a way to return to their original way of life and relearn their connection to Allah – synonymous with the God of the Bible – before the physical and psychological trauma of slavery (Barnett, 2006).

A positive self-image is a central theme within the communal identity of the Nation of Islam, but beyond these aesthetic markers such as wearing suits and white garments, shaven heads and headscarves and following a selective diet, the NOI's internalized identity is 'chosenness' (Barnett, 2006). Having merged biblical and Qur'anic text, both recognized as sacred texts of the aboriginals, the NOI refer to the narrative of the Hebrews in Genesis 15.13–14:

And he said unto Abram, Know of a surety that thy seed shall be a stranger in a land that is not theirs, and shall serve them; and they shall afflict them four hundred years;

And also that nation, whom they shall serve, will I judge: and afterward shall they come out with great substance. (Genesis 15.13–14, KJV)

Believing this scripture to be foresight of the transatlantic slave trade and subsequent subjugation, much like the Rastafari, the NOI follow through the narrative with a communal identity of a 'chosen people', an 'original people', and a' supreme people' from the Afroasiatic region. The NOI were a prominent part of the struggle for freedom during the Jim Crow and civil rights eras; they taught Garvey's Black nationalism alongside submission to Allah. The Nation of Islam established itself as a religion to better Blacks and reunite Black people with their ethno-religious origins. Tynetta Muhammed says:

(NOI) Teach the downtrodden and defenceless Black people through a knowledge of God and of themselves and put them on the road to self-independence with a superior culture and higher civilization than they had previously experienced. (Muhammad, T., 1996)

In an ethnographic study, A. A. Akom explores Black achievement ideology in the Nation of Islam, which stems from this 'chosenness'; Akom can demonstrate that while they are undeniably a separatist religion, they cannot be considered entirely oppositional in culture and orientation because their religious teaching demands that personal and communal achievement, such as in education and industry, be taken seriously. He studied teenage girls from the NOI community in mainstream education. Akom says, 'In short, rigid morals, self-determination, nontraditional Islam, and Black nationalism are the key elements that constitute what I refer to as the NOI's Black achievement ideology' (Akom, 2003, p. 307). The Nation of Islam's teaching about geographic origins generates purpose and direction while in Babylon (America/Britain), revealed in part by high achievement and excellence.

Conclusion

Knowledge was definitely considered power for many among the de-churched; after years of trusting church leadership, parents and Sunday school teachings, self-study has become the vehicle through which many of the de-churched have found a way to fill in the gaps. While the participants demonstrated interest in philosophical and abstract conversation, the necessity to ground truth in concrete realities such as geography, land, ethnic groupings, and ancestors seems to help the de-churched attain the validity, presence and agency they need to pursue a Bible-reading religion. The general promise of heaven in the afterlife as a reward for faith in the Jesus they engage in the mainstream loses gravitas for those who come to realize the Christianity in which they have grown up isn't neutral, objective or transparent but the legacy of colonialism, imperialism and civil/internal conflicts rooted in national interests or excluding African/Black presence and participation.

We can see how the de-churched and Black Bible Religions emerged in similar ways to the evangelical movement, driven by the need to recover autonomy, basic principles and religious epistemologies as outlined in Scripture rather than the traditions of the Church/state. So there is no surprise that we see converging methodologies, the need for measurable evidence, for roots and alternative mythologies that serve as building blocks for Black religious autonomy.

Researcher's reflection, 2016

'White Man's Religion?' had ended, and after a quick debrief with the minister who had allowed me access to his building for the event, I stepped out on to the front steps of the building. It was still sunny and warm. I was exhausted. My husband was standing on the steps with a friend engaged in discussion with the 'Hotep' brothers. What could only be described as a reasoning session was happening: my husband had his phone out looking through scriptures, and one of the other brothers was reading from the Metu Neter. They were standing close together, and there seemed to be mutual respect among the men; although the dividing line was evident on a matter of belief, they all seemed keen to find, establish and teach the truth. It was interesting to visualize this restrained passion. As I approached the gathering, one of the brothers, wearing jeans, a fitted T-shirt, snapback (hat) and a carving of Africa on a chain, was explaining more about what they believe: 'All these hieroglyphs are metaphors that guided our ancestors on right ways of living ... where man and women were equal, where they traded and were educated ... that's what we want – to get back to, a time of peace and order.'

His reference to this egalitarian model struck me. During the event, there was minimal talk about gender roles, gender discrimination – the conversation was so heavily focused on 'race' and 'truth' and 'slavery' that I had yet to consider other social and relational aspects of the alternative Afroasiatic religions that perhaps underpin their decolonization process. It felt like this comment was directed at me as I approached. Perhaps my role as the facilitator indicated that I did not have traditional conservative complementarian values. I decided to remain quiet and listen.

I did not want to disturb the conversation that was in full swing. The conversation quickly moved on to the topic of the Bible and Jesus. One of the brothers was making his case against the legitimacy of the Bible as a plagiarized repackaging of ancient Kemetic religion. He was referring to the teachings in the book in his hand; he seemed so excited to be holding a tool of liberation and so keen to see other brothers and sisters be set free.

Hotep Brother: 'I mean I don't have a problem with Jesus as a man – if he existed, what he had to say, what he did for people was cool, I get the principles. But he was not God, and we cannot rely on the Bible.

Husband: but your ideas are just beliefs, I believe in the Bible, and you believe in the hieroglyphs. You can't read them; you depend on a translation ... at the end of the day, what it boils down to is faith.

Note

1 NOI also teach that before they were established on earth they had extraterrestrial origin.

7

Message to the Mainstream

Participant BJ: I'm, umm, extremely excited; I was hoping it was gonna be like this. I didn't think it was; I was hoping. And, umm, I left church two years ago and didn't know it was something with the word, and I kept on thinking, you know there's so much going out in our community, but the church is here and doesn't actually have anything to do with us; and, umm, then I started looking on YouTube, searching, searching, and there was so many things like wow! And the more I read, the more I wanted to read, and [name] lives next door, and we want (we have been?) to have these discussions for years and years. Like ten years now! And like you said, there's been an awakening because our children, they're not accepting Christ because we haven't been taught right; we have to make sure that we know him before we can actually give them him. So there's so much to learn, from the beginning. (White Man's Religion, 2018)

Since the time of this research, which began in 2016, I have witnessed shifts towards repair and racial justice, anti-discrimination and anti-racism. I've also had the privilege of being a part of developing several resources for the mainstream Church to support those willing and interested (or box-ticking) in their pursuits. I've seen shifts in the colouring of the imagery of Jesus and people from the Bible and more ethnically diverse reading from the pulpit and in the seminaries. There has been growing interest on the internet on dispelling the myth of the White man's religion from people of all backgrounds and positions: laypeople, apologists, scholars, thinkers and pastors. What was available at the beginning of this research process, in terms of resources on this topic, is so different from what one can access today. It is very encouraging to witness.

Generally speaking, the Church is engaged with the world's discussion on what racial justice looks like. However, it still has a way to go in leading the way, in being the salt and light on this topic; so far as I can see, the willing mainstream participants are toeing the line, often combining all types of social justice interests as dictated by secular society.

There is indeed a lack of the Martin Luther King/Malcolm X vigour on what God's justice looks like for people who are discriminated against because of the colour of their skin, on what repair looks like after centuries of sinful engagement and complicity in the oppression, subjugation and brutalization of Black and Brown bodies.

Despite these shifts and the provision of finance and access to develop resources, there is still more work to do. Those who have to disseminate the resources (local ministers or Christian organizations for example) are concerned that the congregations are not developed or equipped enough to engage with them. Congregation members who are interested in developing their knowledge and strategies for engaging claims against Christianity often have to look outside of their local church for input.

For many churches across Britain, it can be understandable that there wouldn't be someone who specializes in Black religion. Not only because it's a niche topic but because the majority of churches across the United Kingdom will be White majority congregations where racism and the legacy of colonialism are not felt by the majority or even half. Nor will they be coming into contact with Black Bible Religions on street corners, as these seem to be mainly located in cities and locations where there are significant concentrations of Black communities.

Black majority churches (BMC) in Britain are growing significantly, while church attendance of White Christians is declining (LSE, 2017). Despite the growth of BMC churches, many discontented Black millennials are severing ties with Christianity and seeking religious movements supporting their desire to be pro-Black and religious. Social media has seen a growing trend in anti-Christian sentiments from within the Black community, often arguing that Christianity is a slave religion that does not benefit the Black community and remains silent on the societal injustices experienced by Black people. Counter-histories support these anti-Christian sentiments, and alternative spiritual belief systems are considered more authentic and beneficial for the Black community. The arguments tend to be spearheaded by the exposure of Christianity as an ongoing colonial enterprise:

- The historical legacy of slavery as endorsed and instituted by the European Church.
- Existential narratives of domination, assimilation and subjugation in contemporary theology and practice.
- The re-packaging of Indigenous African religious systems with white face: White Jesus and the biblical texts as racialized counterfeit tools used to oppress people of colour.

These initial arguments have much broader implications; they speak to the social and political mobilization of the Black-British community against injustice and expose the theological disconnect between the Black theological academy and the Church. While this study has focused on the underlying drives of the de-churched and the ADR rationale, I have not given much attention to some undeniably racist and supremacist attitudes and ideals among the body of ADR teachings. I felt that it was essential to highlight the underpinning drives of these communities to voice their critical capacity to engage with decolonization. From a Christian perspective, one must ask, what does this study mean for Christianity? Are we to accept the de-churched phenomenon as 'for the best'? Is an attempt to 'win them back for the Lord', in fact, a colonial mechanism of control and assertion of undue power? Am I suggesting that Afroasiatic Diasporic Religion is the solution for Christianity's true decolonization?

The Afroasiatic religions I have selected for this study are often negated as reactionary, extremist, racist and anti-intellectual. Despite this reception, my research considers their teachings in raw form; what I mean by this is that I engaged with the teachings as the religious adherents present them, without censorship. I believe that this is the best way for the study to analyse them as indicators of the desires and needs of the Black-British Christians on the fringes of the British church body. My instinct has been that Black Bible Religions are integral to the future of the study of Black Religion as they are rich sources of information about the Black diaspora and globalized reality. During their initial waves of influence in the nineteenth and twentieth centuries, when slavery, racism, segregation and racial discrimination were legal institutions, these religions were active among an already essentially religious (confessional and traditional) Black society. In the twenty-first century these religions, I argue, are still influential in Black communities, which indicates that, although there have been political, philosophical and social advancements in Western society with regards to the Black lived experience undergirded by more humanist and pluralist ventures, they are failing to meet some core desires and needs within Black Britain that must be explored.

The quest toward anti-racism (as pertains to Black people), from an academic perspective, should not ignore the basic premises of Afroasiatic religions because they are unfavourable to the progressive trajectory, but instead should consider how the social mechanism of the ethno-religious institution has perhaps led the way and presents a more viable option for decolonization and Black identity formation.

At the beginning of this work, I set out to answer three questions:

- Why are some Black people becoming disillusioned with the Church in Britain?
- What do Afroasiatic diasporic religions offer that the de-churched believe mainstream British churches do not?
- What is the main strength of Afroasiatic diasporic religious influence, and how best can we understand their rationale?

The data suggest that the de-churched phenomenon is fuelled by the concept 'White Man's Religion' and the negativity the participants have experienced in Christian spaces when presenting their concerns and questions to church leadership. Several participants recalled instances where they brought questions about the credibility of the Bible, interpretation of Scripture, slavery and the Bible (and the resulting loss of ancestral identity) or, more broadly, about racism and discrimination, and were dismissed or ignored. These experiences left them feeling like they did not belong in the church, frustration, confusion and distrust, which also led them to consider a conspiracy against Black people, as taught by Afroasiatic diasporic religions. Some participants suggested that this dismissal covers hidden truths that reveal Black people as the true chosen people of God or demonstrates the churches' reluctance to acknowledge the Afroasiatic origins of Christianity and the Bible.

Further to these ideas, some of the participants felt that the mainstream Church was unsupportive and neglectful of the congregation's needs, contrary to the demands of Scripture. The disconnect between weekly teachings and their own Bible reading, together with the history of both ancient and modern Christianity, is central to the de-churched people's frustrations. The de-churched, then, are no longer satisfied with the role of the mainstream Church for Black people and seek alternative spaces where the teaching makes them feel included, answers their questions and gives them a sense of communal religious identity.

The Afroasiatic diasporic religions' approach to liberation and decolonization is identified by their prioritization of 'knowledge building' and recovery of lost identities. In Chapter 2, I demonstrated the various approaches among the Black Bible Religions to fill the gaps that the mainstream churches seem to negate. Regarding 'knowledge', religions such as the Holy Qubtic Church take an apologetic stance (studying history, archaeology and etymology, for example) combined with the revelatory teachings of their leaders. They distinguish between their religion and the 'White Man's religion' through these mediums. They make sense of the Black identity crisis that has led to the de-churched phenomenon and broader social ills in the Black community; they also encourage regular study and define what *true religion* is in the face of

Colonial Christianity. Making distinctions was a prominent feature in the data; the de-churched are concerned about knowing what is *correct and true*. This focus on knowledge building fuels their identity formation; Black people can learn of and be proud of their rediscovered ethnoreligious heritage, ancestral legacies and the cultures that have survived or developed through the experiences of subjugation.

The Nation of Islam, for example, present many controversial ideas such as Black supremacy, nationalism and separatism; the ADR religious teachings carve out an exclusive religious epistemology which, while it may be considered problematic in a twenty-first-century pluralistic world, seems to be the strength of their influence among the de-churched. When one reflects on the religious teachings alongside the data collected, Afroasiatic Diasporic Religion presents the religious continuity that the de-churched seek. Biblical religious identity is based on ethnicity and nationhood – the descendants of 'God's chosen people' or the 'original man'. Establishing these connections and sites of continuity through mythical/genealogical interpretations of Scripture seems to help validate what would regularly be rejected as racist. What assists in the buy-in is the accessible nature of the reading; ADR adherents do not need a formal education to read the text plainly and in light of their leader's revelation. Once they have been convinced of the appropriate canon, translation and 'lens', the de-churched can pursue individual study to build their own knowledge.

The Afroasiatic diasporic religious paradigm can provide methodological solutions to past hurts and future hopes. First, it centres the Black experiences using Scripture, which explains and offsets the feelings of rejection the de-churched experienced in mainstream Christianity. Second, by pursuing what is *true, correct and authoritative* (rather than reading and applying contextually in a postcolonial sense), the de-churched can participate in rediscovering lost ancestral identity and religious origins, reclaiming the Bible religion. The participants often alluded to the internal transformation that occurs when they deepen their knowledge; for some of the de-churched and many in the ADR, this pursuit reveals the Black man as 'god', a super status or superiority over others as one chosen and designated by 'The Most High'.

There is a tension between Black intellectualism in Britain and Afroasiatic diasporic religions in their 'raw form' because the general ambition is to belong to Britain as British people and citizens, being treated equally and acknowledged for their contribution and suffering, and this cannot easily be reconciled with an exclusive, anti-Babylon rationale. Afroasiatic diasporic religions do not necessarily seek this type of citizenship and acceptance, and their teachings and contributions to scholarship have been considered problematic and non-progressive. To assert Black Religion as political agency, Black Liberation Theology mines religions such as Rastafari as a resource to develop themes and models of liberation, but equally struggles with and resists the divine, ethnocentric, nationalist teachings in their raw form. Reddie demonstrates a common trajectory:

> The use of the term 'Black' in the UK context has invariably been used in a plural sense to connote identities and subjectivities that have transcended the seemingly ethnocentric boundaries that want to police such discourses around Afrocentric or Black nationalistic thought ... Using the term Black is to identify oneself as a socially constructed 'other' when juxtaposed against Eurocentric discourses that dominate the normative gaze and trajectory of what it means to be authentically British. (Reddie and Jagessar, 2007, Chapter 9)

Despite the trend towards social constructivism as a sufficient frame for identity formation in academia and the now well-formed bridges between Black academia and the Black community (due to a high engagement with higher education and social media platforms), in every session that I facilitated there was a recurring theme that was generated by the participants, which I argue has been inspired by Black Bible Religions' teachings on identity: they ask 'Where do we come from?' and believe the answer to be of divine origin. The constructivist position is an outsider position, but this ethnographic study was concerned with the participants' perceptions. The evidence, I believe, demonstrates that Afroasiatic Diasporic Religion adherents and the de-churched participants consider themselves not to have the power to construct identity but to discover it through divine means.

Tariq Modood, in his 1998 article 'Anti-essentialism, multiculturalism and the "recognition" of religious groups', considers the power of essentialist ethnoreligious identities for minority diaspora groups in Britain:

> The identities formed in such processes are fluid and susceptible to change with the political climate, but to think of them as weak is to overlook the pride with which they may be asserted, the intensity with which they may be debated and their capacity to generate community activism and political campaigns. In any case, what is described here as cultural-practices based identities and associational identities are not mutually exclusive. They depict ideal types which are usually found, as in this survey, in a mixed form. Moreover, a reactive pride identity can generate new cultural practices or revive old ones. For some Caribbean

people, a Black identity has come to mean a reclaiming of the African-Caribbean cultural heritage and has thus stimulated among some younger people an interest in Patois-Creole languages, which was not there amongst the migrants. A similar Muslim assertiveness, sometimes a political identity, sometimes a religious revival, sometimes both, is evident in Britain and elsewhere, especially amongst some of the young. (Modood, 1998, p. 386)

In resisting modernity's fixed identifications, postmodern academics put religious, historical institutions, tradition and ancestral culture at risk of being insignificant vehicles for knowledge.

The challenge from the Afroasiatic diasporic religions I have selected for this study lies in rediscovering the true, correct and authoritative interpretation of Scripture and the function of the Bible. Although the religions have doctrinal diversity, what allows them to be placed under a unifying umbrella is their relationship to the Scriptures, a shared historical experience, and a hermeneutical premise that I have conceptualized as *preservation–liberation*. The foundation of the hermeneutical premise can be summarized as a belief that the Bible is the written history, legacy and redemption story of Black people, more specifically, those enslaved and transported from the African continent by European imperial powers in the sixteenth century. Therefore, the biblical Scriptures detail the traditions, instructions, stories, divine revelation and a redemption guide to coming out of the oppression of the Europeans and becoming 'woke' to their true identity, purpose and destiny as designed by the God of the Bible.

Rational choice – God shopping?

Rational Choice Theory is an economic theory that suggests that human behaviour is influenced by getting maximum benefit for the least cost. To understand the human side of religious behaviour, as one cannot quantify the supernatural aspects of religion, scholars have applied Rational Choice Theory (RCT) to the sociology of religion. Following a survivalist and constructivist trend, New Religious Movements can be understood in transactional terms. Arguably, one can suggest that, because people cannot obtain their ultimate desires, such as immortality, they are drawn toward supernaturalism and notions of transcendence through their human ability.

Rodney Stark and Roger Finke, for example, in *Acts of Faith: Explaining the Human Side of Religion* (2000), argue that institution weakens the prospects of religions, so what can be observed is the emergence of new religions – a cycle in which secularization (of which globalization could be considered one aspect) acts as a catalyst. The term 'religious economy' speaks specifically to the competition within the religious framework:

> Each firm seeks to occupy and to consolidate a key 'niche'. Thus it is not church-switching [i.e. changes in the relative demand for various 'brands'] that is the central dynamic in religious change. Rather it is the *shifting of religious firms from niche to niche* that has the greatest impact on the overall religious economy with the consequence that the primary religious suppliers change over time. (Stark and Finke, 2000, p. 196, italics original)

Observing the shift from mainstream churches to these Afroasiatic congregations does provoke questions about religious, social, economic and political needs. Given that these organizations are not as economically prosperous or socially or politically influential as the dominant religions from which they have diverged, one must consider the influence of the genealogical and historical claims they make to support their religious functionality. Do we see this play out in the 'market' of Black religion and their emphasis on particular aspects of social and religious heritage? Can these merely be versions of Christianity that appeal to niche requirements within the Black community? Is there also a connection between the influence of secular philosophies and postmodernism in Black religious and theological discourse and the persistence and flourishing of these 'modernist'/fundamentalist religious groups? What is at stake if we consider these movements solely based on human behaviour – a need to survive, achieve and bank a constructed version of their ultimate desires?

A weakness of Rational Choice Theory is that it does not take into consideration the beliefs of the religious adherents – this is typical of many constructivist responses to a religious phenomenon. Subjecting religious belief to rationality equally negates the unique function that religion plays in society: to embrace a mysterious, mystical or metaphysical reality that transcends our versions of rationality. Andrew M. McKinnon (2013) posits that analysing religion through a capitalist lens using terms such as 'religious economy' and 'the market' for the way that religious people may view God considers society as one-dimensional, naturally self-serving and without the capacity for diverse human action (McKinnon, 2013, p. 542). While Rational Choice Theory flags up some helpful questions for this study, in the broader conversations that seek to define religion, it reduces religion to a mechanism for coping, competing and surviving. The merit of this approach perhaps lies in its ability to critique the overlap of the seeker's quest for a divine purpose and how religions and centres of religion market themselves to appeal to 'customers'.

To this end I suggest the following action points for the mainstream, who seek to build bridges with the de-churched. I first remind the reader that this study has undertaken ethnographic research to understand a particular community's inner mind in response to these questions. I have not sought to authenticate or validate their positions. Good research, however, should develop learning outcomes for interested parties and so for the Church; I consider these lessons derived from my exploration:

- The de-churched have described the Church as an *unsafe space* for asking questions about Black identity concerning faith and Christian/ church history. This study has presented a possible approach to transforming the learning space in a Christian setting.
- The de-churched seek to be heard and acknowledged and guided on their journey to reconcile faith and identity among a community of like-minded people.
- The de-churched are seeking a community that rejects the 'White Man's Religion', rediscovering the true religion and teachings of the Bible and severing ties with Colonial Christianity.

Response from the mainstream

Mainstream Christianity is not a monolith, and so detailing a proposal for a response to the de-churched is not a simple matter. However, as we reflect on what we have learned about the Black, British and de-churched, there are a few responsive actions many mainstream churches can engage in that begin the journey of responding and being reflexive to the challenges presented toward building bridges with the de-churched. Mainstream Christian churches comprise both historical/ institutional European churches, diasporic churches, and independent and free churches, so it must be made clear that many of the claims made against the Church are made with the historical institutional European churches in mind with regard to Colonial Christianity. There is also, however, an issue with Black majority churches, who in their failure to respond to difficult questions adequately caused relational breakdown and disappointment.

Drawing upon the preservation–liberation framework, I suggest that we can achieve decolonization, liberation, preservation and localization through the teaching faculty of the Church (a gift to the Church). Preaching, teaching and discipleship are three target areas that can engage directly with the questions and concerns of the de-churched, engage the claims of Black Bible Religions and eventually build up safe spaces for evangelism and the prophetic and healing ministries in the body of Christ and those on the fringes of local church life.

In summary, the de-churched have posited the following sentiments:

- There are gaps in their Christian education as it relates to the origins of Christianity, early church history and how early believers organized themselves and established doctrine.
- In their church experiences, there has been a silence on the African presence in the Bible as well as the contribution of Africans to the formation of beliefs we hold as central to the Christian faith
- The complicity of the European Church in the enslavement of Black and Brown peoples and the colonization of African and Asian lands and societies is a stumbling block for the de-churched.
- The complicity of European churches in the ongoing legal discrimination of Black and Brown people up until the time of one's grandparents is a stumbling block.
- The de-churched are looking for a religious experience that considers and speaks to the experiences of Black people, providing a hopeful future, justice and judgement for the perpetrators of their oppression or exclusion.
- The de-churched seek to find the final authoritative, true and correct meaning of Scripture rather than a relativized or fluid reading.
- The de-churched are interested in self-study, research, and supporting literature to learn more about the Bible, its history and its ancestral roots, both ethnic and religious.
- The de-churched seek to be a part of a religious community that can support them in multiple aspects of their life, a community that operates as a nation within a nation.
- The de-churched make distinctions between the religion of the Bible and Colonial Christianity; images of a White Jesus, White Bible characters and the dominance of literature written by Europeans provided in seminaries are examples of the legacy of Colonial Christianity – in other words, whitewashing and gatekeeping.

The call to respond to the Black British de-churched and Black Bible Religions isn't a call to accept their doctrine, re-readings and eschatological interpretations. But to engage with them. To discuss them, to have ready a response, and to equip our congregations with the tools, safe spaces and confidence to interrogate challenges to core beliefs with humility and understanding – preserving religious conviction but liberating those responses from the legacy of domination and White hegemony. The Bible says:

> Do your best to present yourself to God as one approved by him, a worker who has no need to be ashamed, rightly explaining the word of truth. (2 Timothy 2.15, ESV)

The KJV reading, more familiar among the de-churched, reads: 'Study to shew thyself approved.' This scripture helps to guide the myriad of feelings on the surface when tackling such challenging issues. On the one hand, there is the legacy of oppression and exploitation that is sinful and a stain on the reputation of the European Church where there is a need for repentance and repair – yet there is no need to be ashamed of being a Christian or of the word of truth. The engagement with the de-churched is not to draw the lost sheep back to the perfect paradise of the mainstream but to work together to build a bridge, a pathway of exchange where both parties are transformed. 1 Peter 3.13–17 says:

> Now, who is there to harm you if you are zealous for what is good? But even if you should suffer for righteousness' sake, you will be blessed. Have no fear of them, nor be troubled, but in your hearts honour Christ the Lord as holy, always being prepared to make a defence to anyone who asks you for a reason for the hope that is in you; yet do it with gentleness and respect, having a good conscience, so that, when you are slandered, those who revile your good behaviour in Christ may be put to shame. For it is better to suffer for doing good, if that should be God's will, than for doing evil. (ESV)

Local mainstream churches must develop an apologetic faculty within their church setting, equipping believers with the gift to learn, reason, teach and defend, creating a space in which the de-churched can explore their questions, develop their research skills and have a deeper understanding of the doctrinal position of that particular church. Thinking back to participant RU, who grew up thinking that all Christians believed the same things only to realize later in life that his own congregation would be considered a cult to the mainstream. Being transparent about the particular leanings of one's local church, and the history and method underpinning these leanings, is one of the ways we can reduce the potential for severe cases of disillusionment.

Apologetics in the mainstream

The field of apologetics within Christian theology is concerned with answering questions about and claims against the faith using evidence, logic and reason. Typical topics include creationism vs evolution, morality, life after death, human experiences and the validity of Scripture. It is philosophically situated in modernist perspectives that value empirical evidence, absolute truths, and high regard for the biblical Scriptures. Apologetics is very popular in conservative, evangelical and reformed denominations of Christianity which, generally speaking, position Scripture and Christ as the revelation of God's authority on all matters. During my research, it has been encouraging to see the growing field of urban apologetics in North America – the arm of apologetics that speaks to the experiences, questions, and needs of Black and Brown urban communities. Christopher Brooks, in *Urban Apologetics,* defines this task as equipping Christians and ministers with the foundational tools for engaging in Urban Apologetics; he says:

> The greatest of these tools are wise and well-framed biblical answers to the questions Urban America is asking of the faith. These issues range from matters of poverty, public policy and personal suffering to those of social justice and sexual identity. (Brooks, 2003, p. 17)

Brooks calls for the role of the apologist to be well resourced with sound theological teaching and support from the local church, and requiring an individual who is spiritually, socially and intellectually gifted to respond to the difficult questions and hostile claims made against the Christian faith. Black Urban Apologetics is based on the same foundation as (Western) apologetics but speaks particularly to the context of Black urban peoples and Black religions often termed mystery cults, such as the Nation of Islam, (Black) Hebrew Israelites, Five-Percenters, Kemetic Scientists and the wider Black Conscious Community.

In its early stages of development, Black Urban Apologists (pastors and teachers) have the task of internal reflection, working through some of the attributes it has inherited from the wider evangelical/conservative apologetic movement. Typically, apologetics has been male-dominated, heavy debate spaces undergirded by 'colourblind', conservative Christian interpretation of Scripture. BUA has employed a more relatable discussion method (rather than debate), has sought to engage women's expertise in theology and religion and is more self-critical of the wider Church, the Black Church, and the Black religious movement in urban communities. BUA has achieved in a decade what Black Theology has failed to do in over half a century – bridge the gap between academia, the Church and the streets – and I hypothesize that it is developing a postcolonial conservative space that meets the spiritual, social and intellectual needs of the Black-British and de-churched.

Lisa Fields, for example, has made a considerable contribution to Black Urban Apologetics in America by developing the Jude 3 Project, which creates content to help Black Christians defend their faith through apologetics, aiming the conversations at historical, political and social issues that affect the African American community. This is particularly exceptional because of the lack of Black and/or female apologists in the wider world of apologetics. She acts as a facilitator and develops a discussion-based style, opposing the confrontational debate style that dominated apologetics. Lisa also takes her work beyond the Urban community. In an interview with *Christianity Today*, she says:

> *Black people in the inner city need apologetics, but black people in the suburbs do too ... We offer apologetics for black people across socio-economic statuses. So that is where I would say Jude 3 is a bit broader. While I want to connect to the black person on the corner, I also want to connect with black people on the Hill in DC who have brunch every Saturday.* (*Christianity Today*, 2018, italics original)

Through online courses, day conferences, speaking engagements and social media, Lisa Fields has contributed to forming a network of Black Christian intellectuals, ministers and teachers. Field's YouTube channel covers key issues and questions to engage the defectors, equip Christians, and inspire all to study further. Although apologetics is historically found in theologically (and often socially) conservative spaces, Fields expands her network beyond this tradition and dialogues with progressive thinkers to provide a transparent discussion of Black God-talk in the twenty-first century.

Dr Eric Mason, Pastor of Epiphany Church and author of *Woke Church: An Urgent Call for Christians in America to Confront Racism and Injustice* (2018), realizes his apologetic enterprise through the pulpit. Mason acknowledges the need for robust theological education in the general discipleship of churchgoers and shapes his sermons with components of biblical studies, theological reflection, and his congregation's lived experiences in Black America. Mason asserts:

> We need textbooks that reflect truth concerning biblical history. The images used should display the richness and diversity of our faith. Practical theology classes need to be developed that focus on the needs

in Black, poor, and middle-class spheres. We must help people to understand how the Bible addresses key questions concerning dignity, identity and significance. (Mason, 2018, p. 149)

Mason is among a throng of ministers who speak out against the whitewashing of Christian education, colourblind and racist attitudes towards colleagues and contextualized theological discussions. Beyond articulate rebuttals, Mason's ministry is an example of how these theologically conservative yet socially conscious churches are engaging in social justice activities, from feeding programmes and career advice to advocating for change in public education policies.

Brother Berean is a YouTube personality who regularly streams live discussions and commentaries about Black consciousness and Christian Faith. As a Pentecostal Christian who grew up in an urban context and has been through his own experience of religious exploration into the mystery cults, Berean's mission is to engage in intellectual debate with claims against the validity of Christianity. This resource is informal and conversational and is aimed at street-level conversations that are often missed by church and intellectual efforts. In this way, Berean has utilized social media to engage with other YouTube personalities who are heavily influential within the Black Conscious Community and debate with some leading critics. Berean is a clear example of how Black Urban Apologetics has developed in-house criticism on several levels: first within the wider apologetics world (often on issues of racism and dominant interpretations); second within the Black Church and academic spheres (often on issues of doctrine and liberal interpretations); and last within the Black religious community (often on issues of pseudo-scholarship, cultish behaviours and integrity).

These are but a few examples of many people who transform how Black people engage with their Black, Bible-based religious traditions. I believe that forming bridges between the academy, the Church, the de-churched and Afroasiatic diasporic religions (as they present themselves), using apologetics in the teaching mechanism of the Church, would facilitate a connection that leads to repentance, understanding and course correction (on both sides). Furthermore, providing more formal education for local discipleship combats the suspicions that things are being hidden or that one must pay or get special access to information that influences and shapes the religion that people submit to in the pew.

Decolonization in the mainstream

Decolonization applied to Christianity and theology helps respond to these issues. Although many sceptics consider complete decolonization as an unattainable and unrealistic goal, few people would argue that there is no room for improvement when considering the equality and visibility of Black and Brown people in established institutions such as the organized Church.

- **Power** – Decolonization calls for the dismantling or reform of historic colonial structures and institutions to share power among all participants from all communities.
- **Presence** – Decolonization calls for the recognition of the presence of the 'other': non-White peoples that have made significant contributions to the shaping of society in the case of British contexts. It also considers ways in which the presence of the 'other' critiques the existing power structures.
- **Participation** – Decolonization demands a seat at the table for the 'other' to shape their experiences in society in a meaningful way. This would be an equal contribution that accepts contextualized and nuanced presuppositions, knowledge forms and outcomes.[1]

The strength of ADR's appeal to the fringes of the Black-British Christian body seems to be rooted in how they establish connections with their ancestors as chosen people of God. This, of course, is exclusive, but it also serves as a corrective. ADR suggests that Christianity or the Bible religion has been birthed from within the Afroasiatic region, among people of colour, cultures, traditions and languages integral to interpreting Scripture. Churches that do not maintain this exclusive view of 'chosenness' based on ethnicity and nation can still employ some of this emphasis in Christian teaching to correct the whitewashed epistemologies that currently maintain a colourblind stance. This begins with acknowledging the sin of whitewashing and correcting the offending cultural and ritual articles that perpetuate the silencing and exclusion of other communities who have been central and integral to the unfolding history of the Church. For the Church to maintain integrity when challenging some of the more controversial, Black supremacist ideologies found within the more extreme ends of Black Bible Religions, it must lead, taking the log of white supremacy from its own eye.

It is safe to assert that Black Bible Religions operate an eisegetical approach to Scripture, nuancing their claims to plain reading and interpretation as well as the progressive revelation afforded to key Black figures in recent history. It is also safe to teach about these methods and their implications in Bible study: teaching the everyday Christian how to exegete and what it means to eisegete is not a distraction from the gospel, from shepherding or building community. It does not just belong in the seminary, and it should cost to engage with these insights; *upskilling the local church* is a form of decolonization. It levels the playing field, necessitates participation and works on the understanding that everyone brings something to the text.

Many mainstream churches teach an inclusive gospel, inclusive in the sense that the gospel is for all and that Jesus Christ died for all and not for a specific ethnic group. One of the ways that we can further display this is by including other cultures and being open to listening to, engaging with, and discussing our perspectives in humility. It is to give people room to express Christianity according to the traditions and cultures they carry with them as a diaspora. Romans 10.8–13 says:

> But what does it say? 'The word is near you, in your mouth and in your heart' (that is, the word of faith that we proclaim); because, if you confess with your mouth that Jesus is Lord and believe in your heart that God raised him from the dead, you will be saved. For with the heart one believes and is justified, and with the mouth one confesses and is saved. For the Scripture says, 'Everyone who believes in him will not be put to shame'. For there is no distinction between Jew and Greek; for the same Lord is Lord of all, bestowing his riches on all who call on him. For 'everyone who calls on the name of the Lord will be saved'.

If the gospel is for everybody – or for all who receive it (leaving the Calvinist–Armenian battle for another time) – then God is speaking to everybody in words and languages and through cultures that they understand. Having a firm dialectical and discussion-based framework, much like we see with Participatory Action Research, will help when, as a congregation, challenging or controversial ideals come to the fore. This is not so that the mainstream can filter the incoming 'foreign' or 'migratory' ideas but so that the difference within certain communities can be an accountability filter for all.

Local churches must upskill their congregants, giving them the opportunity to engage with Biblical Studies (even if only at an introductory level). Broadening the participation across people groups (with the support of ethnically diverse theological input) will, over time, dismantle the hold of European epistemologies, allowing the community of believers to be equal conversation partners in discerning the mind and heart of God, and the revelation of the Gospel in the Scriptures – applying it to the experiences of the everyday, including the experiences of the Black community in Britain.

Localizing in the mainstream

I suggest three Gs that emerge from my research:

- **Get geographic** – Getting geographic refers to the use of maps and detailing of locations. The focus here is on the perspective of the maps and using them to familiarize our listeners with the Afroasiatic world of the Bible – rather than just the 'Bible lands'. By attaching significance to the landscape and trying to understand the relationships between people groups, hearers of the word can in some way draw parallels in their own lives and discover points of application: in every account, the intervention of God was necessary. Further to this, we can use maps to correct the gaze of the listeners, helping them to see that many of the biblical accounts took place on the continent of Africa and that when they read the Bible they are often reading the religious history of Egyptians, Ethiopians, Canaanites, Nubians, Tunisians and Sudanese.
- **Get genealogical** – My second suggestion is to use the genealogies in the Bible. While they can seem like the most tedious part of Scripture, particularly in the case of Yeshua, the Messiah, his documented genealogy shows us how God uses people, ethnicity and lineage to realize his plan for redemption. Redemption is not found in the lofty ideas of present-day prophets and teachers but in the incarnation of Christ, the person – both human and divine. These genealogies together allow people a way to see how Christ, our central figure for redemption, is linked to all people – both mysteriously and physically.
- **Go global** – We must allow the voices of non-White peoples to tell the story of redemption through their own ethnic and cultural perspectives. This creates a sense of democracy, distributing responsibility among other qualified and spiritually gifted brothers and sisters by eliminating the one-sided preaching shaped by the Eurocentric gaze. In this way, the diversity within a multicultural congregation has room to thrive and flourish rather than fall back to the (dis)comfort of the dominant culture.

Another way that we can connect our congregations with the geographic and genealogical aspects of the Bible is to introduce the learning of Hebrew into both children's and adults' education (perhaps as an interest group or featured as a segment in the service). Learning one of the languages used to transmit the revelation given to the Prophets (which I agree to be authoritative and a singular message pointing to the incarnation of God the Son) aids believers in their understanding of the people, places and cultures that inform our understanding of the text. I believe this type of engagement will also help congregants and the de-churched see how God is present among people groups today, able to be understood through their own cultural assets and mechanisms, and how connected we are as humanity with shared hopes, fears and experiences.

This is not about turning churches into seminaries and believers into scholars, nor is it a training manual for new colonial-style Christian soldiers. Rather, given the demand for input we see from the Black de-churched and beyond, boosting the skill set of the congregation – those who are willing – and making that part of the fabric of church life increases their ability to participate, to have presence, and to share the power that God has given to all of us to get to know him, to learn to share with one another and to preach the gospel to diverse people. It develops an accountability mechanism that goes beyond leadership teams. The more people are equipped with the skills to share deeply, with humility and understanding, the more de-churched groups – not just Black, but the atheist de-churched, the LGBTQI+ de-churched – they can engage.

By getting geographic, genealogical and global, churches can begin to overcome the theological conundrums in twenty-first-century society. By embracing an ethnic-centred reading of Scripture, preachers can preserve the religious integrity and authority of Scripture yet liberate our perspectives from the lie of colourblindness and residual colonial attitudes that breed suspicion of the input of the 'other'.

Conclusions

My hope is that you come to the end of this study with a deeper understanding and appreciation for the de-churched and Black Bible Religions and how important their critique of mainstream Christianity is for the pursuit of justice, repair and reconciliation. It was my goal to draw mainstream Christians into my investigation and equip you with tools for adequately responding to these challenges at a local level, but also to develop in-house questions about how mainstream churches, in all their shapes and sizes and methodologies, engage in teaching, preaching and discipleship.

For those who belong to the de-churched, I hope you feel in some way seen and heard.

Considering what has been achieved with this book, future research can be geared to a more exhaustive comparative analysis of twenty-first-century Afroasiatic religions in Britain. I feel there is still room for further documentation and investigation of these religions that would serve British studies as it pertains to religion, culture, theology, identity, politics and sociology. I have demonstrated that these Afroasiatic diasporic religions operate on the sidelines but can generate interest in academic studies and particularly change the shape and culture of more White, male-dominated departments such as Biblical Studies and apologetics.

> But when he saw many of the Pharisees and Sadducees coming to his baptism, he said to them, 'You brood of vipers! Who warned you to flee from the wrath to come? Bear fruit in keeping with repentance. And do not presume to say to yourselves, "We have Abraham as our father," for I tell you, God is able from these stones to raise up children for Abraham. Even now the axe is laid to the root of the trees. Every tree therefore that does not bear good fruit is cut down and thrown into the fire.' (Matthew 3.7–10)

Notes

1 This is a definition I have formalized in the last year of this study. Inspired by this research, I have used this as a quote in other research projects such (1) Visions of Colour, an anti-racism resource I developed for the Baptist Union of Great Britain, (2) 'Children's Christian Resources and Racism', a report developed for the Council for World Missions.

Bibliography

Abarry, Abu Shardow and Asante, Molefi Kete, 1996, *African Intellectual Heritage: A Book of Sources*, Philadelphia, PA: Temple University Press.
Abraham, Susan, 2009, 'Strategic essentialism in nationalist discourses: Sketching a feminist agenda in the study of religion', *Journal of Feminist Studies in Religion*, 25 1, pp. 156–61.
Abrams, Andrea C., 2014, *God and Blackness: Race, Gender, and Identity in a Middle Class Afrocentric Church*, New York: New York University Press.
Adam, A. K. M. et al., 2009, 'Should we be teaching the historical-critical method?', *Teaching Theology and Religion*, 12 2, pp. 162–87.
Adamo, David T., 2001, *Africa and Africans in the Old Testament*, Eugene, OR: Wipf and Stock.
Adams, Tony E., Holmann-Jones, Stacy Linn and Ellis, Carolyn, 2015, *Autoethnography*, Oxford: Oxford University Press.
Adams, Tony E., Holmann-Jones, Stacy Linn and Ellis, Carolyn, 2016, *Handbook of Autoethnography*, Abingdon: Routledge.
Adedibu, Babatunde, 2012, *Coat of Many Colours*, London: Wisdom Summit.
Adeleke, Tunde, 2009, *The Case Against Afrocentrism*, Jackson, MS: University of Mississippi Press.
Adorno, T. W. et al., 1950, *The Authoritarian Personality*, New York: Harper.
Ahluwalia, Pal and Zegeye, Aee, 2010, 'Frantz Fanon and Steve Biko: Towards liberation', *Journal for the Study of Race, Nation and Culture*, 7 3, pp. 455–69.
Akbar, N., 1991, 'Mental disorder among African Americans' in R. L. Jones (ed.), *Black Psychology*, London: Cobb & Henry Publishers, pp. 339–52.
Akom, A. A., 2003, 'Reexamining resistance as oppositional behavior: The Nation of Islam and the creation of a Black achievement ideology', *Sociology of Education*, 76 4, pp. 305–25.
Aldred, Joe, 1999, 'Paradigms for a Black theology in Britain', *Black Theology of Liberation*, 2, pp. 9–32.
Aldred, Joe, 2019, *Pentecostals and Charismatics in Britain: An Anthology*, London: SCM Press.
Aldred, Joe, 2024, *Flourishing in Babylon: Black British Agency and Self-Determination*, London: SCM Press.
Aldred, Joe and Lampard, John S., 2005, *Respect: Understanding Caribbean British Christianity*, London: Epworth Press.
Alexander, Claire, 2002, 'Beyond Black: Rethinking the colour/culture divide', *Ethics and Racial Studies*, 25 4, pp. 552–71.
Allen, Ricky Lee, 2004, 'Whiteness and critical pedagogy', *Educational Philosophy and Theory*, 36 2, pp. 121–36.

Alridge, Derrick P., 2007, 'Of Victorianism, civilizationism, and progressivism: The educational ideas of Anna Julia Cooper and W. E. B. Du Bois, 1892–1940', *History of Education Quarterly*, 47 4, pp.

Alston, William, F., 1991, *Perceiving God: The Epistemology of Religious Experience*, Ithaca, NY: Cornell University Press.

Anderson, Carver L., 2015, Towards a Practical Theology for Effective Responses to Black Young Men Associated with Crime for Black Majority Churches, PhD, The University of Birmingham.

Andrews, Dale P., 2002, *Practical Theology for Black Churches: Bridging Black Theology and African American Folk Religion*, Louisville, KY: Westminster John Knox Press.

Andrews, Edward, 2010, 'Christian missions and colonial empires reconsidered: A black evangelist in west Africa 1766–1816', *Journal of Church and State*, 51 4, pp. 663–91.

Andrews, Kehinde, 2018, *Back to Black: Retelling Black Radicalism for the 21st Century*, London: Zed Books.

Angrosino, Michael, 2007, *Doing Ethnographic and Observational Research*, London: Sage Publications.

Anney, Vicent N., 2014, 'Ensuring the quality of findings of qualitative research: looking at trustworthiness criteria', *Journal of Emerging Trends in Educational Research and Policy Studies*, 5 2, pp. 272–81.

Appiah, Kwame Anthony, 2006, 'The politics of identity', *Daedalus*, 135 4, pp. 15–22.

Arvidsson, Stefan, 1999, 'Aryan mythology as science and ideology', *Journal of the American Academy of Religion*, 67 2, pp. 327–54.

Atkinson, P., 1997, 'Narrative turn or blind alley?', *Qualitative Health Research*, 7, pp. 315–44.

Austin, Algernon, 2003, 'Rethinking race and the Nation of Islam, 1930–1975', *Ethnic and Racial Studies*, 26 1, pp. 52–69.

Bacote, Vincent, Miguilez, Laura and Okholm, Dennis (eds), 2009, *Evangelicals & Scripture: Tradition, Authority and Hermeneutics*, Illinois: InterVarsity Press.

Baker, Christopher, 2007, *Hybrid Church in the City: Third Space Thinking*, Burlington, VT: Ashgate Publishing.

Baker-Fletcher, Karen and Baker-Fletcher, Garth Kasimu, 2002, *My Sister, My Brother: Xodus and Womanist God-Talk*, Eugene, OR: Wipf and Stock.

Baldick, Julian, 1997, *Black God: The Afroasiatic Roots of the Jewish, Christian and Muslim Religions*, London: I.B. Tauris.

Bankole, Katherine Olukemi, 2005, *Africalogical Perspectives: Historical and Contemporary Analysis of Race and Africana Studies*, New York: iUniverse.

Bantu, Vince L., 2020a, *A Multitude of All Peoples: Engaging Ancient Christianity's Global Identity*, Illinois: InterVarsity Press.

Bantu, Vincent, 2020b, *Gospel Haymanot: A Constructive Theology and Critical Reflection on African and Diasporic Christianity*, Illinois: Urban Ministries Incorporated.

Barndt, Joseph, 2011, *Becoming the Anti-Racist Church: Journeying Towards Wholeness*, Minneapolis, MN: Fortress.

Barnes, Sandra L., 2010, *Black Megachurch Culture: Models for Education and Empowerment*, New York: Peter Lang.

Barnett, Michael, 2006, 'Differences and similarities between the Rastafari movement and the Nation of Islam', *Journal of Black Studies*, 36 6, pp. 873–93.

Barratt, Leonard E., 1997, *The Rastafarians*, Boston, MA: Beacon Press.
Bates, Dennis, Durka, Gloria and Schweitzer, Friedrich (eds), 2006, *Education, Religion and Society: Essays in Honour of John M. Hill*, London: Routledge.
Baurmann, Michael, 2009, 'Fundamentalism and Epistemic Authority', https://www.fkop.de/wp-content/cache/mendeley-file-cache/85592fa3-f9d0-371b-b658-548fe9916c72.pdf, accessed 01.07.2020.
Bebbington, David W., 2003, *Evangelicalism in Modern Britain: A History from the 1730s to the 1980s*, Taylor and Francis Routledge e-library, accessed 01.07.2020.
Beckford, Robert, 2006, *Jesus Dub: Theology, Music and Social Change*, Abingdon: Routledge.
Beckford, Robert, 2008, 'More dread: 10th anniversary of Jesus is dread: Black theology and Black culture in Britain', *Black Theology*, 6 3, pp. 291–9.
Beckford, Robert, 2011, *Dread and Pentecostal: A Political Theology for the Black Church in Britain*, Eugene, OR: Wipf and Stock.
Beckford, Robert, 2014, *Documentary as Exorcism: Resisting the Bewitchment of Colonial Christianity*, London: Bloomsbury.
Bedell-Avers, Katrina et al., 2009, 'Charismatic, ideological and pragmatic leaders: An examination of leader–leader interactions', *The Leadership Quarterly*, 20, pp. 299–315.
Bediako, Kwame, 1995, *Christianity in Africa: The Renewal of a Non-western Religion*, Maryknoll, NY: Orbis Books.
Bediako, Kwame, 2004, *Jesus and the Gospel in Africa: History and Experience*, Maryknoll, NY: Orbis Books.
Ben-Jochannan, Yosef, 1970, *African Origins of the Major Western Religions: The Black Man's Religion Volume 1*, Baltimore, MD: Black Classic Press.
Bennet, Herman L, 2003, *African in Colonial Mexico: Absolutism, Christianity and Afro-Creole Consciousness, 1570–1640*, Bloomington, IN: Indiana University Press.
Bergmann, Michael, 2004, 'What's "NOT" wrong with foundationalism', *Philosophy and Phenomenological Research*, 68, pp. 161–5.
Bernal, Martin, 1987a, *Black Athena: The Afroasiatic Roots of Classical Civilisation Volume I*, New Brunswick, NJ: Rutgers University Press.
Bernal, Martin, 1987b, *Black Athena: The Archaeological and Documentary Evidence*, New Brunswick, NJ: Rutgers University Press.
Bernal, Martin, 1992, *Black Athena: The Afroasiatic Roots of Classical Civilisation Volume II*, New Brunswick, NJ: Rutgers University Press.
Bernal, Martin, 2006, *Black Athena: The Afroasiatic Roots of Classical Civilisation Volume III*, New Brunswick, NJ: Rutgers University Press.
Berson, Yair et al., 2001, 'The relationship between vision and strength: Leadership style and context', *The Leadership Quarterly*, 12, pp. 53–73.
Bhabha, Homi K., 1984, 'Of mimicry and man: The ambivalence of colonial discourse', *Discipleship: A Special Issue of Psychoanalysis*, 28, pp. 125–33.
Bhabha, Homi K, 1990, *Nation and Narration*, Abingdon: Routledge.
Bhabha, Homi K., 1994, *The Location of Culture*, Abingdon: Routledge.
Biko, S., 1987, *I Write What I Like*, Oxford: Heinemann Educational Publishers.
Birchett, Colleen, 1995, *Africans Who Shape our Faith*, Illinois: Urban Ministries INC.
Bizumic, B., 2018, *Ethnocentrism: Integrated Perspectives*, London: Routledge.

Blyden, Edward W., 1993, *Christianity, Islam and the Negro Race*, Baltimore, MD: Black Classic Press.
Bobo, Jacqueline, Hudley, Cynthia, and Michel, Claudine, 2004, *The Black Studies Reader*, Abingdon: Routledge.
Bogues, Anthony, 2002, 'Politics, nation and postcolony: Caribbean inflections', *Small Axe*, 6 1, pp. 1–30.
Bowman, Fredrick B., 1993, Exploring Effective Leadership in The Black Church Entering The 21st Century, Dissertation, Candler School of Theology Emory University, Atlanta, Georgia.
Boxhill, Bernard R. 1995, 'Fear and Shame as Forms of Moral Suasion in the Thought of Frederick Douglass', *Transactions of the Charles S. Peirce Society*, 31 4, pp. 713–44
Boys, Mary C., 1999, 'Engaged pedagogy dialogue and critical reflection', *Teaching Theology and Religion*, 2 3, pp. 129–36.
Bradley, Anthony B., 2010, *Liberating Black Theology: The Bible and the Black Experience in America*, Illinois: Crossway Books.
Bradley, Anthony B., 2015, *Black Scholars in White Spaces: New Vistas in African America Studies from the Christian Academy*, Eugene, OR: Pickwick Publications.
Briskin, Linda, 2017, 'Identity politics and the hierarchy of oppression: A comment', *Feminist Review*, 35, pp. 102–08.
Brodber, Erna, 1997, 'Re-engineering Black space', *Caribbean Quarterly*, 43 1, pp. 70–81.
Bromley, David G., 2007, *Teaching New Religious Movements*, Oxford: Oxford University Press.
Brooks, C., 2014, *Urban Apologetics: Why the Gospel is Good News for the City*, United States: Kregel Publications.
Brooks, S., 2009, *Sex, Race and God*, Eugene, OR: Wipf and Stock.
Brotz, Howard, 1965, 'The Negro-Jewish community and the contemporary race crisis', *Jewish Social Studies*, 27 1, pp. 10–17.
Brown, Raymond E., 2008, *The Sensus Plenior of Sacred Scripture*, Eugene, OR: Wipf and Stock.
Bruce, Steve, 2011, 'Defining religion: A practical response', *International Review of Sociology*, 21, pp. 107–20.
Brydon-Miller, Mary et al., 2015, 'Why action research?', *Action Research*, 1, pp. 9–28.
Bujo, Benezet, 1990, 'African morality: Individual responsibility and communitarian dimension' in Bujo, Benezet (ed.), *African Christian Morality at the Age of Inculturation*, Kenya: St. Paul Publications-Africa, pp. 95–102.
Burger, Hans, Huijgen, Arnold and Peels, Eric (eds), 2018, *Sola Scriptura: Biblical and Theological Perspectives on Scripture, Authority and Hermeneutics*, Boston, MA: Brill.
Burke, E., 1790, *Reflections on the Revolution in France: And on the Proceedings in Certain Societies in London Relative to that Event: In a Letter Intended to Have Been Sent to a Gentleman in Paris*, London: J. Dodsley in Pall-Mall.
Burrell, Kevin, 2020, *Cushites in the Hebrew Bible: Negotiating Ethnic Identity in the Past and Present*, Boston, MA: Brill.
Burton, Keith Augustus, 2007, *The Blessing of Africa: The Bible and African Christianity*, Illinois: InterVarsity Press.

Bynum, Edward Bruce, 1999, *The African Unconscious: Roots of Ancient Mysticism and Modern Psychology*, New York: Cosimo Books.
Byron, Gay L., 2012, 'Race, ethnicity, and the Bible: Pedagogical challenges and curricular opportunities', *Teaching Theology and Religion*, 15 2, pp. 105–24.
Byron, Gay L. and Lovelace, Vanessa, 2016, *Womanist Interpretations of the Bible: Expanding the Discourse*, Atlanta, GA: S.B.L. Press.
Calhoun-Brown, Allison, 2000, 'Upon this rock: The Black church, nonviolence, and the civil rights movement', *PS: Political Science and Politics*, 33 2, pp. 168–74.
Campbell, Elizabeth and Lassiter, Luke Eric, 2015, *Doing Ethnography Today*, Chichester: John Wiley & Sons.
Campbell, Heidi, 2007, 'Who's got the power? Religious authority and the internet', *Journal of Computer-Mediated Communication*, 12, pp. 1043–62.
Carroll, Vincent, 2001, *Christianity on Trial: Arguments Against Anti-Religious Bigotry*, New York: Encounter Books.
Carter, Glynne Gordon, 2003, *An Amazing Journey: The Church of England's Response to Institutional Racism*, London: Church House Publishing.
Carter, J. Kameron, 2008, *Race: A Theological Account*, Oxford: Oxford University Press.
Caza, Arran et al., 2015, 'How do you really feel? Effect of leaders' perceived emotional sincerity on followers' trust', *The Leadership Quarterly*, 26, pp. 518–31.
Chike, Chigor, 2007, *African Christianity in Britain: Diaspora Doctrines and Dialogue*, Milton Keynes: Author House.
Chilisa, B. and Preece, J., 2005, *African Perspective in Adult Learning: Research Methods for Adult Educators*, Hamburg: UNESCO Institute of Education.
Chisholm, Clinton A., 2005, 'Afrocentricity & Black consciousness: Challenges for Christianity part 1', *Caribbean Journal of Evangelical Theology*, 9, pp. 1–20.
Christian, Mark, 2008a, 'Introduction to the special issue: Marcus Garvey and the universal negro improvement association: New perspectives on philosophy, religion, micro-studies, unity, and practice', *Journal of Black Studies*, 39 2, pp. 163–5.
Christian, Mark, 2008b, 'Marcus Garvey and African unity: lessons for the future from the past', *Journal of Black Studies*, 39 2, pp. 316–31.
Chryssides, George D. and Benjamin E. Zeller, 2014, *The Bloomsbury Companion to New Religious Movements*, London: Bloomsbury.
Cleage, Albert, 1989, *The Black Messiah*, Toronto: Africa World Press.
Clifford, James, 1997, *Travel and Translation in the Late Twentieth Century*, Cambridge, MA: Harvard University Press.
Coffey, A., 1999, *The Ethnographic Self*, London: Sage.
Coffey, John, 2005, Puritanism, Evangelicalism, and the Evangelical Protestant Tradition, Paper for E.T.S. Conference, University of Leicester.
Cohen, Jere M., 1977, 'Sources of Peer Group Homogeneity Source', *Sociology of Education*, 50 4, pp. 227–41.
Coleman, Monica A., 2008, *Making a Way out of No Way: A Womanist Theology*, Minneapolis, MN: Fortress Press.
Comaroff, Jean and Comaroff, John, 2010, 'Africa observed: Discourses of the imperial imagination in perspectives on Africa: A reader in culture, history and representation' in Roy Richard Grinker, Stephen C. Lubkemann and Christopher B. Stiener (eds), *Perspectives on Africa: A Reader in Culture, History and Representation*, West Sussex: Wiley-Blackwell, pp. 31–43.

Cone, James, 1969, *Black Theology and Black Power*, Maryknoll, NY: Orbis Books.
Cone, James, 1970, *A Black Theology of Liberation*, Maryknoll, NY: Orbis Books.
Cone, James, 1977, 'Black theology and the black church: Where do we go from here?', *Cross Currents*, 27 2, pp. 147–56.
Cone, James, 1984, *For My People*, Maryknoll, NY: Orbis Books.
Conger, Jay A., Kanungo, Rabindra N. and Menon, Sanjay T., 2000, 'Charismatic leadership and follower effects', *Journal of Organizational Behavior*, 21, pp. 747–67.
Cooling, Trevor, 2015, 'Competing imaginations for teaching and learning: The findings of research into a Christian approach to teaching and learning called *What If Learning*', *International Journal of Christianity & Education*, 19 2, pp. 96–107.
Corbin, Juliet and Strauss, Anselm, 1990, 'Grounded Theory Research: Procedures, Canons and Evaluative Criteria', *Zeitschrift fur Soziologie*, 19 6, pp. 418–27.
Corbin, J. and Strauss, A., 1994, 'Grounded theory methodology: An overview', in N. K. Denzin and Y. S. Lincoln (eds), *Handbook of Qualitative Research*, Thousand Oaks, CA: Sage Publications, pp. 273–85.
Cornelius, Janet Duitsman, 1992, *When I Can Read My Title Clear: Literacy, Slavery and Religion in the Antebellum South*, Columbia, SC: University of South Carolina Press.
Cowan, Douglas E. and Bromley, David G., 2008, *Cults and New Religions: A Brief History*, West Sussex: Wiley Blackwell.
Crane, Richard D., 2016, 'Method, MacIntyre, and pedagogy: Inviting students to participate in theology as a living conversation', *Teaching Theology & Religion*, 19 3, pp. 222–44.
Crawford, Anna Elaine Brown, 2002, *Hope in the Holler: A Womanist Theology*, London: Westminster John Knox Press.
Curtis, Edward E., 2002, 'Islamizing the Black body: Ritual and power in Elijah Muhammad's Nation of Islam', *Religion and American Culture: A Journal of Interpretation*, 12 2, pp. 167–96.
Curtis, E. E., 2009, *Black Muslim Religion in the Nation of Islam, 1960–1975*, Chapel Hill: University of North Carolina Press.
Curtis, Edward E., 2014, *The Call of Bilal: Islam in the African Diaspora*, North Carolina: University of North Carolina Press.
Dantley, Michael E., 2005, 'African American spirituality and Cornel West's notions of prophetic pragmatism: Restructuring educational leadership in American urban schools', *Educational Administration*, 41 4, pp. 651–74.
David, Marian, 2016, 'The Correspondence Theory of Truth', *The Stanford Encyclopedia of Philosophy*, https://plato.stanford.edu/archives/sum2022/entries/truth-correspondence/, accessed 17.03.2018.
Davidson, Steed V., 2008, 'Leave Babylon: The trope of Babylon in Rastafari discourse', *Black Theology: An International Journal*, 6, pp. 46–60.
DeHanas, Daniel, N., 2016, *London Youth, Religion, and Politics: Engagements and Activism from Brixton to Brick Lane*, Oxford: Oxford University Press.
Delamarter, Steve, Lutheran, Javier Alanís, Haitch, Russell, Hoffman, Mark Vitalis, Jones, Arun W. and Brent, Austin Strawn, 2007, 'Pedagogy, and Transformation in Theological Education: Five Case Studies', *Teaching Theology and Religion*, 10 2, pp. 64–79.

Dew, Spencer, 2019, *The Aliites*, Chicago, IL: University of Chicago Press.
Dorman, Jacob S., 2013, *Chosen People: The Rise of American Black Israelite Religions*, Oxford: Oxford University Press.
Douglas, Kelly Brown, 1994, *The Black Christ*, Maryknoll, NY: Orbis Books.
Douglas, Kelly Brown, 1999, *Sexuality and the Black Church: A Womanist Perspective*, Maryknoll, NY: Orbis Books.
Douglas, Kelly Brown, 2005, *What's Faith Got to Do with it? Black bodies/Christian Souls*, Maryknoll, NY: Orbis Books.
Du Bois, W. E. B., 1898, 'The Study of Negro Problems', *Annals of the American Academy of Political and Social Science*, 11, p. 8.
Du Bois, W. E. B., 1994, *The Souls of Black Folk*, New York: Dover Publications.
Dumisani, Welcome Methula, 2015, Black Theology and the Struggle for Economic Justice in the Democratic South Africa, Master's Thesis, University of South Africa.
Duncan, G. A., 2014, 'Inculturation: Adaptation, innovation and reflexivity: An African Christian perspective', *H.T.S. Teologiese Studies/Theological Studies*, 70, pp. 1–11.
Dyson, Michael Eric, 1996, *Between God and Gangsta Rap: Bearing Witness to Black Culture*, Oxford: Oxford University Press.
Eck, Earnst van, 2006, 'The word is life: African theology as biblical and contextual theology', *H.T.S. Teologiese Studies/Theological Studies*, 62 2, pp. 679–701
Edwards, Kirsten T., 2013, 'Christianity as anti-colonial resistance?', *Souls*, 15, pp. 146–62.
Elbourne, Elizabeth, 2003, 'Word made flesh: Christianity, modernity and cultural colonialism in the work of Jean and John Comaroff', *American Historical Review*, 108, pp. 435–59.
Enns, Peter, 2003, 'Apostolic hermeneutics and evangelical doctrine of scripture: Moving beyond a modernist impasse', *Westminster Theological Seminary*, 65, pp. 263–87.
Eppehimer, Trevor, 2006, 'Victor Anderson's beyond ontological blackness and James Cone's Black theology: A discussion', *Black Theology*, 4 1, pp. 87–106.
Erskine, Noel Leo, 2008, *Black Theology and Pedagogy*, New York: Palgrave Macmillan.
Eze, Emmanuel Chukwudi (ed.), 1997, *Postcolonial African Philosophy: A Critical Reader*, New Jersey: Wiley-Blackwell.
Fanon, Frantz, 1961, *The Wretched of The Earth*, New York: Grove Press.
Fauset, Arthur Huff, 1944, 2002, *Black Gods of the Metropolis*, Philadelphia, PA: University of Pennsylvania Press.
Feltmate, David, 2016, 'Rethinking new religious movements beyond a social problems paradigm', *Nova Religio: The Journal of Alternative and Emergent Religions*, 20 2, pp. 82–96.
Firth, Rhiannon and Robinson, Andrew, 2016, 'For a revival of feminist consciousness-raising: Horizontal transformation of epistemologies and transgression of neoliberal timespace', *Gender and Education*, 28 3, pp. 343–58.
Fortson, D., 2018, *The Black Hebrew Awakening: The Final 400 Years as Slaves in America*, South Carolina: CreateSpace Independent Publishing.
Foucault, M., 1991, *The Foucault Effect: Studies in Governmentality*, London: University of Chicago Press.

Franks, Mary Anne, 2014, 'I am/am not: On Angela Harris's race and essentialism', *Feminist Legal Theory*, 102 4, pp. 1053–68.
Fredrickson, George M., 1996, *Black Liberation: A Comparative History of Black Ideologies in the United States and South Africa*, Oxford: Oxford University Press.
Freire, P., 1970, *Pedagogy of the Oppressed*, New York: Seabury Press.
Frisk, Lisolette, 2014, 'Globalisation' in Zeller (ed.), *The Bloomsbury Companion to New Religious Movements*, London: Bloomsbury, pp. 273–8.
Ganiel, Gladys, 2021, 'Online opportunities in secularizing societies? Clergy and the COVID-19 pandemic in Ireland', *Religions*, 12, pp. 437–55.
Ganley, Toby, 2003, 'What's all this talk about whiteness??', *Dialogue*, 1 2, pp. 12–30.
Garces-Foley, Kathleen, 2007, 'New opportunities and new values: The emergence of the multicultural church', *American Academy of Political and Social Science*, 612, pp. 209–24.
Gardell, Mattias, 1996, *In the Name of Elijah Muhammad: Louis Farrakhan and the Nation of Islam*, Durham, NC: Duke University Press.
Garvey, Marcus and Garvey, Amy Jacques, 2022, *Africa for Africans: Or, the Philosophy and Opinions of Marcus Garvey*, Berkeley, CA: Mint Editions.
Gellner, Ernest, 1983, *Nations and Nationalism*, New York: Cornell University Press.
Gerloff, Roswith, 2010, *A Plea for British Black Theologies, Volume 1: The Black Church Movement in Britain in its Transatlantic Cultural and Theological Interaction with Special Reference to the Pentecostal Oneness (Apostolic) and Sabbatarian Movements*, Eugene, OR: Wipf and Stock.
Gibson, Dawn Marie, 2012, *A History of the Nation of Islam: Race, Islam and the Quest for Freedom*, Santa Barbara, CA: ABC-Clio.
Gifford, Paul, 1991, 'Christian Fundamentalism and Development in Africa', *Review of African Political Economy*, 19 52, pp. 9–20.
Gifford, Paul, 2008, 'Africa's inculturation theology', *Hakima Review*, 38, pp. 18–34.
Gilroy, Paul, 1993a, *The Black Atlantic: Modernity and Double Consciousness*, London: Verso.
Gilroy, Paul, 1993b, *Small Acts: Thoughts on the Politics of Black Cultures*, London: Serpents Tail.
Gilroy, Paul, 2000, *Against Race: Imagining Political Culture Beyond the Colour Line*, Cambridge, MA: Belknap Press.
Gilroy, Paul, 2006, 'Multiculturalism and the Dynamics of Modern Civilizations: Colonial Crimes and Convivial Cultures', http://rethinking-nordic-colonialism.org/files/pdf/ACT2/ESSAYS/Gilroy.pdf (transcribed talk, accessed 19.02.2018).
Gilroy, Paul, 2009, 'True Humanism?: Civilizationism, securitocracy and racial resignation', *Salem*, 1, pp. 14–22.
Gilroy, Paul, 2013, *There Ain't No Black in the Union Jack*, Abingdon: Routledge.
Gonzalez, Michelle A., 2014, *A Critical Introduction to Religion in the Americas: Bridging the Liberation Theology and Religious Studies Divide*, New York: New York University Press.
Gordon, Lewis, 2021, *Freedom, Justice and Decolonisation*, New York: Routledge.
Gordon, Lewis and Gordon, Jane Anna, 2006, *Not Only the Master's Tools: African American Studies in Theory and Practice*, Abingdon: Routledge.

Gordon, Paul and Rosenburg, David, 1989, *Daily Racism: The Press and Black People in Britain*, London: Runnymede Trust.

Gottdiener, M., 1993, 'Ideology, foundationalism, and sociological theory', *The Sociological Quarterly*, 34 4, pp. 653–71.

Graham, Mekada, 2002, 'Creating spaces: Exploring the role of cultural knowledge as a source of empowerment in models of social welfare in black communities', *British Journal of Social Work*, 3, pp. 35–49.

Grant, Jaquelyn, 1989, *White Women's Christ, Black Women's Jesus: Feminist Christology and Womanist Response*, Atlanta, GA: Scholars Press.

Gregory, Brad S., 2012, *The Unintended Reformation: How a Religious Reformation Secularized Society*, Cambridge, MA: Belknap Press of Harvard University.

Guba, Egon G. and Lincoln, Yvonna S., 1989, *Naturalistic Enquiry*, London: Sage Publications.

Guest, Greg, Namey, Emily E. and Mitchel, Marilyn L., 2013, *Collecting Qualitative Data: Field Manual for Applied Research*, London: Sage Publications.

Gunning, David, 2013, *Race and Antiracism in Black British and British Asian Literature*, Liverpool: Liverpool University Press.

Hadden, Jeffrey K. and Cowan, Douglas E. (eds), 2000, 'Religion on the internet: Research prospects and promises', *Sociology of Religion*, 63 4, pp. 249–76.

Hall, Stuart, 1990, 'Cultural identity and diaspora' in Johnathan Rutherford (ed.), *Identity: Community, Culture, Difference*, London: Lawrence & Wishart, pp. 222–37.

Hall, Stuart, 1991, 'Old and new identities, old and new ethnicities' in A. D. King (ed), *Culture Globalisation and the World-System*, London: Macmillan.

Hall, Stuart, 1992, 'The question of cultural identity' in Stuart Hall, David Held and Anthony McGrew (eds), *Modernity and Its Futures*, Cambridge: Polity Press, pp. 274–316.

Hall, Stuart, 1993, 'What is this 'Black' in Black popular culture?', *Social Justice*, 20, pp. 104–14.

Hall, Stuart, 2014, 'Race, articulation and societies structured in dominance', *Ethnic and Racial Studies*, 37 10, pp. 1667–75.

Hall, Stuart and Geiben, Bram, 1992, *The West and the Rest: Discourse and Power*, Cambridge: Polity Press.

Hamer, Lynne et al., 2013, 'Toward a cultural framework for dialogue about justice', *Journal of Black Studies*, 44 4, pp. 356–75.

Hamilton, Charles and Ture, Kwame, 2011, *Black Power: The Politics of Liberation in America*, New York: Vintage Books.

Hammersley, Martyn, 1992, *What's Wrong with Ethnography?*, New York: Routledge.

Hanciles, Jehu J., 2014, '"Africa is our fatherland": The Black Atlantic, globalization, and modern African Christianity', *Theology Today*, 71 2, pp. 207–20.

Harris, Forrest E., 1993, *Ministry for Social Crisis: Theology and Praxis in the Black Church Tradition*, Macon, GA: Mercer University Press.

Harris, Frederick C., 1999, *Something Within: Religion in African-American Political Activism*, Oxford: Oxford University Press.

Harris, James H., 1991, *Pastoral Theology: A Black Church Perspective*, Minneapolis, MN: Fortress Press.

Hayes, Diana L., 2000, 'James Cone's hermeneutic of language and Black theology', *Theological Studies*, 61 4, pp. 609–31.

Hayes, Diana L., 2010, *Standing in the Shoes My Mother Made: A Womanist Theology*, Minneapolis, MN: Fortress Press.
Hayes, Floyd W., 2000, *The Turbulent Voyage: Readings in African American Studies*, Oxford: Collegiate Press.
Haynes, Bruce D., 2018, *The Soul of Judaism: Jews of African Descent in America*, New York: New York University Press.
Healy, Paul, 2007, 'Rationality, dialogue, and critical inquiry: Toward a viable postfoundationalist stance', *Cosmos and History: The Journal of Natural and Social Philosophy*, 3, pp. 134–58.
Hearn, Mark, 2009, 'Color-blind racism, color-blind theology, and church practices', *Religious Education*, 104 3, pp. 272–88.
Heewong, Chang, 2016, *Autoethnography as Method*, Abingdon: Routledge.
Heim, Joel J., Scovill, Nelia Beth and Wisconsin, Jackson, 2001, 'A spectrum pedagogy for Christian ethics: Respecting difference without resorting to relativism', *Teaching Theology and Religion*, 13 4, pp. 350–70.
Herkovitz, Jean, 2000, 'Review of violence in Nigeria: The crisis of religious politics and secular ideologies', *Journal of Interdisciplinary History*, 30 4, pp. 732–34.
Hill, Robert A., 2006, *Marcus Garvey and Universal Negro Improvement Association Papers Volume X, Africa for the Africans 1923-1945*, California, University of California Press.
Hillborn, David, 2001, *Evangelicalism and the Orthodox Church*, Bletchley: Authentic Media.
Hindmarsh, Bruce D., 2018, *The Spirit of Early Evangelicalism: True Religion in a Modern World*, Oxford: Oxford University Press.
Hodge. Carlton T., 1971, *Afroasiatic: A Survey*, The Hague: Mouton.
Hollon, Bryan C., 2011, 'Knowledge of God as assimilation and participation: An essay on theological pedagogy in the light of biblical epistemology', *Perspectives in Religious Studies*, 38, pp. 85–106.
Holt, Thomas C., 1990, 'The political uses of alienation: W. E. B. Du Bois on politics, race, and culture, 1903–1940', *American Quarterly*, 42 2, pp. 301–23.
Homack, John and Tedlock, Barbara (eds), 1987, *Dreaming: Anthropological and Psychological Interpretations*, Cambridge: Cambridge University Press.
Hood, Robert, E., 1990, *Must God Remain Greek? Afro Cultures and God Talk*, Philadelphia, PA: Fortress Press.
Hook, Derek, 2011, 'Retrieving Biko: A Black consciousness critique of whiteness', *African Identities*, 9, pp. 19–32.
hooks, bell, 1965, *Talking Back: Thinking Feminist, Thinking Black*, Boston, MA: South End Press.
hooks, bell, 1994, *Teaching to Transgress: Education as the Practice of Freedom*, New York: Routledge.
Hopkins, Dwight N. and Lewis, Marjorie, 2014, *Another World is Possible: Spiritualities and Religions of Global Darker Peoples*, Abingdon: Routledge.
Houston, Tom, 2004, 'Biblical models of leadership', *Transformation: An International Journal of Holistic Mission Studies*, 214, pp. 227–33.
Howard, K., 2013, 'Kwame Bediako: Considerations on the motivating force behind his theology and identity', *Global Missiology English*, 3 10, http://ojs.globalmissiology.org/index.php/english/article/view/1186/2735#_ftn95, accessed 10.10.2018.

Howarth, Caroline and Andreouli, Eleni, 2012, 'Has multiculturalism failed?' The importance of lay knowledge and everyday practice', https://ercbgd.org.rs/images/stories/multi-kulti-biblioteka/HOWARTH%20&%20ANDREOULI HAS%20MULTICULTURALISM%20FAILD.pdf, accessed 19.02.2018.

Howe, Thomas, 2015, *Objectivity in Biblical Interpretation*, South Carolina: CreateSpace Independent Publishing.

Howell, Leonard Percival, 1933, 2008, *The Promised Key*, Hogarth Black Ltd.

Howell, Maxine, 2009, 'Towards a womanist pneumatological pedagogy: Reading and re-reading the Bible from British Black women's perspectives', *Black Theology*, 7, pp. 86–99.

Howorth, David, 1997, 'Complexities of identity/difference: Black Consciousness ideology in South Africa', *Journal of Political Ideologies*, 2, pp. 51–78.

Hull, John M., 2010, 'Practical theology and religious education in the pluralist Europe', *British Journal of Religious Education*, 26, pp. 7–19.

Hunt, S. and Lightly, N., 2001, 'The British Black Pentecostal "revival": Identity and belief in the "new" Nigerian churches', *Ethics and Racial Studies*, 24, pp. 104–24.

Huntington, Samuel P., 1957, 'Conservatism as an ideology', *The American Political Science Review*, 51 2, pp. 454–73.

Ilesanmi, Simeon O., 1995, 'Inculturation and liberation: Christian social ethics and the African theology', *The Annual of the Society of Christian Ethics*, 15, pp. 49–73.

Ilo, Stan Chu, 2009, 'Towards an African theology of reconciliation: A missiological reflection on the instrumentum laboris of the second African synod', *The Heythrop Journal*, 53 6, pp. 1–21.

Iqbal, Asep Muhamad, 2016, 'When religion meets the internet (cyber-religion and the secularization thesis)', *Jurnal Komunikasi Islam*, 6 1, pp. 1–28.

Irons, Charles F., 2008, *The Origins of Proslavery Christianity: White and Black Evangelicals in Colonial and Antebellum Virginia*, Chapel Hill, NC: University of North Carolina Press.

Jackson Jr, John L., 2005, *Real Black: Adventures in Racial Sincerity*, Chicago, IL: University of Chicago Press.

Jackson, Robert, 2008, 'From colonialism to theology: Encounters with Martin Wight's international thought', *International Affairs (Royal Institute of International Affairs 1944–)*, 84 2, pp. 351–64.

Jacques-Garvey, Amy (ed.), 2009, *Philosophy and Opinions of Marcus Garvey*, The Journal of Pan African Studies (eBook).

Jalata, Asafa, 2009, 'Being in and out of Africa. The impact of duality of Ethiopianism', *Journal of Black Studies*, 40 2, pp. 189–214.

Jenkinson, Jaqueline, 2009, *Black 1919: Riots, Racism and Resistance in Imperial Britain*, Liverpool: Liverpool University Press.

Jennings, Willie J., 2010, *The Christian Imagination: Theology and the Origins of Race*, London: Yale University Press.

Johnson, Ernest H., 2015, *The Secrets for Motivating, Educating and Lifting the Spirit of African American Males*, Bloomington, IN: iUniverse.

Johnson, George D., 2011, *Profiles in Hue*, Harrisburg: Light of Saviour Ministries.

Johnson, Lemuel A., 1991, 'Inventions of paradise: The Caribbean and the utopian bent', *Afro-Hispanic Review*, 10 2, pp. 3–15.

BIBLIOGRAPHY

Juhrt, Gordon, 2001, *Ministry Issues for the Church of England: Mapping the Trends*, London: Church House Publishing.

Junior, Nyasha, 2015, *An Introduction to Womanist Biblical Interpretation*, Louisville, KY: Westminster John Knox Press.

Kaiser Jr., Walter C., 1982, 'Evangelical hermeneutics: Restatement, advance or retreat from the reformation?', *Concordia Theological Quarterly*, 46, pp. 167–80.

Kalilombe, Patrick, 1997, 'Black Christianity in Britain', *Ethnic and Racial Studies*, 20 2, pp. 306–24.

Kambon, Kobi, 1998, *African/Black Psychology in the American Context: An African-Centred Approach*, New York: Nubian Nation Publications.

Karenga, Maulana, 1986, *Kemet and the African Worldview: Research, Rescue and Restoration*, Timbuktu: University of Sankore Press.

Katongole, Emmanuel, 1998, 'African renaissance and the challenge of narrative theology in Africa', *Journal of Theology for Southern Africa*, 102, pp. 29–39.

Katongole, Emmanuel, 2002, 'A different world right here, a world being gestated in the deeds of the everyday: The church wishing African theological imagination', *Missional*, 30 2, pp. 206–34.

Katznelson, I. and Jones, Gareth S. (eds), 2010, *Religion and the Political Imagination*, Cambridge: Cambridge University Press.

Kaunda, C. J., 2015, 'The denial of African agency: A decolonial theological turn', *Black Theology*, 13, pp. 73–92.

Kaunda, C. J., 2016, 'The wilderness wanderings: A theo-liminal pedagogy for mind decolonisation in African Christianity', *Acta Theologica*, 36, pp. 52–69.

Kay, Roy, 2011, *Ethiopian Prophesy in Black American Letters*, Gainesville, FL: University of Florida Press.

Kebede, AlemSeghed, Shriver, Thomas E. and Knottnerus, J. David, 2000, 'Social movement endurance: Collective identity and the Rastafari', *Sociological Inquiry*, 70 3, pp. 313–37.

Kee, Alistair, 2006, *The Rise and Demise of Black Theology*, Aldershot: Ashgate Publishing.

Kenneh, Kadiatu, 1998, *African Identities: Race, Nation, and Culture in Ethnography, Pan-Africanism, and Black Literatures*, Abingdon: Routledge.

Key, Andre E., 2014, 'Towards a typology of Black Hebrew religions thought and practice', *Journal of Africana Religions*, 2, pp. 21–66.

Killingray, David, 2003, 'The Black Atlantic missionary movement and Africa, 1780s–1920s', *Journal of Religion in Africa*, 33, pp. 3–31.

King, Joyce. E., 2015, *Dysconscious Racism, Afrocentric Praxis, and Education for Human Freedom: Through the Years I Keep on Toiling*, London: Routledge.

Kinnvall, Catarina, 2004, 'Globalization and Religious Nationalism: Self, Identity, and the Search for Ontological Security', *Political Psychology*, 25 5, pp. 741–67.

Kinyua, Johnson, 2015, 'A postcolonial examination of Matthew 16:13–23 and related issues in biblical hermeneutics', *Black Theology*, 13, pp. 4–28.

Kline, David, 2017, 'The pragmatics of resistance: framing anti-blackness and the limits of political ontology', *Critical Philosophy of Race*, 5, pp. 51–69.

Knight, Frank, 1999, 'Eric Williams' inward hunger: The Caribbean as a microcosm of world history', *Caribbean Quarterly*, 45, pp. 78–94.

Komolafe, Sunday Jide, 2013, *The Transformation of African Christianity: Development and Change in the Nigerian Church*, Cumbria: Langham Monographs.

Koning, Lukas F. and Van Kleef, Gerben A., 2015, 'How leaders' emotional displays shape followers' organizational citizenship behaviour', *Leadership Quarterly*, 26, pp. 450–501.

Krause, Neal, 2014, 'Exploring the relationships among humility, negative interaction in the church, and depressed affect', *Aging & Mental Health*, 18 8, pp. 970–9.

Laperriere, Helene, 2018, 'Self-reflection on emancipatory education practices with the "oppressed" in community health', *Reflective Practice*, 19, pp. 14–25.

Lawrence, Van-Anthoney Hall, 2010, *Critical Black Aesthetics: Curriculum for Social Justice*, PhD, University of Illinois Urbana-Champaign.

Lee, Emily S., 2011, 'The epistemology of the question of authenticity in place of strategic essentialism', *Hypatia*, 26 2, pp. 258–79.

Lee, Martha F., 1996, *The Nation of Islam: An American Millenarian Movement*, New York: Syracuse University Press.

Lee, Shayne, 2007, 'Prosperity theology: T.D. Jakes and the gospel of the almighty', *Cross Currents*, 57 2, pp. 227–36.

Leech, Kenneth, 1988, *Struggle in Babylon: Racism in the Cities and Churches of Britain*, London: SPCK.

Lefkowitz, Mary R. and Rogers, Guy Maclean, 1996, *Black Athena Revisited*, Chapel Hill, NC: University of North Carolina Press.

Leonardo, Zeus, 2002, 'The souls of white folk: critical pedagogy, whiteness studies, and globalization discourse', *Race Ethnicity and Education*, 5, pp. 9–50.

Levison, John and Pope-Levison, Priscilla, 1995, 'Global perspectives on New Testament interpretations' in Joel B. Green (ed.), *Hearing the New Testament: Strategies for Interpretation*, Grand Rapids, MI: Eerdmans, pp. 339–48.

Lewis, David Levering, 1984, 'Parallels and divergences: Assimilationist strategies of Afro-American and Jewish elites from 1910 to the early 1930s', *Journal of American History*, 71 3, pp. 543–64.

Lewis, Tyson, 2010, 'Messianic pedagogy', *Educational Theory*, 60 2, pp. 231–48.

Lightsey, Pamela, 2015, *Our Lives Matter: A Womanist Queer Theology*, Oregon: Pickwick Publications.

Lindsay, Ben, 2019, *We Need to Talk About Race: Understanding the Black Experience in White-Majority Churches*, London: SPCK.

Lloyd, Vincent, W., 2017, *Religion of the Field Negro: On Black Secularism and Black Theology*, New York: Fordham University Press.

Locklin, Reid B., 2012, 'Teaching world religions without teaching "World Religions"', *Teaching Theology and Religion*, 15 2, pp. 159–81.

Long, Charles H., 1975, 'Structural similarities and dissimilarities in Black and African theologies', *Journal of Religious Thought*, 33 2, pp. 16–17.

Louis, Eleasah P. and Goodliff, Andy, 2023, *Voicing New Questions for Baptist Identity*, Oxford: Regent's Park College.

Lowe, Frank, 2013, 'Keeping leadership white: Invisible blocks to Black leadership and its denial in white organizations', *Journal of Social Work Practice*, 27 2, pp. 149–62.

Lyon, K. Brynolf, 2007, 'Uses of otherness in group life: Racism, white privilege, and Christian vocation', *Encounter*, 68, pp. 19–32.

Maat, Sekhmet Ra Em Kht (Cher Love Mcallister), 2014, 'Towards an African-centred sociological approach to Africana lesbian, gay, bisexual, transgender, queer and intersected identities and performances: The Kemetic model of cosmological interactive self', *Critical Sociology*, 40 2, pp. 239–56.

Maclean, Iain S., 2004, 'Dangerous memories, daring documents, and the demands of discipleship: The Christian church, racism, and racial justice', *Missiology: An International Review*, 32, pp. 13–35.

MacLeod, E. C., 2014, *Visions of Zion: Ethiopians and Rastafari in the Search for the Promised Land*, New York: New York University Press.

Maddox, Marion, 2016, 'In the goofy parking lot: Growth churches as a novel religious form for late capitalism', *Social Compass*, 59 2, pp. 146–58.

Magazi, Vhumani, 2017, 'Ubuntu in flames: Injustice and disillusionment in post-colonial Africa: A practical theology for new "liminal ubuntu" and personhood' in Jaco Dreyer et al. (eds), *Practicing Ubuntu: Practical Theological Perspectives on Injustice, Personhood and Human Dignity*, Zurich: Lit Verlag, pp. 111–22.

Marcus, George E., 1995, 'Ethnography in/of the world system: The emergence of multi-sited ethnography', *Annual Review of Anthropology*, 24, pp. 95–117.

Markowitz, Fran, 1996, 'Israel as African, African as Israel: "Divine geography" in the personal narratives and community identity of the Black Hebrew Israelites', *Anthropological Quarterly*, 69 4, pp. 193–205.

Marsden, George, 1997, 'Fundamentalism as an American phenomenon, a comparison with English evangelicalism', *Church History*, 46 2, pp. 215–32.

Marsden, George, 2006, *Fundamentalism and American Culture*, Oxford: Oxford University Press.

Martin, C. J., 1990, 'Womanist Interpretations of the New Testament: The Quest for Holistic and Inclusive Translation and Interpretation', *Journal of Feminist Studies in Religion*, 6 2, pp. 41–61.

Martin, Dale B., 2008, *Pedagogy of the Bible: An Analysis and Proposal*, Louisville, KY: Westminster John Knox Press.

Martin, Darnise C., 2005, *Beyond Christianity: African Americans in a New Thought Church*, New York University Press.

Martin, Robert K., 1997, 'Congregational studies and critical pedagogy in Theological Perspective', *Theological Education*, 33 2, pp. 121–46.

Mason, David R., 2000, 'A Christian alternative to (Christian) racism and anti-semitism', *The Journal of Ecumenical Studies*, 37 2, pp. 151–60.

Mason, Eric, 2018, *Woke Church: An Urgent Call for Christians in America to Confront Racism and Injustice*, Chicago, IL: Moody Publishers.

Mason, Eric, 2021, *Urban Apologetics: Restoring Black Dignity with the Gospel*, Grand Rapids, MI: Zondervan.

Mason, Eric, 2023, *Urban Apologetics: Cults and Cultural Ideologies*, Grand Rapids, MI: Zondervan.

Mathison, Keith A., 2001, *The Shape of Sola Scriptura*, Idaho: Cannon Press.

Matthews, Donald Henry, 1998, *Honoring the Ancestors: An African Cultural Interpretation of Black Religion and Literature*, Oxford: Oxford University Press.

Mattis, Jacqueline S., Palmer, Gordon J. M. and Hope, Meredith O., 2019, 'Where our bright star is cast: Religiosity, spirituality, and positive Black development in urban landscapes', *Religions*, 10, pp. 654–78.

Maulana, Kenenga, 2004, *Maat, the Moral Idea in Ancient Egypt: A Study in Classical African Ethics*, London: Routledge.

Maxwell, David, 1998, 'Delivered from the spirit of poverty?: Pentecostalism, prosperity and modernity in Zimbabwe', *Journal of Religion in Africa*, 28 3, pp. 350–73.

Mbuvi, Andrew, 2014, 'Teaching exegesis in historically Black theological schools', *Theology and Religion*, 17 2, pp. 141–64.
McCaulley, Esau, 2020, *Reading While Black: African American Biblical Interpretation as an Exercise in Hope*, Illinois: InterVarsity Press.
Mcclure, Paul K., 2017, 'Tinkering with technology and religion in the digital age: The effects of internet use on religious belief, behavior, and belonging', *Journal for the Scientific Study of Religion*, 56 3, pp. 481–97.
McCray, Walter, 1990, *The Black Presence in the Bible: Discovering the Black and African Identity of Biblical Persons and Nations*, Illinois: Black Light Fellowship.
McCutcheon, Priscilla, 2013, 'Returning home to our rightful place: The Nation of Islam and Muhammed Farms', *Geoforum*, 49, pp. 61–70.
McGrath, Allister, 1993, *Evangelicalism and the Fire of Christianity*, London: Hodder and Stoughton.
McKinnis, Leonard C., 2016, 'From Christ to Black Jesus: Black theology's Christological move as operative in the Black Coptic Church', *Black Theology*, 14 3, pp. 235–51.
McKinnon, A. M., 2012, 'Ideology and the Market Metaphor in Rational Choice Theory of Religion: A Rhetorical Critique of "Religious Economies"', *Critical Sociology*, 39 4, pp. 529–43.
Mcquilkin, Robertson and Mullen, Bradford, 1997, 'The Impact of Postmodern Thinking on Evangelical Hermeneutics', *Journal of the Evangelical Theological Society*, 40, pp. 69–71.
Meyer, J., 2016, '"I am who I am": Deconstructing orphaned boys' references to God: An application of the post-foundational notion of practical theology', *Verbum et Ecclesia*, 37, pp. 1–10.
Michael, Matthew, 2013, *Christian Theology and African Traditions*, Cambridge: The Lutterworth Press.
Miller, Michael T., 2020, 'The African Hebrew Israelites of Jerusalem and Ben Ammi's theology of marginalisation and reorientation', *Religions*, 11 87, pp. 1–21.
Mitchell, Roland W., 2010, 'The African American church, education and self-determination', *The Journal of Negro Education*, 79 3, pp. 202–4.
Mitchem, Stephanie Y., 2014, *Introducing Womanist Theology*, Maryknoll, NY: Orbis Books.
Miter, Sarah et al., 2008, 'An ethic for community-based participatory action research', *Action Research*, 6 3, pp. 305–25.
Modood, Tariq, 1998, 'Anti-essentialism, multiculturalism and the "recognition" of religious groups', *The Journal of Political Philosophy*, 6 4, pp. 378–99.
Mpanga, Denis, 2017, *Towards a Catholic Theology in the African Context: Insights and Reservations from Karl Adam's Theology*, Zurich: Lit Verlang.
Mudimbe, Vumbi Yoka, 1980, *The Invention of Africa: Gnosis, Philosophy and the Order of Knowledge*, Bloomington, IN: Indiana University Press.
Mudimbe, Vumbi Yoki, 1994, *The Idea of Africa*, Bloomington, IN: Indiana University Press.
Muhammad, Elijah, 1973, *Message to the Black Man in America*, Phoenix, AZ: Secretarius MEMPS Publications.
Muhammad, Elijah and Min Nasir Makr, Hakim, 2012, *The God Tribe of Shabazz: The True History*, Phoenix, AZ: Secretarius MEMPS Publications.

Murray, John Courtney, 1944, 'Towards a theology for the layman: The pedagogical problem', *Theological Studies*, 5, pp. 340–76.

Murrell, Nathaniel Samuel, Spencer, William David and McFarlane, Adrian Anthony, 1998, *Chanting down Babylon: The Rastafari Reader*, Philadelphia, PA: Temple University Press.

Nandi, Alita and Platt, Lucinda, 2013, 'Britishness and identity assimilation among the U.K.'s minority and majority ethnic groups', *Understanding Society Working Paper Series*, 8, https://www.understandingsociety.ac.uk/wp-content/uploads/working-papers/2013-08.pdf, accessed 09.05.2019.

Nel, Marius, 2018, *An African Pentecostal Hermeneutics: A Distinctive Contribution to Hermeneutics*, Eugene, OR: Wipf & Stock.

Nelson, Lynn Hankinson, 1990, *Who Knows: From Quine to Feminist Empiricism*, Philadelphia, PA: Temple University Press.

Neville, Robert Cummings, 2018, *Defining Religion: Essays in Philosophy of Religion*, New York: University of New York Press.

Nichols, Austin Lee and Cottrell, Catherine A., 2014, 'What do people desire in their leaders? The role of leadership level on trait desirability', *The Leadership Quarterly*, 25, pp. 711–79.

Nisbet, Robert, 2017, *Conservatism: Dream and Reality*, London: Routledge.

Nobles, W., 2006, *Seeking the Sadhu: Foundational Writings for an African Psychology*, Chicago IL: Third World Press.

Noddings, Nel, 2005, 'Can spiritual/theological discourse guide curriculum and pedagogy?', *Journal of Curriculum and Pedagogy*, 2 2, pp. 21–3.

Nwatu, Felix, 1994, '"Colonial" Christianity in post-colonial Africa?', *The Ecumenical Review*, 46 3, pp. 352–60.

Nyengele, Mpyana Fulgence, 2004, *African Women's Theology, Relations and Family Systems Theory: Pastoral Theological Considerations and Guidelines for Care and Counselling*, New York: Peter Lang.

O'Hara, Kieron, 2016, 'Conservatism, Epistemology and Value', *The Monist*, 99 4, pp. 423–40.

O'Neill, William R., S.J., 2001, 'African moral theology', *Theological Studies*, 62, pp. 122–39.

O'Niell, Daniel, 2016, *Edmund Burke and the Conservative Logic of Empire*, Oakland: University of California Press.

O'Reilly, Karen, 2008, *Key Concepts in Ethnography*, London: Sage Publications.

Odozor, Paulinus Ikechukwu, 2008, 'An African moral theology of inculturation: Methodological considerations', *Theological Studies*, 6 3, pp. 583–609.

Ojo, Sanya, 2018, *The Evolution of Black African Entrepreneurship in the U.K.*, Hershey, PA: IGI Global.

Omenyo, Cephas, 2011, 'Agenda for a discussion of African initiatives in Christianity: The west African/Ghanaian case', *Missiology*, 39 3, pp. 373–89.

Omulokoli, Watson, 1986, 'The quest for authentic African Christianity', *East Africa Journal of Evangelical Theology*, 5 2, pp. 22–55.

Osler, Audrey, 2009, 'Patriotism, multiculturalism and belonging: Political discourse and the teaching of history', *Educational Review*, 61, pp. 85–100.

Ospino, Hosffman, 2010, 'Theological horizons for a pedagogy of accompaniment', *Religious Education*, 105 4, pp. 413–29.

Oss, Douglas A., 1988, 'Canon as context: The function of sensus plenior in evangelical hermeneutics', *Grace Theological Journal*, 9, pp. 105–27.

Owens, Michael L., 2007, *God and Government in the Ghetto: The Politics of Church–State Collaboration*, Chicago: University of Chicago Press.

Oyewumi, Oyeronke, 2002, 'Conceptualizing gender: The eurocentric foundations of feminist concepts and the challenge of African epistemologies', *Jenda*, 2 3, no page given.

Page Jr., Hugh R. (ed.), 2009, *The Africana Bible: Reading Israel's Scriptures from Africa and the African Diaspora*, Minnesota: Augsburg Fortress.

Park, S.-K., 2010, 'A postfoundationalist research paradigm of practical theology', *H.T.S. Teologiese/Theological Studies*, 66 2, pp. 849–55.

Parratt, John, 2004, *An Introduction to Third World Theologies*, Cambridge: Cambridge University Press.

Partridge, C., 2004, 'Alternative spiritualities, new religions and the re-enchantment of the west' in J. Lewis (ed.), *The Oxford Handbook of New Religious Movements*, Oxford: Oxford University Press, pp. 39–67.

Patton, M., 1990, *Qualitative Evaluation and Research Methods*, Beverly Hills, CA: Sage Publications.

Peck, Gary R., 1982, 'Black radical consciousness and the Black Christian experience: Toward a critical sociology of Afro-American religion', *Sociological Analysis*, 43 2, pp. 155–69.

Perkinson, James W., 2011, 'How I came to be christened "Bird": Christian baptism, white racism, and theological passion in the 21st century', *Anglican Theological Review*, 93 4, pp. 599–618.

Perkinson, James W., 2012, 'Pedagogy beyond piracy: Un-learning the white body to recreate a body of learning', *Teaching Theology and Religion*, 15 4, pp. 323–47.

Perrin, Ruth H. and Bielo, James S., 2016, *The Bible Reading of Young Evangelicals: An Exploration of the Ordinary Hermeneutics and Faith of Generation Y*, Oregon: Pickwick Publications.

Petrella, Ivan, 2017, *The Future of Liberation Theology: An Argument and Manifesto*, London: SCM Press.

Petterson, Christina, 2012, 'Colonial subjectification: Foucault, Christianity and governmentality', *Cultural Studies Review*, 18 2, pp. 89–108.

Phillips, Peter, 1988, 'Race, class, nationalism: A perspective on twentieth century social movements in Jamaica', *Social and Economic Studies*, 37 3, pp. 97–124.

Pinn, Anthony B., 2004, 'Black is, Black ain't': Victor Anderson, African American theological thought and identity', *Dialog: A Journal of Theology*, 43, pp. 54–62.

Pinn, Anthony B., 2007, 'Jesus and justice: An outline of liberation theology within Black churches', *CrossCurrents*, 57 2, pp. 218–26.

Pinn, Anthony B., 2008, 'Black theology: A survey of its past, present and future', *Religious Compass*, 2 2, pp. 160–79.

Pinn, Anthony B., 2010, *Embodiment and the New Shape of Black Theological Thought*, New York: New York University Press.

Plantigua-Pauw, Amy and Jones, Serene, 2006, *Feminist and Womanist Essays in Reformed Dogmatics*, London: Westminster John Knox Press.

Pobee, John, 1979, *Towards an African Theology*, Nashville, TN: Abingdon Press.

Posnock, Ross, 1997, 'How it feels to be a problem: Du Bois, Fanon, and the "impossible life" of the Black intellectual', *Critical Inquiry*, 23 2, pp. 323–49.

Prentoukis, Marina, 2012, 'The construction of the black British community in The Voice and the New Nation', *Journalism*, 12 6, pp. 721–49.

Prevost, Elizabeth, 2008, 'Married to the mission field: Gender, Christianity, and professionalization in Britain and colonial Africa, 1865–1914', *Journal of British Studies*, 47 4, pp. 796–826.

Price, Charles, 2009, *Becoming Rasta: Origins of Identity in Jamaica*, New York: New York University Press.

Price, Charles, 2014, 'Cultural production of a Black Messiah: Ethiopianism and the Rastafari', *Journal of Africana Religions*, 2 3, pp. 418–33.

Price, Charles Reavis, 2003a, '"Cleave to the Black": Expressions of Ethiopianism in Jamaica', *New West Indian Guide / Nieuwe West-Indische Gids*, 77, pp. 31–64.

Price, Charles Reavis, 2003b, 'Social change and the development and co-optation of a Black antisystemic identity: The case of Rastafarians in Jamaica', *Identity*, 3, pp. 9–27.

Principe, Walter H., 1987, 'Catholicity, inculturation, and liberation theology: Do they mix?', *Franciscan Studies*, 47, pp. 24–43.

Quirin, James, 2011, 'W.E.B. Du Bois, Ethiopianism and Ethiopia, 1890–1955', *International Journal of Ethiopian Studies*, 5 2, pp. 1–26.

Rah, Soong-Chan, 2009, *The Next Evangelicalism: Freeing the Church from Western Cultural Captivity*, Downers Grove, IL: InterVarsity Press.

Raschke, Carl, 2004, *The Next Reformation: Why Evangelicals Must Embrace Postmodernity*, Michigan: Baker Academic.

Reason, P. and Bradbury, H., 2001, *Handbook of Action Research: Participative Inquiry and Practice*, Thousand Oaks, CA: Sage Publications.

Reason, Peter and Wicks, Patricia Gaya, 2009, 'Challenges and paradoxes of opening communicative space', *Action Research*, 7 3, pp. 243–62.

Reddie, Anthony, 1998, 'Towards a Black Christian education of liberation: The Christian education of Black children in Britain', *Black Theology in Britain: A Journal of Contextual Praxis*, 1, pp. 46–58.

Reddie, Anthony G., 2003, *Nobodies to Somebodies: A Practical Theology for Education and Liberation*, Peterborough: Epworth Press.

Reddie, Anthony G., 2009, 'Exploring the workings of Black theology in Britain: Issues of theological method and epistemological construction', *Black Theology*, 7, pp. 64–85.

Reddie, Anthony, 2011, 'If Heaven is such a wonderful place, then why would white people tell Black people about it??: Problematising Black Christian confessional belief in postcolonial Britain', *Discourse*, 10, pp. 29–54.

Reddie, Anthony, 2012a, 'Being the enemy within: Reasserting Black "otherness" as a riposte to homogeneous construct of whiteness', *Modern Believing*, 53, pp. 408–18.

Reddie, Anthony, 2012b, *Black Theology: A Reader*, London: SCM Press.

Reddie, Anthony, 2012c, 'Christianity tu'n mi fool: Deconstructing confessional Black Christian faith in postcolonial Britain', *Black Theology*, 10, pp. 49–76.

Reddie, Anthony, 2012d, 'The quest for liberation and inclusivity', *The Ecumenical Review*, 64 4, pp. 530–45.

Reddie, Anthony G., 2014, *Working Against the Grain: Re-imaging Black Theology in the 21st Century*, London: Routledge.

Reddie, Anthony G., 2016a, *Black Theology, Slavery and Contemporary Christianity: 200 years and No Apology*, Abingdon: Routledge.

Reddie, Anthony, 2016b, 'The quest for a radical black Jesus: An antidote to imperial mission Christianity' in Jawanza Eric Clark (ed.), *Albert Cleage Jr. and the Black Madonna and Child*, London: Palgrave Macmillan, pp. 285–300.

Reddie, Anthony G., 2019, *Theologizing Brexit: A Liberationist and Postcolonial Critique*, Abingdon: Routledge.

Reddie, A. G. and Jagessar, M. N., 2007, *Black Theology in Britain: A Reader*, United Kingdom: Equinox.

Reddie, Anthony, Ackah, William and Smith, R. (eds), 2014, *Churches, Blackness and Contested Multiculturalism: Europe, Africa and North America*, New York: Palgrave Macmillan.

Reddie, Richard, 2009, *Black Muslims in Britain*, Oxford: Lion Hudson.

Rex, John, 1997, 'The problematic of multinational and multicultural societies', *Ethnic and Racial Studies*, 20 3, pp. 455–73.

Riad, Sally and Jones, Deborah, 2013, 'Invoking Black Athena and its debates: Insights for organization on diversity, race and culture', *Journal of Management History*, 19 3, pp. 394–415.

Richardson, Christopher, 2006, 'A nonfoundationalist approach to education in religion', *Religious Education*, 101 2, pp. 292–303.

Rieger, Joerg, 2004, 'Theology and mission between neocolonialism and postcolonialism', *Mission Studies*, 21 2, pp. 201–27.

Robbins, Thomas and Lucas, Phillip Charles, 2007, 'From "cults" to new religious movements: Coherence, definitions and conceptual framing in the study of new religious movements' in James A. Beckford and Jay Demerath (eds), *Sage Handbook of the Sociology of Religion*, Newburyport Park, CA: Sage Publications, pp. 227–47.

Roberts, J. Deotis, 1987, *Black Theology in Dialogue*, Philadelphia, PA: Westminster Press.

Roberts, J. Deotis, 1989, 'A Christian response to evil and suffering religious education', *Periodicals Archive Online*, 84, pp. 68–71.

Roberts, J. Deotis, 2005, *Liberation and Reconciliation: A Black Theology*, Louisville, KY: Westminster John Knox Press.

Ruether, Rosemary Radford, 1972, *Liberation Theology: Human Hope Confronts Christian History and American Power*, Mahwah, NJ: Paulist Press.

Saliba, John A., 1995, *Perspectives on New Religious Movements*, London: Bloomsbury.

Salter, Richard C., 2005, 'Sources and chronology in Rastafari origins', *Nova Religio: The Journal of Alternative and Emergent Religions*, 9, pp. 5–31.

Sanders, Bo S. and Woodley, Randy S., 2020, *Decolonizing Evangelicalism*, Oregon: Cascade Books.

Sanou, Boubakar, 2015, 'Ethnicity, tribalism and racism: A global challenge for the Christian church and its mission', *The Journal of Applied Christian Leadership*, 9, pp. 94–104.

Sarid, Ariel, 2012, 'Systematic thinking on dialogical education', *Educational Philosophy and Theory*, 44 9, pp. 926–41.

Sawyer, Mary R., 1996, 'The Black church and black politics: Models of ministerial activism', *Journal of Religious Thought*, 52/53, pp. 45–62.

Sayyid. S., 1998, 'Anti-essentialism and universalism', *Innovation*, 11 4, pp. 377–89.

Scheid, Anna Floerke and Vasko, Elisabeth T., 2014, 'Teaching race: Pedagogical challenges in predominantly white undergraduate theology classrooms', *Teaching Theology and Religion*, 17, pp. 27–45.

Schultz, Thom and Schultz, Joani, 2013, *Why Nobody Wants to Go to Church Anymore: And How 4 Acts of Love Will Make Your Church Irresistible*, Colorado: Group Publishing.

Scott, W. R. and Shade, W. G. (eds), 2000, *Upon these Shores: Themes in the African-American Experience 1600 to the Present*, New York: Routledge.

Seabright, Paul and Raiber, Eva, 2020, 'U.S. Churches' Response to Covid-19: Results From Facebook', *CEPR*, https://repec.cepr.org/repec/cpr/ceprdp/DP1566.pdf, accessed 08.01.2021.

Shannahan, Chris, 2013, *A Theology of Community Organizing: Power to the People*, London: Routledge.

Shepperson, George, 1953, 'Ethiopianism and African nationalism', *Phylon*, 14, pp. 9–18.

Shilliam, Robbie, 2016, 'Ethiopianism, Englishness, Britishness: Struggles over imperial belonging', *Citizenship Studies*, 20 2, pp. 243–59.

Shor, Ira and Freire, Paulo, 1987a, *A Pedagogy for Liberation: Dialogues on Transforming Education*, London: Bloomsbury Academic.

Shor, Ira and Freire, Paulo, 1987b, 'What is the dialogical method of teaching?', *The Journal of Education*, 169 3, pp. 11–31.

Shore, Megan, 2016, *Religion and Conflict Resolution: Christianity and South African's Truth and Reconciliation Commission*, Abingdon: Routledge.

Shukra, Kabir,1998, *The Changing Pattern of Black Politics in Britain*, London: Pluto Press.

Siker, Jeffery S., 2007, 'Historicizing a racialized Jesus: Case studies in the "Black Christ", the "Mestizo Christ" and white critique', *Biblical Interpretation: A Journal of Contemporary Approaches*, 15, pp. 26–53.

Simpson, George Eaton, 1985, 'Religion and justice: Some reflections on the Rastafari movement', *Phylon*, 46 4, pp. 286–91.

Singer, Merrill, 1988, 'The social context of conversion to a Black religious sect', *Review of Religious Research*, 30 2, pp. 177–92.

Singer, Merrill, 2000, 'Symbolic identity formation in an African American religious sect: The Black Hebrew Israelites' in Yvonne Patricia Chireau and Nathaniel Deutsch (eds), *Black Zion: African American Religious Encounters with Judaism*, New York: Oxford University Press, pp. 55–72.

Skinner, Tom, 1974, *If Christ is the Answer, What Are the Questions?*, Grand Rapids, MI: Zondervan Publishers.

Smith, M. G., Augier, Roy and Nettleford, Rex, 1967, 'The Rastafari movement in Kingston, Jamaica. Part 1', *Caribbean Quarterly*, 13 3, pp. 3–29.

Smith, Mitzi J., 2015, *I Found God in Me: A Womanist Biblical Hermeneutics Reader*, Oregon: Cascade Books.

Smith, R. Drew et al. (eds), 2015, *Contesting Post-Racialism: Conflicted Churches in the United States and South Africa*, Mississippi: University of Mississippi Press.

Smith, R. Drew and Harris, Fredrick C., 2005, *Black Churches and Local Politics: Clergy, Influence, Organizational Partnerships and Civic Empowerment*, Maryland: Rowman and Littlefield Publishers.

Smith, Timothy L., 1972, 'Slavery and theology: The emergence of Black Christian consciousness in nineteenth-century America', *Church History*, 414, pp. 497–512.

Smith, W. G., 2017, 'A postfoundational ubuntu accepts the unwelcome (by way of process transversality)', *Verbum et Ecclesia*, 38 3, pp. 79–91.

Spry, Tami, 2016, *Autoethnography and the Other: Unsettling Power Through Utopian Performatives*, New York: Routledge.
St. Clair, Raquel Annette, 2008, *Call and Consequences: A Womanist Reading of Mark*, Minneapolis, MN: Fortress Press.
Stalker, Carol A. et al., 2005, 'The case for integrating grounded theory and participatory action research: Empowering clients to inform professional practice', *Qualitative Health Research*, 15 8, pp. 1129–40.
Stanley, Brian, 2013, *The Global Diffusion of Evangelicalism: The Age of Billy Graham and John Stott*, Illinois: InterVarsity Press.
Stark, Rodney and Finke, Roger, 2000, *Acts of Faith: Explaining the Human Side of Religion*, California: University of California Press.
Stewart, Dianne, M., 2004a, 'Womanist God-talk on the cutting edge of theology and Black religious studies: Assessing the contribution of Delores Williams', *Union Seminary Quarterly Review*, 58, pp. 65–83.
Stewart, Dianne M., 2004b, 'Womanist theology in the Caribbean context: Critiquing culture, rethinking doctrine, and expanding boundaries', *Journal of Feminist Studies in Religion*, 20, pp. 61–82.
Strange, Jill M. and Mumford, Michael D., 2005, 'The origins of vision: Effects of reflection, models, and analysis', *The Leadership Quarterly*, 16, pp. 121–48.
Sugirtharajah, R. S., 2002, *Postcolonial Criticism and Biblical Interpretation*, Oxford, Oxford University Press.
Sugirtharajah, R. S. (ed.) 2016, *Voices from the Margin: Interpreting the Bible in the Third World*, Maryknoll, NY: Orbis Books.
Sumner, William G., 1906, *Folkways: A Study of the Sociological Importance of Usages, Manners, Customs, Mores and Morals*, New York: Mentor.
Sundstrom, Ronald, 2005, 'Frederick Douglass's longing for the end of race', *Philosophia Africana*, 8 2, pp. 143–70.
Tafari, I. Jabulani, 1980, 'The Rastafari – successors of Marcus Garvey', *Caribbean Quarterly*, 26 4, pp. 1–12.
Taylor, Michael, 2016, 'British proslavery arguments and the Bible, 1823–1833', *Slavery & Abolition*, 37, pp. 139–58.
Taylor, Wayne, 2005, 'Premillennium tension: Malcolm X and the eschatology of Nation of Islam', *A Critical Journal of Black Politics, Culture and Society*, 7, pp. 52–65.
Teel, Karen, 2014, 'Getting out of the left lane: The possibility of white antiracist pedagogy', *Teaching Theology and Religion*, 17, pp. 3–26.
Thomas, Linda E., 2004, *Living Stones in the Household of God: The Legacy and Future of Black Theology*, Philadelphia, PA: Fortress Press.
Thomas, Stacey Floyd, 2006, *Deeper Shades of Purple: Womanism in Religion and Society*, New York: New York University Press.
Thomas, Stacey Floyd et al., 2007, *Black Church Studies: An Introduction*, Nashville, TN: Abingdon Press.
Thompson, Deloris A., 2001, 'The need to belong: A theory of the therapeutic function of the black church tradition', *Counselling and Values*, 46, pp. 40–53.
Thompson, Krista A., 2004, 'Black skin, blue eyes': Visualizing blackness in Jamaican art, 1922–1944', *Small Axe*, 16 8, pp. 1–31.
Thorsell, Rix, 2009, Theory of the Black Christ, Dissertation, Drake University.
Thumma, Emory, 1991, 'Negotiating a religious identity: The case of the gay evangelical', *Sociological Analysis*, 52 4, pp. 333–47.
Thurman, Howard, 2012, *Jesus and Disinherited*, Boston, MA: Beacon Press.

Tillotson, Michael, 2010, 'A critical location of the contemporary Black church finding a place for the word church formation', *Journal of Black Studies*, 40 5, pp. 1016–30.
Tinaz, Nuri, 2006, 'Black Islam in diaspora: The case of Nation of Islam (N.O.I.) in Britain', *Journal of Muslim Minority Affairs*, 26 2, pp. 151–70.
Tokunboh, A., 2010, *Africa Bible Commentary*, Grand Rapids, MI: Zondervan.
Toll, William, 1982, 'Rehabilitation and revitalization: Black perspectives on race relations', *Humboldt Journal of Social Relations*, 10, pp. 301–19.
Torrey, R. A., 2015, *The Fundamentals: A Testimony to the Truth*, Los Angeles, CA: Delmarva Publications.
Treier, Daniel J., 2008, *Introducing Theological Interpretation of Scripture: Recovering a Christian Practice*, Grand Rapids, MI: Baker Academics.
Tribble, J., 2005, *Transformative Pastoral Leadership in the Black Church*, New York: Palgrave Macmillan.
Trible, Phyllis, 1984, *Texts of Terror: Literary-Feminist Readings of Biblical Narratives*, Minneapolis, MN: Fortress Press.
Troyna, Barry, 2010, *Racial Inequality in Education*, Abingdon: Routledge.
Unesco, 1980, *Sociological Theories: Race and Colonialism*, Paris: Unesco.
Van der Walt, J. L., 2015, 'Education from a post-post-foundationalist perspective and for post-post-foundationalist conditions', *Koers–Bulletin for Christian Scholarship*, 80, pp. 1–8.
Van der Westhuizen, Z., 2010, 'Transversality and interdisciplinary discussion in postfoundational and practical theology – reflecting on Julian Muller's interdisciplinary guidelines', *H.T.S. Teologiese Studies/ Theological Studies*, 66 2, pp. 1–5.
Venn, Couze, 2000, *Occidentalism: Modernity and Subjectivity*, Newbury Park, CA: Sage Publications.
Vietze, Deborah L., Jones, James M. and Dovidio, John F., 2014, *The Psychology of Diversity: Beyond Prejudice and Racism*, West Sussex: Wiley-Blackwell.
Wadsworth, Nancy D., 1997, 'Reconciliation politics: Conservative evangelicals and the new race discourse', *Politics & Society*, 25 3, pp. 341–76.
Wald, Kenneth D., Owen, Dennis E. and Hill Jr, Samuel S., 1990, 'Political cohesion in churches', *The Journal of Politics*, 52, pp. 197–215.
Walford, G., 2004, 'Finding the limits: Autoethnography and being an Oxford University proctor', *Qualitative Research*, 4, pp. 403–17.
Walker, Alice, 1983, *In Search of our Mother's Gardens: Womanist Prose*, Sandiego, CA: Harcourt Publisher.
Walker, D., 1830, *Walker's Appeal in Four Articles: Together with a Preamble, to the Coloured Citizens of the World, But in Particular, and Very Expressly to Those of the United States of America*, United States: D. Walker.
Walker, Theodore, 1991, *Empower the People: Social Ethics for the African American Church*, Maryknoll, NY: Orbis Books.
Walters, Ron, 2007, 'Barack Obama and the politics of Blackness', *Journal of Black Studies*, 38, pp. 7–29.
Walton, John H., 2002, 'Inspired subjectivity and hermeneutical objectivity', *The Master's Seminary Journal*, 13, pp. 65–77.
Wangenen, Aimee Van, 2007, 'The promise and impossibility of representing anti-essentialism: Reading Bulworth through critical race theory', *Race, Gender & Class*, 14, pp. 157–77.

Ware, Frederick L., 2008, *Methodologies of Black Theology*, Oregon: Wipf and Stock.

Warnock, Raphael G., 2014, *The Divided Mind of the Black Church: Theology, Piety, and Public Witness*, New York: New York University Press.

Webner, Prina and Muhammad, Anwar, 1991, *Black and Ethnic Leaderships in Britain: The Cultural Dimensions of Political Action*, London: Routledge.

Weems, Renita J., 2016, 'Re-reading for liberation: African American women and the Bible' in Rasiah S. Sugirtharajah (ed.), *Voices from the Margin: Interpreting the Bible in the Third World*, Maryknoll, NY: Orbis Books, pp. 27–39.

Weisenfeld, Judith, 2017, *A New World – A-Coming: Black Religion and Racial Identity during the Great Migration*, New York: New York University Press.

Weller, Paul, 2004, 'Identity, politics, and the future(s) of religion in the U.K.: The case of the religion questions in the 2001 decennial census', *Journal of Contemporary Religion*, 19, pp. 3–21.

West, Cornel, 1979, *Black Theology and Marxist Thought*, Issue 10 of Documentation series – Theology in the Americas, Theology in the Americas.

West, Cornel, 1988, *Prophetic Fragments: The Crisis of Theological Education*, Grand Rapids, MI: William B. Eerdmans.

West, Cornel, Glaude, Eddie S., 2003, *African American Religious Thought: An Anthology*, Kentucky: Westminster John Knox Press.

West, G. O. and Dube, M. W. (eds), 1998, *The Bible in Africa: Transactions, Trajectories and Trends*, Leiden: Brill.

West, Russell, 2002, 'Middle passages: Negotiating multicultural identities in contemporary Britain: David Dabydeen's "The Intended"', *Arbeiten aus Anglistik und Amerikanistik*, 27 2, pp. 221–36.

White, Carol Wayne, 2016, *Black Lives and Sacred Humanity: Toward an African American Religious Naturalism*, New York: Fordham University Press.

Williams, Al-Yasha Ilhaam, 2003, 'On the subject of kings and queens: "Traditional" African leadership and the diasporal imagination', *African Studies Quarterly*, 7, pp. 95–101.

Williams, Delores Foster, 2011, *Institutional Racism and the Catholic Church*, Wisconsin: Heritage Press.

Williams, Delores S., 1993a, *Sisters in the Wilderness: The Challenge of Womanist God-Talk*, New York: Orbis Books.

Williams, Delores S., 1993b, 'A womanist perspective on sin' in Emile M. Townes (ed.), *A Troubling in My Soul: Womanist Perspectives on Evil and Suffering*, Maryknoll, NY: Orbis Books, Chapter 8.

Williams, Heather A., 2005, *Self Taught: African American Education in Slavery and Freedom*, Chapel Hill, NC: University of North Carolina Press.

Williams, Joan C., 1991, 'Dissolving the sameness/difference debate: A postmodern path beyond essentialism in feminist and critical race theory', *Duke Law Journal*, 1 2, pp. 296–323.

Wills, Garry, 1990, *Under God: Religion and American Politics*, New York: Simon & Schuster.

Wilmore, Gayraud S., 2004, *Pragmatic Spirituality: The Christian Faith through an Afrocentric Lens*, New York: New York University Press.

Wimbush, Vincent L., 2012, *African Americans and their Bible: Sacred Texts and Social Textures*, Eugene, OR: Wipf and Stock.

Wright, J. A., 1995, *Africans Who Shaped Our Faith*, United States: Urban Ministries.

Wünch, Hans-Georg, 2015, 'Learning from African theologians and their hermeneutics: Some reflections from a German Evangelical theologian', *Verbum et Ecclesia*, 36, pp. 1–9.

X, Malcolm, 1971, *The End of White Supremacy*, New York: Seaver Books.

Yancy, George (ed.), 2001, *Cornel West: A Critical Reader*, New Jersey: Wiley-Blackwell.

Yeager, Jonathan, 2008, 'Puritan or enlightened? John Erskine and the transition of Scottish evangelical theology', *EQ*, 80 3, pp. 237–53.

Yeager, Jonathan, 2011, *Enlightened Evangelicals: The Life and Thought of John Erskine*, Oxford: Oxford University Press.

Young, Amos and Alexander, Estrelda Y., 2011, *Afro-Pentecostalism: Black Pentecostal and Charismatic Christianity in History and Culture*, New York: New York University Press.

Zackariasson, Ulf, 2009, 'A critique of foundationalist conceptions of comprehensive doctrines in the religion in politics-debate', *International Journal for Philosophy of Religion*, 65, pp. 11–28.

Zerubavel, Eviatar, 2016, 'The five pillars of essentialism: Reification and the social construction of an objective reality', *Cultural Sociology*, 10, pp. 69–76.

Websites

Appiah, Kwame, 2020, 'Time to Capitalize Black and White', *The Atlantic*, https://www.theatlantic.com/ideas/archive/2020/06/time-to-capitalize-blackand-white/613159/, accessed 01.05.2022.

Barton, Cassie, 2020, 'GE2019: 'How did demographics affect the result?', *UK Parliament*, https://commonslibrary.parliament.uk/ge2019-how-did-demographics-affect-the-result/, accessed 01.05.2022.

Bible Gateway, Genesis 15:13–14 King James Version, *Bible Gateway*, https://www.biblegateway.com/passage/?search=Genesis%2015:13-14&version=KJV, accessed 01.01.2017.

Davis, Caleb, 2018, 'Understanding and reaching the de-churched in your city', *Acts 29*, https://www.acts29.com/understanding-and-reaching-the-de-churched-in-your-city/, accessed 15.12.2020.

Eisenhart, Margaret, 2019, 'The Entanglements of Ethnography and Participatory Action Research (PAR) in Educational Research in North America', *Oxford Research Encyclopedia of Education*, 26 April, https://oxfordre.com/education/view/10.1093/acrefore/9780190264093.001.0001/acrefore-9780190264093-e-324, accessed 17.05.2020.

Farrakhan, Louis, 2002, 'In the Name of Allah, the Beneficent, the Merciful', *Nation of Islam*, https://noi.org/christians-muslims-jews/, accessed 01.01.2017.

Fields, Lisa, 2018, 'Rethinking apologetics for the Black church', *Christianity Today*, https://www.christianitytoday.com/2018/07/rethinking-apologetics-for-black-church, accessed 01.01.2018.

GOCC Twelve Tribes, https://gatheringofchrist.org/twelve-tribes/, accessed 09.05.2022.

Harris, Brian, 2015,' Churched, Un-Churched or De-Churched', https://brianharrisauthor.com/churched-un-churched-or-de-churched/, accessed 01.12.2020.

Holy Qubtic Church of the Black Messiah and the Journey Home Group, http://www.journeyhomegroup.com/about, accessed 01.07.2020.

The Holy Qubtic Church, *Our Scriptures*, https://www.holyqubticchurch.com/, accessed 01.12.2020.

Igielnik, Ruth and Budiman, Abby, 2020, 'The Changing Racial and Ethnic Composition of the U.S. electorate', *Pew Research Centre*, https://www.pewresearch.org/2020/09/23/the-changing-racial-and-ethnic-composition-of-the-u-s-electorate/, accessed 01.05.2022.

Israel United in Christ, https://israelunite.org, accessed 15.12.2020.

Israel United in Christ , 'Nehemiah 13:25–26 K.J.V', https://israelunitedinchrist.tumblr.com/post/143140527236/nehemiah-1325-26-kjv-25-and-i-contended-with, accessed 01.01.2022.

LSE, 2018, 'How are black majority churches growing in the UK? A London Borough case study', https://blogs.lse.ac.uk/africaatlse/2017/02/20/how-are-black-majority-churches-growing-in-the-uk-a-london-borough-case-study, accessed 07.02.2018.

Muhammed, T., 1996, 'Brief History on Origin of the Nation of Islam', *Nation of Islam*, https://noi.org/noi-history/, accessed 01.01.2017.

Southern Evangelical Seminary and Bible College, 2020, 'What is Objectivity and Why is it Important for Bible Study?', https://ses.edu/what-is-objectivity/, accessed 01.05.2022.

Sproul, R. C., 2005, Ancient Promises, *Ligonier*, https://www.ligonier.org/learn/articles/ancient-promises, accessed 01.06.2022.

Walker, David, 'Walker's Appeal, in Four Articles; Together with a Preamble, to the Coloured Citizens of the World, but in Particular, and Very Expressly, to Those of the United States of America, Written in Boston, State of Massachusetts, September 28, 1829', *Documenting the American South*, http://docsouth.unc.edu/nc/walker/walker.html , accessed 01.01.2017.

White, Ismail K. and Laird, N. Chryl, 2020, 'Why are Blacks Democrats?', *Princeton University, Press*, https://press.princeton.edu/ideas/why-are-blacks-democrats, accessed 01.05.2022.

YouTube Videos

aGATHERING144, 2015, 'GOCC Bible Teachings – Overcoming the Curse', https://www.youtube.com/watch?v=WygB6hGy9IM, accessed 01.06.2020.

Black Butterfly Channel, 2010, 'Ancient Africans in the Bible', https://www.youtube.com/watch?v=zF2RPj4cjRw, accessed 01.11.2020.

The Holy Qubtic Church Bahamas, 2016, 'Genesis Revisited through African Eyes – Holy Qubtic Church – KaHun: Anju Sa Ra', https://www.youtube.com/watch?v=o2dhu6GRUls&t=136s, accessed 01.06.2020.

The Israelites: 'Cutting the Christian Lies', https://www.youtube.com/watch?v-i6UHxTAPIVw&t=121s,

Kimbunga Media, 2019, 'The Holy Qubtic Church London – Kahun Montu Tar – Under the Collar', https://www.youtube.com/watch?v=zC5m290Mntw, You Tube, accessed 01.06.2020.

Kimbunga Media, 2020, 'Reclaiming our religious heritage. Rev AJ Varmah |

BIBLIOGRAPHY

K.U.S.H Communiversity', https://www.youtube.com/watch?v=cHfOvFoaXyk&t=177s, accessed 01.12.2020.

Mignolo, Walter D. 2021, 'The politics of decolonial investigations', Theory from the Margins, https://www.youtube.com/watch?v=qDEEbVcxmRU&t=1109s, accessed 03.03.2021.

Muhammad, Leo, 2018, 'The Beginning', P.O.W.E.R LSG, https://www.youtube.com/watch?v=zLYeBNbQ5YY, accessed 16.12.2020.

P.O.W.E.R LSG, 2019, 'Leo Muhammed – The Hijacking of Religion', https://www.youtube.com/watch?v=aAUOXPa7l4s&list=PLi4LBNx_4xA-tWmek3QeKeuWlLZVOFTgx, YouTube, accessed, 01.06.2020.

www.ingramcontent.com/pod-product-compliance
Lightning Source LLC
Chambersburg PA
CBHW022054290426
44109CB00014B/1095